NEXT GENERATION
REAL ESTATE ★

NEW RULES FOR SMARTER HOME BUYING & FASTER SELLING

BRENDON DeSIMONE

CHANGING LIVES PRESS

The advice and information contained in this book is for informational purposes only. The strategies presented in this book are based upon the research
and experiences of the author in his many years as a real estate professional.
Should the reader have any questions about how to proceed with a real
estate matter, the author and publisher strongly suggest consulting appropriate professionals in the fields of law, real estate, and finance.

Changing Lives Press
50 Public Square #1600
Cleveland, OH 44113
www.changinglivespress.com

**Library of Congress Cataloging-in-Publication Data is available
through the Library of Congress.**

ISBN: 978-0-9849400-5-9

Editor: Michele Matrisciani • www.bookchic.net
Project editor: Carol Killman Rosenberg • www.carolkillmanrosenberg.com
Cover designer: Roman Pietrs • www.globalpopstar.com
Interior designer: Gary A. Rosenberg • www.thebookcouple.com

Printed in the United States of America

10   9   8   7   6   5   4   3   2   1

Contents

Introduction: My Message, 1

PART I   REAL ESTATE THEN AND NOW

1. **The More Things Change, the More They Stay the Same, 11**

    A Changing Process, a Changing People, 13

PART II   SMARTER BUYING

2. **Does Buying a Home Make Sense for Me Now?, 19**

    Your First Real Estate Revelation, 20

    First Things First, 23

    Does Buying a Home Make Sense for Me Financially?, 25

    Does Buying a Home Make Sense for Me Practically?, 27

    Does Buying a Home Make Sense for Me Emotionally?, 31

    Next Generation Real Estate Fact:
        Real Estate Is a Long-Term Investment, 34

3. **Virtual Real Estate: Home Buying Starts Online, 35**

Next Generation Real Estate Fact: Data Collection in Olden Days, 37

Meet the Real Estate Syndicators, 37

Enter the Online MLS, 39

The IDX, 40

How to Get the Most out of the Syndicator's Search, 41

Next Generation Real Estate Fact: The Syndicators Are Not Perfect, 43

4. **Team Sport: Why You Still Need a Real Estate Agent, 46**

What to Expect from a Real Estate Agent, 48

How to Find an Agent, 54

Next Generation Real Estate Fact: The Advent of Agent Advertising, 57

How to Work Well with an Agent, 59

Understanding the Real Estate Agent-Buyer Relationship, 60

The Myth of Multiple Agents, 62

Act Locally, 64

5. **What Can I Really Afford? Building Your Financial House, 67**

The Role of a Mortgage Professional, 70

Next Generation Real Estate Fact: Online Mortgage Banking May Not Be the Way to Go, 74

What to Expect from Your Mortgage Professional, 75

The Differences between Prequalification and
   Preapproval, 77

What Does Your Financial House Look Like?, 78

Great Rate?, 80

What's the Best Loan for You?, 86

How Mortgage Lending Has Evolved, 91

Next Generation Real Estate Advice:
   Go for 30!, 92

6. **Game On! Let the Search Begin, 93**

To Have or Have Not: The Question of Criteria, 93

How to Stay the Course during Your
   Learning Curve, 98

Next Generation Real Estate Fact: There Are
   Five Types of People Who Visit Open Houses, 109

The Psychology of the List Price, 111

New Construction: Function or Dysfunction?, 114

7. **Putting Your Money Where Your Mouth Is:**
Formulating and Presenting Your Offer, 118

Before You Make an Offer, 118

Next Generation Real Estate Fact: Conduct
   Reconnaissance through the Listing Agent, 121

Preparing the Offer, 125

Right Price or Bad Offer?, 126

Yes, You're Really Doing This: Submitting
   the Offer, 129

Why Terms Matter, 130

How to Know When to Walk away from
   a Negotiation, 133

8. **Ready for Action! The Anatomy of the Real Estate Transaction, 134**

Real Estate Roll Call, 134

Make an Offer and Write up a Contract, 136

Disclosure Review, 137

Due Diligence Next Generation Style, 142

Appraisal, 145

Next Generation Real Estate Fact: Dispute
a Bad Appraisal, 150

Loan Approvals or Commitment, 152

Inspection, 153

Walk-through, 158

The Closing, 159

9. **Diamonds in the Rough: What You Need to Know When Thinking about Buying a Distressed Sale, 164**

Short Sales, 164

Foreclosures: Sales on the Courthouse Steps, 165

REO, 166

What to Know When You Want to Buy a
Short Sale, 167

What to Know about Auctions on the
Courthouse Steps, 169

What to Know When You Want to Buy
an REO, 170

Next Generation Real Estate Fact: Forget
Face Value; Do Your Due Diligence, 173

PART III FASTER SELLING

10. Does Selling Make Sense for Me Right Now?, 179

The Difference between a Seller and a Buyer, 180

Next Generation Real Estate Fact: Sellers Are Sellers
Who Sell, 183

Two Reasons a Home Sits on the Market, 184

Two Common Seller Screw-Ups Due to Emotional
Attachment, 185

Am I Resisting My Sale?, 187

Can I Afford to Sell My Home Now?, 189

Plan B: Accidental Landlord, 190

Plan B: Negotiate with Your Bank, 192

Plan B: The Short Sale, 192

Plan B: Roll the Dice, 195

**11. The Price Is Right! Four Steps for Understanding
& Maximizing Your Home's Worth, 196**

Step 1: Conduct Initial Research—Understand
the Market, 196

Step 2: Understand Pricing, 201

Step 3: Engage an Agent, 203

Step 4: Gather Some More Nuts and Sit on Them, 205

Next Generation Real Estate Fact: When Setting
the Price, Slow and Steady Wins the Race, 206

12. **The Gist before You List: Choosing the Right Agent, 207**

Changing the Hat You Wear, 207

What to Expect from a Listing Agent, 209

Unrepresented Seller: When to Go For Sale by Owner (FSBO), 212

How to Find a Real Estate Agent, 214

Next Generation Real Estate Fact: Combine Listing Agent Interviews with the Home Tour, 218

Entering into a Listing Agreement, 223

13. **Prepping Your Listing: How to Stay One Step Ahead of the Next Generation Buyer, 226**

Give the People What They Want, 227

Next Generation Face-off, 228

Next Generation Real Estate Fact: Inspect Your Property before You List It, 235

Disclosure and Property History, 237

Why You Shouldn't Disclose Square Footage in Your Listing, 242

14. **Seeing Is Believing: Transforming Your Home with the Art of Staging, 245**

The Psychology of Staging, 246

From Couch Appeal Back to Curb Appeal: Property Presentation at Its Most Powerful, 248

Turning Your Home into a Product, 251

Next Generation Real Estate Fact: When All Else Fails, Call in the Professionals, 254

15. Showtime! Tips and Tricks for Going Live on the Market, 257

Final List Price, 257

Approval of Listing Photos and Marketing Copy, 260

Potential Showing Schedule, 260

Next Generation Real Estate Fact: Open Houses
   Are Necessary, 264

16. Closing Time: How to Negotiate, Accept, and Close a Buyer's Offer, 270

How to Know if You Are Dealing with a Buyer
   Who Is the Real Deal, 271

What Is the Earnest Money Deposit?, 272

Negotiations Round 1, 273

Under Contract, 275

Inspection Planning and Strategy, 277

Negotiations Round 2, 278

Next Generation Real Estate Fact: Be Aware
   of the Loan and Appraisal Contingency, 279

Contingencies Removed: Moving toward
   Closing, 286

Appendix

Real Estate Technology Companies
   and Services, 289

Index, 293

My Message

My name is Brendon DeSimone. In 2004, after actively selling real estate in California for three years, I decided it was my turn to join the ranks of other single 30-somethings who were finally dipping their toes in the pool of adulthood: homeownership. I'd been guiding clients through the home-buying process, and I thought it was only appropriate that I become a homeowner myself. Renting seemed foolish for someone in my profession, especially given the real estate market at the time. Things were moving fast. It seemed like everyone was getting in and making a quick buck. I'd experienced a similar phenomenon a few years earlier, working in Silicon Valley before, during, and after the dot-com bust. Then, it seemed as though everyone was working for a new start-up; ideas and subsequent business plans were flying, as were the stock options offered to the young entrepreneurial idealists heading for gold in California. Surely, I'd take advantage of another boom.

Single, with no immediate plans for a family, I set pen to paper to sign the contract for a two-bedroom fixer-upper in the heart of San Francisco. My stomach dropped, and I had some apprehension. *Wait, is this the right time to buy? Did I see enough properties? Am I overpaying? Is this the best location for me? Can I really afford this home? What if the market crashes?*

Then, the inevitable question: *What would my dad say?*

1

I called my dad, and he listened to my trepidations as I ran down my laundry list of what-ifs and responded with, "What's the rate on a 30-year fixed?"

What a bizarre thing to ask, I thought. Not one of my buyer clients had taken out a 30-year mortgage. Everyone was purchasing homes with five-year, fixed-rate, interest-only loans. A 30-year fixed seemed as obsolete as a rotary telephone or a television antenna. His question led me to dismiss him as out of touch with my lifestyle, my needs, and my priorities—my entire generation's way of life! I was in California. This was 2004.

He was a baby boomer, whereas I was a high-tech boom of Silicon Valley. I worked insane hours at a software start-up before embarking on my second career as a real estate agent at an exciting time in real estate. I surely knew more than he did. Didn't my father realize that I didn't know where I would be in five years—much less 30? Travel and mobility were high on my priority list. I was buying a fixer-upper and was already seeing similar renovated apartments selling for a lot more money than mine cost, so maybe I'd just flip it and move on to the next project. Or maybe I'd move back to the East Coast. I didn't know what was in my future.

All I knew was that the interest rate for a 30-year fixed loan, and therefore my monthly payment, was considerably higher in 2004 than most other types of mortgages. The thought of committing 30 years to my first home seemed ridiculous. I was moving fast; we all were. People overbid on homes, and sellers often received multiple offers. Properties appreciated 10 percent a year (or more), and there didn't appear to be any limits. It was the Wild West, and we were blazing trails.

Real estate, once synonymous with terms such as *settling down* and *planting roots,* was replaced with an ease in snatching up a property, getting a cheap bank loan, or flipping a shack. This created a whimsical climate in which there was no focus on the long term—just an American dream for the taking. This was the world as I knew it. Absent a larger life experience, I didn't have any sort of frame of reference.

Conversely, when my father was my age some 30 years earlier, he and my mother already had three kids under the age of 10. He was building a thriving small business and was focused on supporting his family. When he bought a home, he took into account the community in which the house was located, the school district's reputation, and how far he was willing to commute to work. He viewed homeownership as having two purposes: the starter home and the home to die in. In that context, why would he consider anything *but* a 30-year fixed mortgage?

My father's inquiry about the mortgage rate wasn't about his cluelessness after all; rather, it pointed to a generational shift in real estate, and as I explored the causes for the disconnect, I discovered they went far beyond personal economics. For decades, buying and selling a home was pretty much the same: You stayed close to home, bought something you could afford, and aimed to own full-out by retirement age. However, that was real estate then, and this is now.

The years that followed my dad's first home purchase have been jammed with upswings, downturns, housing style changes, demographic shifts, and of course the huge onslaught of technology. The Internet has changed everything, including how consumers choose properties, how they choose an agent, and how they know what we can afford. The efficiencies created by technology have changed our lives forever.

As I balked at my father's antiquated mind-set, I signed the paperwork for a three-year, interest-only loan with ambitions to fix up the house and sell it before the rates ballooned. I was building a successful real estate practice and was on the front lines. But time flew faster than I expected, and by the time I'd made my mark on the San Francisco real estate market, it was the fall of 2008. My personal Western was taken over by a horror flick in the form of a real estate market crash. By late 2008 the bubble had officially burst. Clients who needed to relocate with their companies, wanted to have another baby, or hoped to start renovating that fixer-upper found themselves stuck in their homes, unable to sell or refinance because their mortgage was underwater.

Now, the tables had turned, and the real estate decision—whether buying or selling—seemed obsolete and became a thorn in the side of seemingly everyone I spoke to on the subject. The new world was negative toward real estate and didn't seem to share the long-term view or ideal that folks such as my dad had so effectively embraced as a practical bet for so many years—that a home was the only real safe place to put your money. Now it was no longer your easy street to great profits or the American dream. Nobody wanted to be involved in real estate. In fact, even if you wanted to buy a home, it became nearly impossible to get a loan, as banks tried to figure out how to get out of their own messes.

For the first time ever, renting became a safer, more secure option than owning, especially when a growing number of people were out of work and couldn't be approved for loans. Because of all of this and much more, real estate practices once considered antiquated emerged as the new normal. By 2011, nearly everything we thought we knew about real estate had changed. Again. Would I have to tell dear old Dad that he was . . . *right*? Not so fast? Fast-forward just a few years, and the real estate market was now hot again. In the spring of 2013, real estate was back in the headlines, this time with stories about historically low interest rates, multiple offers on homes, and double-digit increases in values in some parts of the country. Just nine months later, interest rates had ticked up a point, and there was talk of another real estate bubble, that rates would bring things crashing down. These changes were so abrupt that the consumer didn't know how to respond. Was it suddenly a seller's market? *Should I sell my home now? Have I missed the bottom?* These were all questions I was asked by clients, friends, and family. Was this just a changing market, and we now had to adjust?

But there was more to it. Real estate markets had always risen and fallen. These booms and busts were surely just another part of the cycle of real estate; at least this was the hope when many clients, friends, and colleagues approached me for second opinions on their next steps in buying or selling in the new world. But something seemed bigger this time around, and as I searched for the right solutions and spot-on advice for these folks, I had to take into account that the new buying and selling zeitgeist was not just about economics, unscrupulous mortgage agents, and the idea of being too big to fail. The rise was so fast and the fall so hard, and the world was amidst a rapid change not only physically and behaviorally but also sociologically and technologically. These changes would surely have an impact not only on how we viewed homeownership or what the new idea of home was but also on how we approached real estate as an investment, both when buying and selling. *Next Generation Real Estate* brings to the forefront these major changes in our culture and society to empower you to consider them when thinking about buying or selling a home.

The rules of buying and selling real estate had to adapt to our new transparent world—a world in which buyers and sellers are savvier and more serious about smarter buying and faster selling. That's where *Next Generation Real Estate* comes in.

MY MISSION IN WRITING THIS BOOK

Next Generation Real Estate is about teaching different generations how to speak the same language—the new language of real estate. It is my hope that what you find inside these pages will demystify the new normal and provide you with contrarian approaches and revolutionary ideas about all stages of the real estate process. Use this book as your go-to guide, and consider me as your real estate agent on the page (or on the screen), who can help you start thinking about your buying or selling (or both) journeys.

Because real estate is conducted differently in every state and even varies by town and county, admittedly I can't possibly be an expert in how real estate is done everywhere. I do, however, share my experiences with many types of clients, as well as my tips and advice based on those particular experiences. Your best bet will always be to turn to a local real estate agent, but I hope that this book will plant many seeds or spark a discussion about smarter buying or faster selling.

Throughout this book, you will meet buyer and seller clients I've personally worked with in the new era of real estate. Ultimately, *Next Generation Real Estate* will give you a new perspective and knowledge of what worked before, what works now, and what's likely to work tomorrow so that you can achieve your ultimate goals of smarter buying and faster selling.

I set out to understand who the Next Generation buyer sand sellers are. I'll discuss this at length in Part I, "Real Estate Then and Now," but it must be noted that being a part of the Next Generation has little to do with the year you were born, the amount of income you take in, or what demographic you fall into. In its simplest term, buyers and sellers of the Next Generation are people who are looking to the next phase of their lives. The eclectic nature of that next phase is not only stunning and unprecedented but also the crux of this book.

In Part II, "Smarter Buying," a plethora of information and easy-to-understand translations of what is going on in the world of buying will help you learn how to handle the financial, practical, and emotional issues surrounding home seeking, including:

- How to uncover the hidden value of a home

- How to use Google Street View to discover the truth about a property you might not discover otherwise

- How your smartphone can tell you if a neighborhood is safe

- Why you should never buy the first home you see

- How to determine whether you should buy a short sale or foreclosure

- How to get a refund on your nonrefundable deposit

- How pricing is determined

- What the new mortgage guidelines are and how to work with a bank to get the best rates

- How appraisals have changed and the new role of the appraiser

- Why it's risky to ask for credits during escrow

- How square footage is measured and why you need to know the square footage before you make an offer

- Why buying a home isn't about return on investment anymore (Hint: Say goodbye to the value increases of the old days.)

- Why real estate is still a good *long-term* investment

- What you should know about buying a distressed sale

Part III, "Faster Selling," is dedicated to the financial, emotional, and practical issues facing—you guessed it—sellers in today's economic and social climates, including:

- Which renovations will increase the value of a home and which ones are usually a waste of money

- What boomers need to know about selling to generations X and Y

- What to do if you become an accidental landlord

- What you need to know when you put your house back on the market after a selling hiatus

- How a designer or stager can help increase your sale price

- How your neighbors can help sell your home

- Why it makes sense to get an inspection *before* putting your house on the market

- What you need to know about the new psychology of pricing and negotiation

- Whether open houses are necessary today

- What you need to know about property disclosures

- Why your first buyer is nearly always your best buyer

- What you need to do to avoid a lowball offer

- What you need to know about the rise and risks of the appraisal contingency

For the purposes of this book, I've interviewed trailblazers and experts, who have directly or indirectly helped set the new standard in real estate, so look for featured sidebars throughout from:

Barbara Corcoran, of ABC's *Shark Tank* and Real Estate Expert; **Spencer Rascoff**, CEO of Zillow; **Lockhart Steele**, Founder of Curbed; **Richard Florida**, Senior Editor, *The Atlantic*, and Founder of the Creative Class Group; **Vera Gibbons**, Personal Finance Expert; **Jonathan Miller**, President and CEO of Miller Samuel Appraisers;

Maxwell Ryan, CEO and Founder of Apartment Therapy, **Pete Flint**, CEO of Trulia; and **Greg McBride**, Vice President, Senior Financial Analyst, Bankrate.com. I believe what they have to add to the dialogue surrounding the next generation of real estate will help you along your buying and selling journeys.

No matter what you can accomplish with a keypad, when it comes to making one of the biggest financial, practical, and emotional decisions of your life, it's difficult to imagine not wanting an expert by your side, acting as your sounding board, research center, advisor, protector, negotiator, watchdog, and second opinion. We're made to connect. We need that human-to-human, *mano-a-mano* exchange. I wrote this book to provide you that second opinion. Whether it's in buying or selling, I want you to benefit from cutting through the real estate rules of *then* and customizing your own real estate rules of *now*. That's *Next Generation Real Estate*.

PART I

REAL ESTATE THEN AND NOW

The More Things Change, the More They Stay the Same

When I began to examine the differences between real estate then and now, I couldn't help but first zero in on my own peer group.

Older agents I spoke to had tales of prospecting clients and neighborhoods by cold calling out of the phone book. The successful agents literally walked door to door, knocked, and asked the stranger on the other side, "Are you interested now or in the near future in selling your home?" They kept in touch with the office from phone booths.

These nostalgic agents described how in the 1980s and before, this is how they would build their client base. Additionally, the sales process and timeline back then was a slow process because information wasn't accessible at the touch of an iPad. If agents wanted the stats, price reductions, the days on market, or any other information that would help them better help a seller or buyer, it needed to be scoured in printed reports or in books that were circulated every few weeks. Surely if this was the experience of the agent then, the experience of yesterday's buyer had to tell a compelling story.

Fast-forward 30 years. Real estate agents are no longer slaves to an antiquated system. Agents around the country find clients of all types through Internet advertising, blogging, and social media. But the one thing that hasn't changed is the good old reliable referral. Referrals—whether they come over an e-mail or through two cups connected by a string—are still a method from days gone by that have remained effective for buyers, sellers, and agents.

The passing of time didn't just change how agents operated our businesses, but also the types of people *with whom* we do business. In fact, that's the most dramatic transformation of all. Although there would always be buyers and sellers, what had changed were their priorities: their wants and needs, lifestyles, personal economics, and career goals. On top of all of this, technology was still making an incredible impact on how we do business. The changing of the guards was dramatic, and it was happening on so many levels.

Let's take members of baby boomer generation, who are next generation buyers *and* sellers, as an example. We reveal much if we compare them to their parents' generation. Today, boomers are dreaming of a new lifestyle and what they want their lifestyle to be, which ties strongly into their home search. On the other hand, when their parents became empty nesters, there wasn't much dreaming or researching on the Internet to figure out their next phase. They either downsized or somehow made their home work for them. There weren't many other options.

Across the country, I've seen many cases of boomers moving out of single-family homes in suburbia after 30 years. They are moving into urban environments; into well-appointed full-service buildings, complete with cooking classes and wine tastings. The clients I worked with told me they no longer want to take care of the lawn or a house that has too many unused rooms. They want to go to the theatre and enjoy city life before they feel they are too old. Now that their kids were grown, they wanted to experience something new and exciting. They just weren't ready for the retirement community on the golf course.

Thanks to the information we have access to today, all buyers and sellers out there can see what options are available and how other people with different lifestyles live. Sometimes they didn't know that there were such things as these types of full-service buildings. I once heard of a couple who, while looking on the Internet, noticed that a 55-and-older community was located a block from a dog park in a small city. This actually prompted them not only to buy the home but also to get a dog. The technology we have today is what intertwines people and their decisions.

Buyers 20 years ago walked into the office of their agent and told him or her what kind of home they wanted. The agent looked in the Multiple Listing books, chose a few listings that met their criteria, and made appointments to look at them, and the buyers ultimately bought a home that way. Now when buyers go online, they're looking at neighborhoods, at schools, at whether there's a Starbucks nearby, or at what the culture is like. This dreaming phase, the ability to get lost online and stumble accidentally onto different sites, makes you realize what you can have, and more important, what you can be.

A CHANGING PROCESS, A CHANGING PEOPLE

Yes, the process has certainly changed. There are so many cultural, generational, economical, and personal differences that have affected how we do business and with whom. Three cheers for that! I am lucky to have so much diversity in my clientele, their needs, and what's available now in terms of homes that allow us to help them accomplish their buying and selling needs. Consider these five next generation trends. Maybe you'll see yourself in one, or a few:

1. **Living away from home:** Today, it's less common and not expected for a young person to settle down in the town in which one grew up. A career opportunity or just the quest for the exploration is more likely to dictate where one lives today than in the past. The growth of the economy, the radical change in industry, the mainstream nature of travel, the necessity to chase scarce jobs, and the ubiquity of the Internet, as well as the competitive nature of the marketplace, have required companies to move quicker, faster, and better—or die. That means workers have to be nimble, quick to relocate, and have the resilience to face the unknown.

2. **Renting versus owning:** The decision to rent or buy today is just one dramatic illustration of how things have shifted in recent years. For decades, renting was the only affordable housing option for young people starting out in their careers. They saved for the down payment for years until they could finally buy a home and achieve the American dream. Today, with historically low mortgage rates, and rising rents, renting can actually be more expensive

than owning. For example, according to an online calculator, at an interest rate of 4.5 percent, the total cost of owning a $172,000 home after six years is $76,777. The total cost of that same home at $1,100 per month? $94,179.[1]

3. **Urban expansions and suburban exodus:** My parents' generation and the generation before them fled crowded, expensive urban areas to buy homes in the suburbs. Fast-forward to the present, in which a growing number of homeowners are forsaking the suburbs and moving back to the city, often to live in transit-oriented developments near train stations.[2] Why is this happening? A shift in culture and society is present and having a huge effect on lifestyle and home life.

4. **Lifestyle changes have emerged:** Getting married at 23 and moving to the suburbs for the next 30 years isn't as common anymore. Instead, divorce rates are high, many people stay single well into their 30s or get remarried at 40, women staying in the workforce is commonplace, and so-called "alternative" lifestyles aren't so alternative anymore. For all of these reasons, many people are turning to urban areas and want the freedom to define what home means to them.

5. **Technology:** Let's not forget the Internet's impact on home buying and selling. Real estate agents once held all the keys, literally, to buying and selling. My parents relied on a real estate agent to drive them around, get them information on new homes for sale, and supply them with the background or supporting information they needed to make a decision. Now, buyers flip through properties for sale on an iPad and check out neighborhoods on Google Street View without even contacting an agent—or getting off the couch, for that matter. There is so much more information available to consumers today.

---

1. Kevin Quealy and Archie Tse, "Is It Better to Buy or Rent?" *New York Times,* last modified 2012, www.nytimes.com/interactive/business/buy-rent-calculator.html?_r=0.]

2. Dawn Wotapka, "Suburban Swap: Trading a Backyard for a Train Station," *Wall Street Journal,* May 1, 2012, online.wsj.com/article/SB10001424052702304811304577370044093629550.html.]

6. **A disconnected society:** Although we have Facebook and Twitter to thank for putting us back in touch with old friends and as a way of connecting to the masses, many people these days prefer their personal space. Living alone is more common today than ever. In fact, some people would say that it's more appealing than ever.

I believe that these cultural, technological, and behavioral changes, coupled with giant economic forces, have completely transformed the way people have approached a real estate transaction for the past 50 years. But when it comes to how they approach their agents, it seems nothing has changed at all.

Through my discovery process I thought a lot about real estate brokerages and the role of the real estate agent in this transformed age. Given the demise of the travel agent and changes to so many industries because of the Internet and new technology, most people would assume that we, as real estate agents, would be obsolete. New Internet companies, backed by huge venture capitals, have popped up, but the local real estate agents are still there, working right alongside buyers and sellers. I wondered, *Why isn't the Internet and technology killing off this industry? How has it stood the test of time?*

To understand this, I brainstormed about the motivations, concerns, fears, and trepidations of today's buyers and sellers. There had to be a reason why they still reached out to agents. If it were that easy just to go online and buy or sell a home, surely they would have by now. But they weren't. Something was stopping them, and I started to uncover what it was.

What drives a buyer to buy or a seller to sell is still the same as it always has been: a life change, such as a marriage, divorce, new baby, job transfer, death, or need for expansion. What concerns people and what prompts their decisions to buy and sell are evergreen. Whether it's 1957, 1983, or 2014, real estate transactions represent an enormous life change—the beginning of a new journey, the ending of an era, and the closing of an important chapter in life.

Unlike purchasing an airline ticket on Hotwire or selling your old guitar on eBay, buying or selling a home is a special experience that can't be commoditized—because it can't be duplicated. I came to the realization that whether the client is a Gen X divorcée looking for a condo with a view, a recently engaged millennial couple, or a golf-obsessed boomer desiring a new construction on the ninth hole, real estate will always be driven by three forces:

- Financial implications

- Practical considerations

- Emotional responses

That's right; no matter the decade, the interest rate, or the crime rate, these three factors will always rule buying and selling. We need to step back and go deeper, beyond the circumstances surrounding a sale or a purchase. Whether it's our parents, a newlywed couple, a gay couple, a family looking to plant roots, a recent college graduate, or a single mom, buying and selling will always be governed by financial, practical, and emotional issues.

Many people don't realize all of the issues involved until they are in the thick of a real estate transaction. That's what agents are for. The information in this book is plentiful, and the tips and advice hard earned and learned. The rules of next generation buying and selling found throughout this book are the same ones that I share with my clients and the people who reach out to me online each week.

I have made a point of highlighting throughout the book when an issue is a financial, a practical, or an emotional one. That's because all decisions made in real estate will always have origins in one of these factors. If you become uncertain or feel indecisive or even scared during your home buying or selling process, take a breath and ask yourself, *Is this a financial implication, a practical consideration, or an emotional response?* Simply identifying and then prioritizing the issue that is most influencing your decisions will ultimately help you buy smarter and sell faster.

The changes we have seen in the past three decades of real estate have no doubt left indelible marks on the business, but so have the things that have remained the same. Put then and now together, and you have *Next Generation Real Estate.*

PART II

SMARTER BUYING

Does Buying a Home Make Sense for Me Now?

Remember word association back in grade school? I say a word or phrase, and you tell me the first thing that comes to your mind. What's the first thing you think of when I say *the American dream*?

The fact that you are reading this book tells me there's a good chance that the first image you conjured might be that little Cape Cod in the suburbs, a midcentury raised ranch on a cul-de-sac, or a turn-of-the-century farmhouse on 3 acres in the country. Let's face it; earning a little slice of the real estate pie has been synonymous with the American dream since the first suburb was conceptualized in Levittown, New York, after World War II. And I'm here to tell you that the American dream is still very much alive.

For some people, however, that same dream comes with servings of a huge financial commitment, lack of flexibility, and maintenance that simply aren't alluring enough to throw down a good portion of their life savings or be indebted to a bank for the next three decades.

🏠 EXPERT Barbara Corcoran, Real Estate Expert

"The real estate market is always on a roller coaster ride. Over the last decade we've gone from healthy growth to a bubble to a total collapse of values," Barbara told me. "Now our market is once again on the upswing."

There is a group of buyers that concerns me most of all—the one composed of those who think they are ready to make the leap but learn too late that they didn't quite realize how much goes into the financial, emotional, and practical aspects of buying a home, especially a first home. Can you say buyer's remorse?

I decided to open the section on smarter buying by urging you to ask yourself the all-important question, "Should I buy a home now?" I am not trying to take the wind out of your sails, but through my experiences as a real estate agent, I have seen what happens when all things are *not* considered. *Smarter buying* simply means knowing yourself, your circumstances, and your desires inside out; turning every scenario around in your head; and heading confidently and purposely toward homeownership. Simply said, smarter buying means you know *what to consider.* It's also about knowing your finances inside and out. It's about knowing if you have the down payment saved or what the minimum down payment is. Will you have additional savings to cover a leaky roof, the garden upkeep, or the rainy-day fund? It's about knowing your local economy and starting to understand the housing market where you live.

Buying a home comes with lots of downsides. You are now responsible for fixing your own leaks, paying property taxes, and dealing with homeowner's insurance claims. It may not be for you right now, and that's fine. It may be possible that, after a little bit of research online or talking to a local agent or a mortgage professional, you decide you need to wait. For some people, renting may be a better short- or long-term option. Buying a home doesn't happen overnight, nor is it a simple transaction. From the first time people get the idea about buying a home until they close, it could be at least six months, up to two years.

YOUR FIRST REAL ESTATE REVELATION

The home-buying process can reveal itself in a number of ways, at breakneck speed or over long periods. When potential buyers seek out real estate agents, it's because there has been some sort of catalyst or impetus: nagging parents, lack of privacy, an unexpected rent hike,

---

🏠 *EXPERT*   Vera Gibbons, Personal Finance Expert

"I think one of the biggest mistakes I see people make when they are figuring out whether it's a good time for them to buy is not factoring the total cost of owning a home, plus the worst-case scenario," Vera told me. "You have to figure in what heating a three-bedroom would cost and then add on 10 percent, just in case the winter is a long one. Or how many times a week you might go out to dinner now that you are considering moving in walking distance of a lively downtown. It's not just about the affordability of the mortgage—it's also about homeowner's insurance and home maintenance like gardening, painting, or renovating. Or it's those unforeseen issues like a leaky roof or broken oil tank. But, then it's also things like gas and car insurance, if you have a new commute. The list can go on and on. Figure out if you are ready to afford a home and all its responsibilities by treating it as an *additional* part of your life, not as if it were the *only* part of your life. Doing so will ensure you are never scrimping and moving money around to pay for unexpected things, or worse, missing a mortgage payment."

---

an unresponsive landlord, a new baby on the way, a hot war with a neighbor, loss of a job, and on and on. This may inspire their very first consideration of becoming an owner—and for good reason.

My friends Rick and Sarah decided to call me after living in the same rental for years. Things kept breaking, and the landlord was not responsive. They were getting frustrated with having to rely on someone else to make their home life better. They'd been lured in by cheap rent all these years. They knew it's been somewhat of a deal, but they also understand the concept of, "You get what you pay for." A crappy landlord, a leaky basement, or nosy parents can most definitely spoil people's experience and prompt them to do the math or start to imagine the possibilities of what they could do if their domain were truly theirs. *What if we changed out those cabinets, or if we ripped up the carpets and put in hardwood floors? Can I imagine a life where I didn't share a front door with Mom?*

Even in great rental circumstances or living quarters, big life changes can prompt people to open their eyes about the reality of becoming a homeowner. For individuals in their early to mid-20s, it could be a roommate moving out, or they finally saved enough money to get out of their childhood bedroom or say good-bye to the basement. For others, it could be a breakup or a divorce that brings housing front and center.

Finally, there are outside influences that propel people to start thinking about owning real estate. They could receive a monetary gift, get a new job or a salary increase, or have that serious talk with their parents about getting into the market. They may meet with their accountant, who reminds them of the tax benefits of owning a home. Often, these events happen at year-end, when people take stock or assess their tax or financial situation and set new goals. The New Year, New You phenomenon that attracts millions of people to fad diets on January 1 is the same one that attracts them to real estate.

Every January I see an increase in the number of calls from potential clients asking to meet with and discuss the possibility of buying real estate. These don't include the follow-up calls from folks with whom I've worked previously but who hadn't bought for one reason or another. Maybe it's your own resolution that inspired you to pick up this book, and if so, I'm glad. However, I'd be remiss if I didn't tell you that any real estate agent you work with should first help you determine whether buying a home makes sense for you *right now*. The

---

🏠 EXPERT　　Barbara Corcoran, Real Estate Expert·

When it comes to outside influences, the media reports information that keeps buyers and sellers apprised of market conditions. According to the *Today Show* real estate expert, Barbara Corcoran, "Just a few years ago, buyers—that is, those buyers who could get their hands on financing—had an embarrassment of riches to pick from. But today, prices are bouncing back, inventory is tight, and most markets across the country have bidding wars just like in the good old days of seven to ten years ago."

reason is that no matter the situation, it is rare for a home purchase to happen immediately as a direct result of one of the preceding scenarios. Rather, the events bring the option of housing front and center. They plant the seed. Taking it slowly and introspectively will prevent haste and waste and lead you to smarter buying, whether it's right now or in the future.

FIRST THINGS FIRST

Deciding to purchase a home is a long process composed of three factors that you should always consider separately and then together: financial, practical, and emotional. So much is at stake and so many considerations are to be made that it's never a good idea to jump right in. Instead, take cues from your experience, and start thinking about buying. Many buyers spend months, if not years, looking at homes, running mortgage calculators (see the sample below), and engaging a real estate agent before they ever sign on the bottom line. That's smart buying.

MORTGAGE CALCULATOR

What will your monthly mortgage payment be? Use this mortgage calculator
A house is the largest purchase most of us will ever make so it's important to calculate what your payment will be and how much you can afford. The mortgage calculator will show you how much your monthly payment will be. It can also show the effect of adding extra payments. Watch our "How To" video on how to use a mortgage calculator.

Mortgage Calculator	Mortgage Payment Calculator

Mortgage amount:	$ 165000.00
Mortgage term:	30 years or 360 months
Interest rate:	7.00 % per year
Mortgage start date:	Jan ▾ 14 ▾ 2014 ▾
Monthly payments:	$ 1097.75

Calculate

Extra payments

Adding:	$ 0	to your monthly mortgage payment
Adding:	$ 0	as an extra yearly mortgage payment every Jan ▾
Adding:	$ 0	as a one-time payment in Feb ▾ 2014 ▾

Changes paid off date to: Jan 14, 2044

Show/Recalculate Amortization Table

On the flip side, it could be that you dive in now and learn in two days, two weeks, or two months that homeownership is not right for you right now. Renting can actually be a better option than buying. You may need to save more money, fix some things on your credit report, or realize that, for whatever reason, homeownership is not worth the trouble. That's okay, because not buying can be smart buying, too. In fact, renting can sometimes be smarter than buying.

I am the first person to admit that I turn potential homebuyers away. You would think that a real estate agent would do nothing but encourage someone to buy. But I'd rather see people buy the right home at the right time than be bogged down by a home they can't afford or stuck trying to sell a home and losing their down payment or selling at a loss. Your agent should be asking you a variety of questions, and you should be asking them yourself when considering venturing into the world of real estate. That's why we encourage you to consider some fundamental financial, emotional, and practical questions.

🏠 EXPERT   Vera Gibbons, Personal Finance Expert

"When thinking about buying a home, the first thing buyers—new or veteran—should do is check their annual credit reports. When you do check it, read it carefully," warns Vera Gibbons. "The report can be erroneous. It's not unheard of for a credit history to list a credit card in your name that you do not own or an account still joint with an ex who continues to make late payments, which affects your credit rating. Removing these errors can make big differences in your score."

And, if you still don't like your credit score, Vera says the quickest and easiest way to increase one's credit score is to pay bills on time.

"Approximately 60 percent of the credit score is based on timely bill payments," she says. "Within six to eight months you can see your credit score go up by simply being more disciplined. So if you check your credit score before you embark on a home search, you'll know ahead of time what you can do to build up your credit score."

DOES BUYING A HOME MAKE SENSE FOR ME FINANCIALLY?

What we hear most people ask early on in the process is, "Is it cheaper to rent or buy?" It makes complete sense. You want to leave your parents' home and go out on your own or escape your long-term roommate. However, you need to know your financial options. At a time when interest rates for mortgages are so low, it's not uncommon to see great numbers, such as these:

Purchase price of home: $350,000

Rent on the same home: $1,500

If you look at the graph from Hotpads.com below, you'll see that with a 30-year loan at a rate of 4.0 percent, after more than six years in the home, the cost of owning is cheaper than renting. This sounds like great news and all the more reason to buy, but this should just be the impetus for you to consider homeownership more. You need to factor in a down payment and maintenance costs, as well as the emotional and practical considerations of homeownership. So before you go off

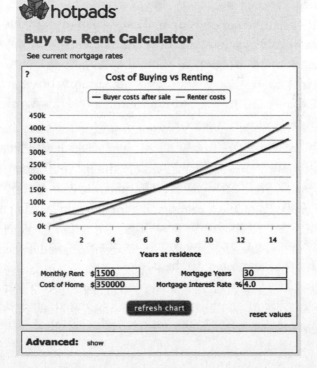

to look at open houses, take a step back. Use this graph to inform yourself and as a tool to get the homeownership juices flowing and your interest piqued.

What Is Happening Locally?

Knowing the politics and economics of your local community should help inform you in the process of deciding whether it's the right time for you to buy. Are companies in your local area hiring, or are they laying people off? Is there a building boom happening, or are there tons of vacancies both in commercial and residential real estate? If you are going to become a homeowner, you will be settling and establishing yourself in a local community. You will literally be invested in it. Find out more about it. Are the politics in your town pro development? Are they pro real estate or something else? If you don't do so already, start to read the local paper. Informing yourself about the political, economic, and financial health of your local community will inform you vis-à-vis your internal guideposts.

If you need a tax break, buying might make sense for you. There are other financial benefits of owning real estate. An undeniable benefit is the tax benefit. Simply put, the government allows homeowners to write off the interest portion of their mortgage payment, dollar for dollar, against their salary. We have seen many buyers (even the savviest of them) fail to really understand how this works, so let's break down the following scenario:

Imagine someone with a monthly mortgage payment of $1,500. Did you know that $1,200 of that is interest paid to the bank and $300 goes toward paying down the actual principal? Over the course of the time of the loan (10-year, 20-year, 30-year, etc.), an owner will pay less interest and more principal (see Chapter 5). But for the sake of this exercise, consider that over the course of one year, the owner will pay $14,400 in mortgage interest to the bank.

If the owner earned $60,000 per year, he can immediately deduct $14,400 off his income, and instead of being taxed on $60,000, he is taxed on an income of $45,600, which reduces what is potentially owed to Uncle Sam.

What Is Home Equity?

Don't forget that unlike an automobile, which loses value the second you drive it off the lot, real estate is an investment. It is an asset that appreciates. You can make your home more valuable by improving it. If you buy a fixer-upper or a home that needs some cosmetic work, you can make it more valuable by fixing it up. Building equity in your home is essentially making it more valuable. Sure, in the middle part of the early 2000s, homeowners' equity was increasing without any improvements. The market was a bubble. It's true that some folks realized 10 or 20 percent of their home's value within just a couple of years. However, when the bubble burst, some folks lost all of that equity and more.

The long-term investment and the equity upside is one of the huge financial benefits to owning real estate. Some folks will scrape together every penny of their savings for a down payment, just to own—to have an asset that appreciates. My parents bought their first home in the mid 1970s for $58,500. After a kitchen renovation, back deck addition, and new siding, they sold it thirteen years later for $275,000. It was a smart investment.

Sure, you can make money on real estate. There are times and situations when it is cheaper to rent than to buy and the government will incentivize you to own a home. However, there are more than just financial considerations when thinking about jumping into the real estate market.

DOES BUYING A HOME MAKE SENSE FOR ME PRACTICALLY?

If you don't see yourself sticking around for at least five years, buying might not make sense for you because of the transactional costs associated with both buying and selling. On the purchase side you will have closing costs. These include an inspection, an appraisal, title insurance, and loan fees. When you go to sell a home, you have to pay a real estate commission plus other fees, even if you are selling for a profit. To cover both the buy and sell costs, a good rule of thumb is to imagine taking nearly 7 percent off the purchase price the minute you

When Buying Makes Sense

In many parts of the country, it makes more financial sense to purchase than to rent. Zillow has some great statistics regarding renting versus buying in major metro areas around the country. They are called the breakeven horizon. Zillow reviews average mortgage payments based on home values and current interest rates, and compares those numbers to rental prices for comparable homes in that market. For instance, the stats take the mortgage payment on a three-bedroom home in Cleveland and determine how long it would take to break even had the rental payment gone toward a down payment.

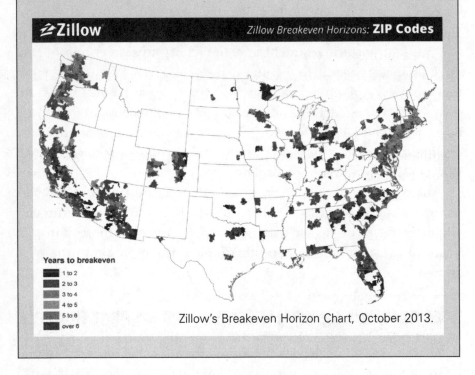

Zillow's Breakeven Horizon Chart, October 2013.

close, almost as if you are driving a brand-new Volkswagen off the lot. This is a conservative number, and it may vary by location. However, there are costs to entering and exiting the market that you must factor in before you start.

Therefore, think seriously about the following questions. Do you like the town where you live, but you don't love it? Do you have the itch to move out of your hometown and start anew? Do you miss your family in the Midwest? Conversely, do you wish that you lived farther away from Mom and Dad? Have you developed allergies in the area to which you just relocated? Is your company growing and opening up new offices in other places where you would rather live? Has your boss ever broached the idea about accepting a transfer? Have there been layoffs, a slew of bad quarterly reports, or the infiltration of a tough business competitor? Have the kids left home? Are you expecting the kids to come back? Whatever the situation, if you simply can't imagine yourself living in this area for at least five years, you might reconsider making a purchase.

Many people who purchase do so because they want to put down some roots and solidify their attachment to a community. They are involved or interested in local politics. They volunteer for local charities or are active in philanthropy. Sometimes they closely follow the restaurant or entertainment scene, or they have children in the public schools and are active in the school association. These people are establishing friendships and networks in the community. If they have the financial wherewithal, have stable jobs, and are creditworthy, they would be good candidates for home buying.

On the other hand, if this just a crash pad community where you are doing your time until something better comes along, then don't think that buying is a good idea, even if it is financially alluring. In the housing boom years, when it seemed like increases in value were par

---

🏠 **EXPERT**   Greg McBride, Vice President,
Senior Financial Analyst, Bankrate.com

"When people consider home buying, it's important to avoid limiting their financial flexibility by buying a house before they are truly ready," Greg told me. "Ideal homeowner candidates have a track record of saving money, pay their bills on time, and have a considerable down payment. A bank will find home owners favorable when they financially aren't biting off more than they can chew."

for the course or expected, it might have made sense. But I am telling you that in the next generation real estate, you simply can't count on it. You've got to play it safe.

Are you there only for a job? Is this somewhere you've been for many years just because? As we get older, we tend to want to gravitate toward our roots. It's common for people today to go off to college, move out of the community where they grew up, spread their wings, and find a new life, but consider whether over time, you might miss home. Have these internal conversations with yourself before entering the housing market.

If you are new to the area, buying probably will not make sense for you. It always makes sense to rent first. Why? Often people will move across the country or across their state for a job transfer, for a life change, or to join a spouse or partner. Until you've lived in an unknown territory for some time, you cannot know if the community suits you. The excitement of the adventure tends to get the best of these types of clients, and the emotions of the new opportunity sweep away their practical needs. Some people become caught up in the excitement of discovering a new community that they want to dive into immediately. Buying a piece of real estate is not the way to do it.

My client Sam moved to San Francisco for a job transfer in the Silicon Valley, some 30 miles south of the city. All of Sam's friends lived in the north end of town. It was close to the jogging trails and had great access to the Golden Gate Bridge National Park. However, was it practical to own a home in the north part of town? What Sam didn't realize, but quickly learned after just one month, was that the commute through the city of San Francisco, just to get to the freeway in the south part of town, would be at least 25 minutes each way, every day. After nine months in San Francisco and on the job, Sam called to say he was ready to buy—on the south end of town.

Lesson learned: You need time to learn a new area. You don't know where you will spend your time, what house of worship you will join, where your kids' friends will live, and so on. When moving to a new place, it simply makes sense to rent first. Learn the area, get to know it, and get to know how you fit into the community. You don't know what you don't know, so you need to take some time to learn. Making a home purchase prematurely could not only cost you financially but could also have a horrible effect on your life, both practically and emotionally.

In general, a move to someplace new brings up all kinds of uncertainty. Moving across the street can be stressful enough for many people. However, discovering a new town, taking on a new job, and choosing schools, not to mention the chaos of planning, packing up, and unpacking, can be stressful enough. As you plan the move, you will likely have so many things on your mind. Will I like it there? How will I deal with the weather? How will the children deal with the transition? I don't know anyone there. How will I meet people? What if I am taking the wrong job? Maybe in preparing for the move, you are in the process of selling your current home. There is so much uncertainty when moving to a new place that adding a home purchase into the equation will add unnecessary stress.

If you sense your job might not be secure, buying might not make sense for you. After the financial collapse of 2008, I saw so many folks stuck with mortgages and tax payments after losing their jobs. To make matters worse, the real estate market unraveled before their very eyes. I always ask buyers about their professions and what they do for a living. For people who work for themselves, I ask, "How long have you been self-employed? Is the business established? Where do you get your customers from, and are those referrals solid? How are your expenses? Are you saving money?" For folks who work at a company or for someone else, the questions are usually, "Are you happy in your job? Do you like your boss? Is it a good company? Is there room for advancement?" Asking these questions for yourself will prompt you to think deeply about your employment situation and take stock of not only your happiness in your current job, but also of job security.

DOES BUYING A HOME MAKE SENSE FOR ME EMOTIONALLY?

If you need more control, buying might make sense for you. Aside from the tax benefit, there is the obvious benefit of being free to make changes to your home. Absent the restrictions of a landlord, homeowners are free to create their dream homes. Inspired by cable television shows and magazines, new homebuyers can relish in picking out new appliances for their kitchen, experimenting online with paint colors for their bedrooms, or planning an entire home expansion. Love seeing a spa-like bath on TV? It, too, can be yours. Living in a cramped apartment without any room for storage? A new home with your very own basement *is* possible. Can you imagine a full-blown home automation system or a built-in entertainment system that you can control from your mobile phone or tablet? You can install these in a home that you own, without needing permission from a landlord.

If you are in a long-term relationship, buying might make sense. If you are in a relationship and considering a purchase together, is the relationship new? Do you live together currently? Have you ever lived together? Getting involved in someone's personal situation can be intrusive and the conversation tricky and uncomfortable. However, as a real estate agent, I sometimes serve as a therapist or even a marriage counselor. A new relationship takes time to build. It doesn't happen overnight. I always encourage younger people in newer relationships to consider renting and living together first.

I once sold a condominium to a couple in their mid-20s who had married after two years of dating. Ted was on the commercial side of the real estate business, understood the benefits of real estate and wanted to own, and was hell-bent on buying a place. He was aggressive and pushed ahead, while his wife, Jordee, didn't seem excited or interested in the prospect. No apartment I showed Jordee stood out, and she simply lacked motivation to invest emotionally. When the time came to write an offer on a home, I saw how disengaged she was and asked her, "Do you have any issues with this place?" She answered no, so with a pit in my stomach, I presented the offer anyway.

Three months after closing, Jordee called. "We're getting a divorce," she said. "We need you to come over and talk about selling."

This was the worst call and the worst meeting I ever had. Jordee said that Ted had pushed her to buy a place because they were having marital problems. In some ways, she admitted, they thought that if they bought a place together, the issues would go away and that a home would solidify the relationship.

Although this may be an extreme (but true) example, it could cut in many different ways. On the flip side, imagine a couple that has been dating for five years. One is ready to buy, but the other is not there yet. Imagine if one-half of the couple decides to buy a small one-bedroom because she wants to get in the market. What happens if marriage happens within one year and they end up moving in together? The couple could quickly outgrow that small apartment. Might it make more sense to save up some money and put a more long-term plan in place?

Nobody likes to be the one in the relationship to have the talk about the future, but when thinking about investing in a home, I am afraid this is one talk you cannot afford to avoid. Imagine your relationship, and therefore your housing situation, two, four, and five years from now. Don't be afraid to ask yourself or your partner the tough questions. Don't feel pressured by your spouse, or even worse, by yourself. Listen to that little voice inside.

What If Things Change?

Enough can happen in one year's time that will help you empirically figure out what is right for you. What if you hate the job? What happens if your old employer tries to lure you back, or your presence in a new town gets you a job offer with another company? What if you realize, as Sam did, that the commute is horrible? What if you simply do not like the town? What if you get homesick or a parent gets sick? What if your car breaks down? Could you afford to buy a new car? Could you afford public transportation if it's available? Buying is an awesome time in anyone's life, but smarter buying means you've exhausted every scenario, worst case or best, and are prepared to be accountable with a backup plan in case of fall out. Asking "What if?" is not intended to close the door but to hold it open long enough so that you can proceed with caution and confidence that it won't be slamming you in the face on moving day.

NEXT GENERATION REAL ESTATE FACT: REAL ESTATE IS A LONG-TERM INVESTMENT

If you are less concerned about a return on investment and more inter-ested in planting roots, then you are ready to buy. In the sky-high real estate market in the early 2000s, when home values increased as much as 20 percent in less than one year, many buyers felt a fever to get in the game. These buyers were practically guaranteed a quick return on their investment. Unfortunately, this was not reality, and we saw an inflated market take a turn for the worse and take many homeowners down with it.

Real estate was never meant to be a place to make a quick buck. It is a place to live first and an investment second. You should want to purchase because you intend to plant roots, make memories, and build a life around a new home for the next 5 to 10 years. Doing small improvements, large renovations, or even taking up gardening allows you to nest in your home, settle in, and get comfortable. These are the emotional benefits of homeownership that can't be bought or sold, and nobody can take these experiences away from you.

So much information is available to us now that it's hard not to be enticed by tracking home values. However, monetary value is not something you should be concerned with on a weekly, monthly, or even yearly basis. Sure, it's nice to know that your neighbor's home sold for a great price, but if that seems to be your sole motivator, con-sider staying out of the market until more of a holistic need emerges.

If you have the littlest amount of doubt about your personal situa-tion as it pertains to housing, it may be better to keep renting until these things are more certain, until you have the confidence you need in your personal and professional life. If you feel pretty stable about your practical, financial, and emotional situation, then you're ready to begin your search online.

Virtual Real Estate:
Home Buying Starts Online

Google your hometown and the word *real estate*, and you'll get hundreds of pages of real estate websites, listing photos, blogs, and real estate agent head shots—mine included! You can take virtual tours, receive offers for mortgages and just about anything else you can think of related (or not) to real estate in your town. This is enough information and response to overwhelm anyone who innocently dipped a toe in the water. With so much information out there, and with technology changing hour by hour, how do you begin your online home search? Who are the major players, and how should you break them all down? Who and what are relevant and trustworthy?

Most people begin their search organically, without an agent, and simply let some of the top online search results lead the way. It's like any Web search: You might assume the first few at the top of the page are the best, or your search can become like a Twitter rabbit hole, one in which you drop in without a parachute and then meander about, confused, exhausted, and about to go mad. Can you imagine there was once a world that didn't afford people this luxury?

Not too long ago, before the advent of the Internet, there existed a vanilla world in which online searches, individualized auto alerts, digital photos, virtual tours, and online floor plans didn't exist. As few as 15 years ago, it was rare that potential buyers could snoop around, observe a selling cycle, and scour listings on their tablet, all from the comfort of the living room.

Before such armchair buyers, people's first foray into the real estate world was in response to bunches of brightly colored balloons flailing on street corners next to a sign that read, "Open House." Of course, technology has changed everything drastically, and in terms of the real estate world, it has transformed not only the role of the agent, but also the way buyers buy. Today, instead of spending a weekend morning doing drive-bys of random open houses, buyers are afforded more focus, streamline, and control. In March 2013, the California Association of Realtors conducted a survey of 1,400 home-owners who had bought in the previous six months. They found that most homebuyers used the Internet and researched independently before contacting an agent for assistance (see the figure below).

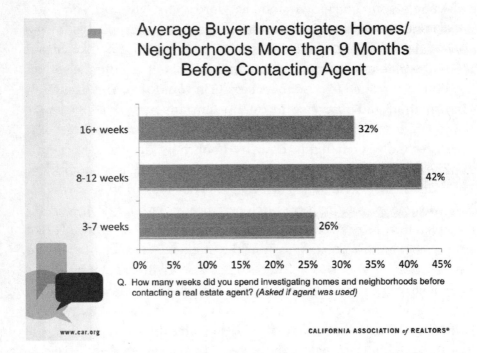

Average Buyer Investigates Homes/ Neighborhoods More than 9 Months Before Contacting Agent

- 16+ weeks — 32%
- 8-12 weeks — 42%
- 3-7 weeks — 26%

Q. How many weeks did you spend investigating homes and neighborhoods before contacting a real estate agent? *(Asked if agent was used)*

www.car.org

CALIFORNIA ASSOCIATION *of* REALTORS®

There are tools today that make it so that smart buying begins with the right online search. However, before I get to the best uses of these tools that put buyers in the driver's seat with their agents riding shotgun, it is important to consider how far we've come.

NEXT GENERATION REAL ESTATE FACT: DATA COLLECTION IN OLDEN DAYS

The art of the open house used to act somewhat like a moth to a flame. Once potential buyers realized the benefit of seeing what they could get for their money (or not), they were drawn to view more houses. Ultimately, the open house was a vehicle that provided buyers tangible data with which they could make informed and confident decisions.

If you have never conducted a job search using the classified ads, then the next data collection vehicle will really seem antiquated—the real estate section of the local Sunday newspaper. Unless buyers were working closely with a real estate agent, these listings were the only source of information buyers could track. With such few options, real estate agents used to hold all of the cards, and buyers *needed* a real estate agent to *find* the listings, conduct and provide research on the local market, and offer advice about how to get started. Because he or she had information, the agent was the gatekeeper of the listing; therefore, a relationship between buyer and agent began much earlier in the process than it does today.

Today the search process begins online. Although you might think that this is to the dismay of the agent, I'm here to tell you that buyer awareness in fact makes for an effective collaboration that can move you from the preparatory data collection phase to the real doing with the help of a professional partner, your agent.

MEET THE REAL ESTATE SYNDICATORS

Founded in 2006 by the people responsible for online travel websites like Expedia and Hotwire, Zillow.com made waves with its automated valuation model called the Zestimate. Zillow, followed by its peers, Trulia.com and Realtor.com, set out to revolutionize the real estate industry by collecting metadata based on public records to estimate the value of homes (otherwise known as automated valuation models or AVMs), whether on the market or not. They made information about homes, listings, and sales more easily accessible to the consumer and lifted the veil on a seemingly proprietary industry.

Known as real estate syndicators, Zillow, Trulia, and Realtor.com are not agents or brokerages; they are portals that collect listings *from* a variety of sources including real estate agents and broker websites as well as multiple listing services (MLS) from around the country. Essentially, these syndicators provide a one-stop shop for home listings by concentrating the listings to one website location.

For instance, a homebuyer in Toledo, Ohio, who is beginning a search most likely will open a search engine and simply type in the words *Toledo real estate*. The first search results that will appear will typically be homes for sale on the syndicator's websites. This is not because they have the most access to inventory but because of marketing. These companies have poured millions of dollars into search engine optimization (SEO) so that their websites come up first in searches. It's worked, for better or for worse, the worse being for local real estate agents and brokerages across the country that prefer their own listings pop up at the top of the page in a Google search.

Much like a single person who uses online dating to flirt with the idea of entering a committed relationship, syndicator's websites are a terrific spot for buyers to settle in for a while, especially when they know they are not quite ready to purchase a home, let alone contact an agent. I've had clients who had searched online for months before they ever reached out to me. Before we began our work together, these savvy buyers had tracked listings anonymously and watched them go from active to pending to closed. They basically watched the selling cycle in real time and started to learn about how their local market worked.

The syndicators offer map searches and filters that make it easy to navigate and search. You can search homes for sale, homes for rent, foreclosure homes, or homes that have recently sold, because they've incorporated data of the recorded sale prices from local town records offices. The listings are displayed easily, and the information for each listing is immediate and accessible and includes historical data. Buyers like to see that home they are interested in was actually listed two years ago but at a much higher price. Tracking history helps facilitate smarter buying.

ENTER THE ONLINE MLS

According to the National Association of Realtors, the MLS concept was born in the late part of the 19th century when agents met with one another to share listings. In the event an agent helped the listing agent unload the property, the brokers agreed to provide compensation. It was a formalized use of "I'll scratch your back if you scratch mine." Eventually, these incentives gave way to different forms of multiple listing services across the country. Before the computer, the MLS came in the form of large books that were printed every two weeks. The MLS was handed out only to local agents every two weeks. Slapped on its cover was, "For Members Only. Do Not Distribute." A seller would list a home with an agent, who would in turn get the property listed in these books and pore over the books with his or her buyer clients.

Given the changing face of the Internet, these MLS books eventually took the form of password-protected websites that agents use to access the database and interact with each other. The MLS provides the real estate communities with a great database it can use to create reports, interact with and send listings to clients, and pull comparable sales. It's where agents can go to look at new listings, do research for similar properties, get the pulse of the market at any one time, and most important, collaborate with their buyer clients about the knowledge and information they collect.

When you enter the market as a buyer, your real estate agent will almost definitely not be the same agent as the one on the seller's side. A buyers' agent (your agent) helps buyers learn the market and understand comparable home values and advocates for buyers in the negotiation process. Although agents might be representing and advocating two different sides of the transaction, they are not pitted against one another. In fact, the MLS makes it possible for the sellers' and buyers' agents to share their listings, solicit each other's clients, and make great matches. The MLS allows market transparency across multiple real estate brokerages in a community.

If I have a great listing for a three-bedroom home, it is shared with another agent, who can present that home as an option to her buyer client. Rarely are these listings for just one agent. Rather, they are shared listings for all brokerages and their agents to freely market to their buyer clients. Real estate was always meant to be collaborative among agents. Sure, there is some competition, but the agents work together in a local community to help facilitate the home buying and selling process for their clients.

The biggest consumer misconception is that if you look at a local brokerage's website, you are only going to see its listings, not all the listings of the competing brokerages, and are therefore not getting a true sense of what's available in your community. However, most local real estate brokerage websites actually display not only their firm's listings but also the listings of the competing firms in town, who are also members of the local association of Realtors and the MLS. It is not just about exclusive listings, and here's why. One of the largest benefits of MLS is that it exchanges data and feeds local websites through an Internet Data Exchange (IDX). You can search any local website and have access to all the listings of all the local companies in the community. People don't typically know this. Because of great SEO and commercial marketing tools, such as apps and blogs, buyers are lured only to the syndicators, but all along IDX makes it possible for local listings to be even more accurate and up to date than Zillow, Trulia, and Realtor.com.

THE IDX

As a dues-paying member of the local association of Realtors, your local brokerage can access the public MLS listings, photos, descriptions, and basic data from the local MLS via an Internet Data Exchange, known as an IDX feed. Quite simply, when searching for listings on Broker A's website, you will likely see not only their listings but also the listings of Broker B's and many others. Because we all share listings via the IDX, you can actually visit one website and potentially see the listings of every company in town. You may see a listing of a home on one website, but somewhere down below it will say, "Listing courtesy of Brendon DeSimone, Paragon Real Estate

> **🏠 EXPERT   Spencer Rascoff, CEO of Zillow**
>
> Online searching has gone mobile. "On weekends, 70 percent of usage of Zillow is on mobile devices, and throughout the week, 60 percent of Zillow usage is mobile," said Spencer. "Fast-forward a few years and 80 or 90 percent will be on mobiles. And using Zillow on an iPad will give you the best experience. Zillow's tools can be used in conjunction with an agent, but buyers shouldn't leave the selection and home vetting to the agent. Nobody knows what you are interested in more than you do."

Group." It's a way of indicating that it's not the listing of the website you are on and giving credit to the other brokerage.

Thanks to the IDX, real estate brokerages cooperate and work together. Some call it coop-petition.

HOW TO GET THE MOST OUT OF THE SYNDICATOR'S SEARCH

Because the first result most buyers find when they search online is one of the syndicator's websites, it's likely that buyers will end up spending some time on them, largely in part because of their value-adds and features, which assist the home buyer in the research and discovery phase of their search.

Zillow, for example, has a feature called Make Me Move. This allows a homeowner to "claim" their home, even if it is not for sale, and list a price that would get them to sell. Often times, their Make Me Move price is a little higher than what the market would bear. But, I know sellers who successfully sold their home off the market, as a result of their Make Me Move listing.

Zillow also has a feature called the Zestimate, on just about every home in America. A Zestimate is an estimated value of the home, and to calculate it, Zillow takes into account prior sales information for that home, if available, and neighboring similar homes, as well as the local city or town data about it (number of bedrooms and baths, square footage, property taxes, etc.), and comes up with an estimate, of the home's value. The other syndicators and websites have followed suit, creating their own automated valuation models (AVMs) to come up with an estimate of that home's value. (See more in Chapter 9 about using these tools in the negotiation process.) Currently, the syndicators have built smartphone and tablet apps to allow buyers to search listings on the go. For example, you can use your phone's GPS to look at nearby homes for sale or recently sold homes.

Buyers can use these apps in conjunction with their Sunday open house tour. Did you like a home you saw at an open house in a new neighborhood and think it was a good price? You can open up one of these apps and quickly, in real time, get a sense for what is for sale, what recently sold in the neighborhood, or what other homes are having open houses that day. All of the data that you can find on the website is generally available in an easy-to-use interface right on your mobile device.

🏠 EXPERT   **Maxwell Ryan, Apartment Therapy,**
www.apartmenttherapy.com

Just as online real estate blogs and syndicators help connect a large audience interested in real estate, the blog Apartment Therapy, connects people to resources as well as to one another. Maxwell says, "People want to make their homes better. At Apartment Therapy, we give them the tools they need to do it. Decorators tend to gravitate to the high end, but online we can stay within the broad middle of people who care about their homes but are not going the route of private decorating services. We inspire DIY projects and ideas, creative and cost-effective ways to enhance their rooms, furniture, and even outdoor spaces. We are the place to go online to make homes more beautiful, organized, and happy, connecting people with problems with people with solutions."

The syndicator's websites have pages and pages of useful real estate content in the form of Q&As, blogs, advice columns, and tons of great content about buying and selling a home. More recently, Zillow has introduced "Zillow Digs," a home renovation and remodeling section for folks who've taken the plunge and now want to renovate.

Finally, you can find an agent on a syndicator's because agents buy advertising on the websites. When these syndicator's websites display listings, there tend to be photos of agents alongside these listings. (These are not always the actual agents who represent the sellers or the listings. Sometimes they are advertisements purchased by local agents, who pay the syndicators to put their faces, phone numbers, e-mails, and other contact information alongside listings in certain zip codes.) You can read agent reviews, make your own comments about an experience with an agent, and read agents' posted tips and advice, deal information, activity, and real estate philosophies.

NEXT GENERATION REAL ESTATE FACT: THE SYNDICATORS ARE NOT PERFECT

The information on the syndicators' websites can be inaccurate and outdated. For instance, a home may have sold already but is listed as active. This could lead to disappointment to buyers, who are relying on one of these websites as their sole research vehicle. This is precisely why a homebuyer needs an agent. Technology is very helpful, but it may not always be the most reliable. These websites, with all of their tools, features, and content are undeniably awesome, but they shouldn't replace working with an agent. Conjunction is key.

Additionally, there may be delays in uploading new listings. An agent may input a new listing, complete with description and photos into his or her local MLS on Monday morning, but it won't sync with syndicators' websites for a day. If you are a serious buyer, who's active in the market, you might miss this home because of this type of information lag.

Because they rely on automated feeds as well as a variety of websites and databases on the Web, it's nearly impossible for syndicators to get every piece of information accurately displayed online, but they sure try. They work closely to partner with local MLS's and encourage real estate agents and brokerages to contact them directly to update listings and verify the information. Syndicators want to be partners with the real estate community and have reached out to work closely to deliver consumers the best possible home search experience.

Many agents believe that the AVMs don't accurately display true market value of a home. A buyer who is looking online for the first time or is seriously interested in a home for sale may see the Zestimate is 10 percent lower than what the seller has listed the home for and therefore deem the home overpriced; or, what's worse, the Zestimate number might be 10 percent higher than the listing price, and the buyer concludes it's a great deal. The AVM is not based on anything more than public records and owner input. A good local agent is the only one who will be able to help buyers (and sellers) determine the true market value, which, as Chapter 5 will discuss, is determined by much more than listing history, criteria, and other objective data. An AVM is only an estimate but still a great starting point to get an idea of how a home is priced.

🏠 EXPERT   **Lockhart Steele, founder of Curbed**

According to Lockhart, Curbed is where education merges with entertainment. "We receive Dozens and dozens of e-mails a day, from 'what are my rights,' all the way to funny urban stories, like "I saw someone selling meat out of the backseat of a car. When our readers start reading Curbed as part of their home search, we provide ambience to their learning. If you read it every day, it will make you laugh more than it will tell you how to negotiate a closing, although we have that information too. The main point is that because we deal in local markets, readers get more comfortable about what things costs and learn how to make comparisons. It's an education every day, without it being an education."

It's my opinion that, for buyers who are just starting out in the process, the syndicators' websites are a fine way to test the waters and look at dozens of photographs and listings to get a general understanding of price, inventory, and types of homes for sale in an area.

Because the next generation of real estate starts online, I always encourage buyers at all stages of the process to look at all types of websites. You have to start somewhere, so it might as well be with the game rules, which are sprawled out in interactive, informative, and unique ways all over the Web. Knowing the rules of the game before you get on the field is a win-win for both buyer and agent.

Team Sport: Why You Still Need a Real Estate Agent

With so much information online nowadays, many buyers don't quite understand why they need a real estate agent. Surely, the Internet has cut out the intermediary in other industries, such as travel. If you can search for homes using syndicate websites and search words, why on earth would you need an agent? It's a valid question and one that we hear all the time. In fact, it's a question that Sara and her husband, Gordon, asked when they first met me at a showing for a house on which they were interested in making an offer.

Sara called after being referred to me by a coworker. "My husband and I have been fishing online for a home for about three months now, and we finally found one we think we want to make an offer on," Sara said.

After I met with them at the property, which Sara and Gordon loved, we had coffee to discuss the next steps. At this point, though, Sara and Gordon did everything on their own, so they wondered why they should work with me when all I did was meet them at the property.

But not so fast. Upon further discussion, Sara and Gordon revealed that this was the first home that they'd seen and liked and, of even more interest, that this was the first home they had visited together. After further probing I wanted to understand how much experience Sara and Gordon had in the current market. I wanted to get a sense of how far along they were in the process. Had they seen X, Y, and Z properties, which recently sold in the neighborhood? These were comparable sales that would help inform them all on the value of this home.

Other questions I asked Sara and Gordon included where they currently lived and how long they'd lived there. They lived on the other end of town, and the property visit was the first time they'd seen the new neighborhood. The kitchen in the subject property needed some work. Also I knew, because of my experience with the area, that the list price was atypically low. Suspecting more than a motivated seller, I asked the listing seller's agent, with whom I'd worked before, for the story. "The home has some termite issues and the plumbing is old galvanized steel," explained the seller's agent. Knowing how eager Sara and Gordon were to write an offer, I asked them to expect a hefty renovation, from anywhere between $20,000 and $50,000.

The couple was drawn to the price and location. The price seemed too good to be true, and I discovered that it was. I recognized the look of disappointment in their faces, but saw the glimmer of excitement as well. They had caught the bug. By beginning passively snooping around, they were able to cross the threshold into serious territory and move out from behind their smartphones and tablets. Now, they were really in the market.

I sensed that Sara and Gordon were comfortable with my knowledge and trusted me. I had just told them the honest truth about why that home wouldn't work for them. They had assumed a real estate agent would just want to close the deal, but now they were confident that aligning themselves with me would help them get the job done. Our newly formed team agreed to step back and discuss the market, the home-buying process, and loan preapproval, and we began to work together to find an even better home.

Nine months later, Sarah and Gordon wrote offers on three other homes, none of which were accepted. Able to stay positive and learn from the other dead deals, a new offer was finally accepted. Their new home—a town house condo—is twice as big as the initial house. It took them some time and was a bit of an evolution, but in the end they felt that having an agent was like having a watchdog on their side 24/7, like a pair of eyes that was trained to see what their eyes couldn't. This is not propaganda that says we agents are the all-knowing, omnipotent ones. However, when it comes to betting your entire hand on one big transaction in the game of life, as is the case for so many first-time homebuyers, wouldn't you want a dealer who knows how the game is won?

At the end of the transaction, Sara and Gordon figured out that, throughout the nine months together, I had completed 10 other sales. It hadn't occurred to her that they weren't my only clients. It made sense now why using an agent was so valuable. She realized that by doing this over and over with buyers and sellers, agents earn their keep and gain an incredible amount of intellectual capital.

★

The next generation of real estate doesn't look at the role of the agent as an intermediary. Instead, agents are allies. Although there is nothing wrong with having an abundance of accessible information at your fingertips, there is sometimes a downside—lots of noise. Aligning with an agent helps you cut through the extras that sidetrack you from your original mission so that you make the best financial, practical, and emotional decisions for smarter buying.

WHAT TO EXPECT FROM A REAL ESTATE AGENT

In the case of the majority of buyers, there always comes a time when a wave of doubt will test them. *Is this the right house? Is this priced right? Is this too good to be true?* Despite the fact that buyers today can read comments about the property on a blog, research the home's previous sales, look up tax records, and even use mortgage calculators to run the numbers, most buyers decide the investment is too steep to go it alone. Only when buyers move beyond the idea that an agent is there simply to show the listing can they expect more from the ally that they now call their agent. Now that you know you need one, what should an agent be capable of?

Good Agents Have Their Fingers on the Pulse of the Local Playing Field

Real estate agents do dozens of transactions each year. While you spend your day working in your profession, good local agents are shoring up their knowledge base with vast amounts of market information and equity. This means they know the players and other agents in town, how they work, what their reputations are, and how they like to do business.

Buyers could never know that Agent Joe has a history of pricing his sellers' listings too low and that they always immediately sell, that Agent Mary tends to work exclusively in one neighborhood and despises open houses, or that Agent Suzy has a legal background and is strict about disclosures. However, a good local agent would know specifics such as these and many more.

An active local agent can tell you that Agent Joe does not have a good reputation and has had ethical complaints brought up against him by the local association of Realtors. Having insider knowledge such as this, especially when in the presence of a prospective home you love, helps you tread cautiously.

Although there is so much information online, when it actually comes to the house that the buyer ends up buying, it's their agent who finds it. Once connected and working closely with a good local agent, you know they are keeping a lookout for listings while you go about your life. As a part of their 2013 home-buyer survey of 1,400 new homeowners, the California Association of Realtors found this to be true as illustrated in the figure on the following page.

Good Agents Are Members of the Local Board of Realtors and Have Access to the Local Multiple Listing Service (MLS)

Every local board of Realtors agrees to collaborate by sharing information, business tools, education, and codes of ethics. Ninety-nine percent of the time, you will meet an agent who is a member of the local board of Realtors. What this tells you is that the agent is dedicated to advancing his or her career knowledge while enhancing your home buying or selling experience.

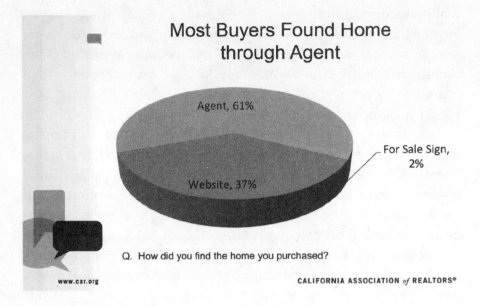

Most Buyers Found Home through Agent

Agent, 61%

For Sale Sign, 2%

Website, 37%

Q. How did you find the home you purchased?

www.car.org

CALIFORNIA ASSOCIATION *of* REALTORS®

Good Agents Work with Other Good Local Professionals

From attorneys to engineers, inspectors, escrow officers, and many others, good agents have a network of professionals they consult to help them help you complete the purchase of your home. For instance, if you're buying a home that is over 100 years old and needs to be inspected as part of the process, are you going to call an inspector out of the phone book? That's not very Next Generation. However, your agent likely has a great inspector or two, who, in a market with limited inventory, can get out to see the place within a day or two.

Imagine that you are in a competitive market, and the seller accepts your offer. However, there are people hot on your tail. You need to have your inspection within the first few days of getting your offer accepted. Who would you call? Would you go through Yelp and look at reviews? What if the inspector you reached out to was on vacation? Then whom would you call? This is an important part of the transaction. You have to make sure you thoroughly inspect the place. A good local agent will have a relationship with a handful of reputable local inspectors. Having done business in this community for a while, the inspector knows this agent and relies on him or her for business. In a pinch to get an inspection completed before someone swoops it out from someone else? A good local agent will whisk you through this process.

Good Agents Have the Inside Track on the Market

Broker caravans, or broker open house tours, are opportunities for agents to invite each other into their listings to preview potential places for their buyer clients. They are basically open houses for agents, and you should expect your agent to attend them. This is a great way for a good agent to not only keep up with the market but also get the inside scoop on the circumstances of the home sale. You may enter the market in March and want to write an offer on the home of your dreams. The same house, two doors down, may have sold last fall for 25 percent less, but you don't have any idea why. A good local agent will know that the house was sold because of a

---

🏠 EXPERT   Pete Flint, CEO of Trulia

"Buyers today are presented with much more information than ever before about market conditions, neighborhoods, schools, crime statistics, commutes, as well as large photos and details about millions of homes. There is more information available to buyers now than at any other time in the history of real estate," Pete told me. "Savvy buyers are well informed because they know exactly where to find the information they need. But the challenge now for the industry is to help buyers wade through the massive amount of information that is now available. That's why, while much has changed, working with a smart and experienced broker or agent is still essential for people who want to have the best home buying experience."

divorce, that there was a big crack in the foundation, and that it sold to an all-cash buyer as is. Behind-the-scenes information such as this can really serve you when it's time to make your offer on the right home for the right price. We'll address this more in Chapter 8.

Early in my career I met a Silicon Valley engineer in his mid-20s, named Brian, who was interested in seeing a loft in San Francisco's South of Market district. The listing agent was on vacation, and I was covering for him. I knew the loft well. Overpriced, it had been on the market for an extensive period of time. After he saw the place, Brian said that he didn't want or need to use an agent. He was tech savvy, and he had all kinds of property searches going online. Brian decided that he knew the loft was a great deal and that he was going to make an offer.

After the showing I e-mailed Brian an unsolicited list of some comparable lofts in the area. Sure, the price per square foot seemed great compared to the rest of the area, but there was a catch. This loft was at the back of the complex, and a local developer had bought up the land behind it. He would likely build because this area was experiencing huge growth. If this happened, the loft would lose light and views. Although this information surely would have come out in the disclosure review process, Brian, without a good local agent, would have spent a lot of his time searching the comps online, looking at recent sales, and scratching his head as to why this was such a great deal. He may have even gone as far as making an offer, only to find out in the disclosure review about the possible worst-case scenario. Luckily for him, I saved him time and energy.

When agents stay on top of listings, they can also become privy to homes that are not yet on the market. Real estate agent offices generally have frequent sales and marketing meetings at which agents discuss the market and the details of events week to week. This is when agents will announce new sales or the number of offers received on a sale in a hot market. Agents will also review price reductions of homes that have been sitting for a while. Additionally, these meetings include announcements of upcoming listings that are not yet on the market or haven't yet hit the MLS, which allows agents to get up-to-the-minute market intelligence and share it with their buyers.

Good Agents Want to Meet with You before Working Together

Sometimes buyers think they are ready to buy, and practically and financially, they are. They're tired of paying too much in rent and have a good-sized down payment ready to go. However, emotionally, they may not be ready to give up relying on the good old landlord or to commit to a home, new commute, or reduction in a savings account. These may be subconscious issues that typically go unrevealed when buyers make initial contact with an agent.

Though it's tempting, easy to do, and often the case, we recommend against an agent and buyer jumping into a relationship during an open house, via e-mail, or online. We advise buyers, particularly first-time buyers, to sit down and meet with an agent and talk about real estate, the market, and their current situation. A good agent will want to have you come to his or her office, and you should expect an agent to do more listening than talking. This is an agent's chance to be formally interviewed for the job. You, as a buyer, should make it clear that you are getting more serious about entering the market and are now talking to agents about building a relationship. You shouldn't disclose this as a threat that you are interviewing multiple agents, although some people do that. Instead, convey in some way that you are serious about finding a home and want to collaborate with the best local agent in the process.

Sitting down with an agent early on benefits both the buyer and the agent. This is someone you are going to be working closely with. Do you have same communication style? Do you think the agent shares your values and would be looking out for you? You have to make sure that you jive with this person, that you find him or her trustworthy and competent to advise you and take you through what can be a very stressful and emotional process. It's not always about how much experience an agent has but rather how likeable he or she is. Additionally, some buyers may want to move slowly. They may be more analytical, may like to mull things over, and won't work well with a fast-moving, fast-talking agent. Other buyers may appreciate the fast approach, and the analytical and methodical thinker may frustrate them. Meeting with an agent is also a great opportunity for the agent to interview you, the buyer. It's helpful for an agent to know where you are in the process, how much experience you have, and what your timing is. Some agents may not have the time to educate new buyers or work with them too early in the process. If good agents sense this, they will give you homework to help you start and keep the door open for when you get serious.

If you find yourself unwilling to meet and sit down with an agent to speak about the home buying process and the possibility of working together, sit on the sidelines for a bit longer. An experienced agent will be aware of this reality; a trustworthy agent will be honest about that recommendation, if it's an appropriate one. Words matter. Putting your thoughts, ideas, values, and emotions out there for the first time will help you sort through where you are and how far you want to go in your home buying process.

HOW TO FIND AN AGENT

There is no right or wrong way to meet an agent. Here are some of the most common ways we think you can partner with someone who is right for you and your situation: referrals, open houses, online, and ads.

Referrals

The best way to go find a good local agent is through a referral of a friend, family member, or coworker who recently (within the past year) bought or sold a home. I emphasize *recently* because markets move and change so quickly that someone who helped your cousin sell her home 10 years ago may not be the absolute best person to assist you in buying a home today.

Agents work mainly on referrals; therefore, satisfied clients become our bread and butter instead of the commission on the sale. If I was your agent, and I was unresponsive or just didn't seem to have your best interests in mind, the bad news could get back to the person who referred me to you. The last thing I wants is to lose this source of referrals.

If you have ever referred someone, you can see how potentially damaging this relationship could be to an agent. You don't want to swear on a hairdresser's talents and then have your friend call you, crying because she has pink hair. You'd feel responsible, and you'd never refer that hairdresser again. The same would go for my business. If your newlywed friends hired me and thought I did a less-than-spectacular job, it would be a double whammy to my business. Talk about burning bridges. I'd lose those potential buyers plus the referral source—you!

The real estate agent you choose will be someone that you work intimately with for the next three, six, or nine months or, in some cases, for more than a year. You will take a call from this person at all hours of the day. For a high-level executive, this person may be the only one who gets past their assistant. Buying a home is an emotional and personal process. Many details are revealed along the way, and there are a variety of surprises and disappointments. Realizing all of this makes it imperative that you feel comfortable with this agent as a person and ally, primarily, even if he or she doesn't have the most knowledge and activity in your local real estate market.

If you don't mesh with your friend's referral or don't feel the agent is knowledgeable and versed in your specific criteria and situation, stop. Don't assume that you will automatically love this agent as much as your friend or coworker did.

Everyone's real estate experience is different. Some people are more hands on; others, more hands off. It's not always the best fit and that's okay. Just realize that up front and don't move ahead. Plan B is right around the corner.

Plan B: The Open House

Going to open houses is a great way not only to get a feel for the market and see homes that you like but also to interview agents. Use these open houses as opportunities to gauge what kind of agent personality type and professional style might work best for you. Ask agents open-ended questions, including, "How's the market?" Try to engage them and understand their experience level. Ask them what neighborhoods they work in. A good agent will engage you first by asking you questions. You should never feel obligated to sign in or give your contact information. If you feel like the agent is pushing you to write it down and refuses to take no for an answer, either before or after you see a home, give a fake name, number, and e-mail. Only in the case of luxury homes will an agent insist on having your contact information for security reasons. At the end of the day, it's unlikely there will be an open house for a $14 million listing anyway.

The next generation buyer may not be the type to be chatty with agents at an open house. You might prefer to walk through anonymously and keep to yourself. At any one open house with 10 buyers, it's likely that only three or four will speak to the agent at all. Of those three or four, two might ask a question, and one may be more communicative. Some may be tentative about entering the buying phase, or they could be further along but still may be interested in staying independent. Good agents know that people approach their housing situation in the same way that they approach their business and professional lives. A good agent will find out what that style is and adapt his or hers to meet the comfort levels of the prospective buyer client.

Many times the agent who is hosting the open house is not necessarily the agent who is representing the seller. Because some agents will have multiple listings at one time, they simply cannot be in two (or more) places at one time. This is a great opportunity for an agent, who wants to meet new buyers, to step in and conduct the open house on behalf of the listing agent. Called the showing agent, this person can now interface and connect with potential new clients. I actually started my business by doing other people's open houses. On Sundays, I was out there with zeal, and my future clients appreciated that about me. At the end of the day, they decided their comfort level with an agent superseded a résumé .

I want you to know this fact in the event an agent at an open house can't answer a question about the property (for example, how old the roof is, how long the sellers have lived there, or how big the attic is). The showing agent may not know this because it is not their listing, but a good agent will take your name, number, or e-mail and follow up to get you the answer.

Online

Even though you might not want to chat up agents at open houses, you could very well be comfortable connecting with real estate agents online. I've been known to e-mail with people I've never met. Sometimes exchanges can go on for a few weeks. You may have a question about a property, and you should feel free to e-mail the agent and ask a zillion questions. Years ago, nothing would be strange abut calling a phone number on a for sale sign, so there is nothing to shy away from in the next generation of real estate. Nowadays, agents' bios, most recent sales, and previous listings are all out there for the world to see, but taking the next step and inviting an e-mail exchange can offer you boatloads about the agent even while you are browsing. Going through agents' real estate websites and following them on Twitter or their Facebook pages are other surefire ways to get a sense of who they are, how they work, and whether they'd be a good fit. Maybe you did get referrals for agents from your coworkers. First things first, look them up, see their track records, read their bios, and take a look at their past listings and social media.

> **🏠 EXPERT**   Spencer Rascoff, CEO of Zillow
>
> "In addition to learning what's for sale, days on market, and a home's worth, Zillow's users can read reviews of real estate agents," Spencer told me. "On Zillow right now, there are more than 250,000 reviews of agents."

NEXT GENERATION REAL ESTATE FACT: THE ADVENT OF AGENT ADVERTISING

So far I've covered three ways to find an agent: referrals, open houses, and online. This last way is the newest and certainly a popular choice by next generation real estate professionals—advertising on real estate syndication websites. I give ads a thumbs-up because they're a great tool when looking to stay local and when you need an agent with expertise in a particular zip code. A local agent, strong in one town or neighborhood, may pay for advertising to get more buyer or seller clients. In days gone by, maybe agents placed their ads on grocery store shopping carts, on the sides of busses, in movie theaters, or in the real estate sections of the local Sunday newspapers or penny savers. You still see all of this today, and some of it works.

However, the Internet has enabled agents to advertise their services in a more targeted way, which has a better return on the investment of the cost of the ad. To attract clients, agents place ads on some of the syndicate websites because this is where the majority of buyers today begin their search. It would make complete sense to advertise there because they can advertise in specific targeted areas, in which they have plenty of outreach and success.

If agents are particularly strong in one part of town, they can buy ads based on zip codes. Note that if you see a home that is interesting online, you might notice, off in the corner, a couple of head shots and language, such as, "Contact a buyer's agent," or "Connect with a local agent to find out more." Some consumers assume that the picture next to the listing is of the actual agent who is representing the seller. He or she might be, but I'd would be remiss if I didn't tell you that in other cases, the pictures are paid advertisements that have no direct association with the listing.

If you look closely below the property listing, the name of the listing brokerage or the agent appears. If you have serious questions or need detailed information about this listing, the three or four agents whose photos are there may not be the most knowledgeable about every little detail on this particular listing, but they could serve as impartial advisors to provide guidance about this house and others. Also, given that they are experts in this zip code, they could be great resources for information about the market in general. Through the years, I've heard many agents telling me about how many successful transactions they've completed or the dozens of buyers they've met, thanks to advertising on syndicate websites.

No matter what, trust your gut. Whether you meet by referral, online, through an ad, or at an open house, if you feel comfortable with this person and he or she seems to be knowledgeable, send an e-mail or take a business card. Let the relationship begin.

HOW TO WORK WELL WITH AN AGENT

Believe me, I wish the only things that I learned about my buyer clients were their salaries and credit scores, but that is just not the case. I've broken up fights between husbands and wives, been the shoulder for a pregnant woman to cry on, and been the vault in which people confess their true feelings about home buying.

Because home buying is such an emotionally charged activity, it is common for agents to find themselves smack dab in the middle of the drama. The husband loves the home, but the wife can't stand it. The girlfriend asks the sellers for a large credit based on an inspection report and risks losing the deal. The boyfriend is furious. One man wants a fixer-upper and sees the positive, but his partner doesn't. Two brothers have opposing visions on what kind of place to invest in. The point is, a great agent should expect these situations, know how to handle them, and act as a nonpartisan sounding board while helping the buyers stay focused on their original goals and priorities. If the time comes, a good agent will also know when to dump you.

Contrary to popular belief, not all real estate agents are desperate for a buck. The relationship is an intense one, and there are difficulties. Often, buyers lose a house and become upset with the market or its competitive nature, or they become frustrated with a seller or the results of an inspection. In these instances, they sometimes take it out on the agent. They may lash out, get mad at the agent, or blame him or her for something. We get it. Things get frustrating, and we are nothing more than the closest target. However, some buyers may either take it too far or begin to treat their agent unfairly. This is when the agent just doesn't believe it makes sense to continue working with certain people. The cons begin to outweigh the benefits for both agent and buyer.

A next generation buyer won't let this happen. If you met an agent through an online ad, through a referral, or at an open house, ask to meet in person. A good local agent will absolutely love the opportunity to meet with you.

UNDERSTANDING THE REAL ESTATE AGENT-BUYER RELATIONSHIP

Rarely is there any type of contractual agreement between a buyer and a buyer's real estate agent. Instead, both parties agree to work in good faith with the common goal of purchasing a home. From time to time a real estate agent will ask a buyer to sign a buyer-broker agreement, which binds the buyer to work with that agent, and that agent only, for a specified period. Most buyers shy away from this. The

---

Conversation Starters

Here are some smart questions to ask a potential agent:

1. What kind of mortgages do most people do in this community?

2. What do mortgage rates look like? Are they going up or down?

3. Is this a buyer's market or a seller's market?

4. Are some areas selling faster than others?

5. How long will it take me to find a home?

6. What is the number of days on market for the average home?

7. Are most homes selling well below the list price, at the list price, or over the list price?

Good local agents will have their pulse on the market and can give you the types of stats, data, and input that you just can't find online. Use this meeting to make sure that they are competent in the market and comfortable. If you aren't comfortable with the experience level or simply the personality of the agent, it's very easy to say that you are still working independently and that you haven't committed to a local agent.

home-buying process is fluid and can take a long time, and many buyers prefer to work independently for a while. I generally discourage buyers from entering into this type of agreement. Instead, I prefer them to work and communicate closely with their agent. Immediately after an initial meeting with potential buyer clients, I always explain to them how I am paid. We then agree to work together exclusively but have an open and communicative relationship. I always say, "If at any point it's not working out for either of us, let's just talk about it." Most of the time, the issue is small, and agreeing to anticipate glitches along the way helps keep it from escalating.

It's helpful to understand how real estate agents are paid and what goes on behind the scenes. Nearly all agents are commission only. That is, we don't receive salaries, and we are paid only once a real estate transaction closes. When it does close, a real estate agent commission, generally 6 percent, is paid by the seller. That commission is split between the seller's brokerage and the brokerage of the agent who brought the buyer to the transaction, so there is no cost to buyers to have an agent represent their interests in a transaction.

Having said this, be mindful that some agents will work with buyers for six months or even more, previewing and showing properties, reviewing disclosures, writing contracts, and doing inspections, and some buyers don't end up buying anything. Although it is par for the course for a self-employed agent, we do spend a lot of time and energy working with buyer clients. I once spent 18 months working with a couple. For a good while they were aggressively looking at properties and even presented an offer before going lukewarm again, only to return to the table, writing six more offers and entering into a contract once, only to have a poor inspection kill the deal. Then they decided to move out of state, so the home search was completely off.

With no paper or ink between them, the buyer and agent should enter into the partnership with good intentions and agree to work together in good faith. If you begin to feel as if the relationship is not working out, do not hesitate to let your agent know early in the process. Your relationship could begin like a whirlwind romance, a perfect fit, but as you get deeper in the process, things may change.

Because there isn't a legal document tying you together, either of you can choose to leave at any point. However, should you agree, at the end of the first meeting, that you will work together, you should commit to your agent exclusively while he or she focuses all of his or her energy toward your home search. As I will discuss next, getting immersed with multiple agents is a lose-lose situation for everybody.

THE MYTH OF MULTIPLE AGENTS

As you now know, agents are paid by commission only. Agents get paid only once a seller sells a home with them or a buyer purchases a home through us. It is possible that things happen, and buyers end up not buying with their agents. Situations such as my 18-month fiasco happen all of the time. One of the most frustrating things for an agent and a huge misconception among buyers is that they shouldn't have just one buyer's agent, that they need multiple agents to help them find a home. Multiple agents do not mean multiple results. This is worth repeating.

For starters, nearly every community across the country uses an MLS. All agents who are members of the local association of Realtors have access to all of the same listings. Although there are always exceptions, rarely are there secret listings that aren't on the market. If you have multiple agents looking at the same database and sending you the same listings, it won't do you any good. An agent who doesn't have a committed buyer working to find a home is less motivated to work with that buyer. Why would we want to answer lots of phone calls, communicate via e-mail, and show properties for months on end, only to find out that the buyer we are working with could purchase a property using another agent? If we know that this is the case, we are less willing to commit our time and resources to that buyer. Agents, or any professional for that matter, delegate their hours in the day and energies toward folks who want to commit to working with them in the process.

At the end of the first meeting with potential homebuyers, I lay this fact out there. I explain what the MLS is, how agents are paid, and

My Tale of Woe: Fired by a Buyer Client

I worked for months with a couple but began to sense that I wasn't meeting their expectations. My investment in time and resources kept me dedicated to pursuing the relationship and the home search. After all, no client or scenario is perfect. Sure enough, after some time and the disappointment of losing out on a great home, the buyers asked to meet in person. No doubt, there is never a right time to have the talk, the "It's not you; it's us" speech, but nonetheless, I sat over my latte, left cold. "It's just not working out," they told me. "We're going to take a break and reconnect with another agent going forward."

I was disappointed but looked at the bright side—at least they felt comfortable enough to tell me how they felt and to be honest and up front.

If you are working with agent and sense that it's not working out, raise a red flag sooner rather than later. Before you engage the agent and take up too much of his or her time, either jump ship or find a constructive way to make it known that you are unhappy or that things aren't working out. If it's possible, offer guidance and see if the agent can turn things around. If the agent is unresponsive or unreasonable, then turn the tables and do the dumping. We're all grownups here.

how the business works. I explain that I work only with buyers who work with agents exclusively. I assure them of the opportunities afforded to them because there is no contractual agreement; that is, you can opt out at any time. Should things go the wrong way, and either of us feels the partnership is not working out, we will agree in advance to communicate the issue. We can part ways in the event there is no resolution. If your agent doesn't have a similar conversation with you, don't be afraid to bring it up. I find that most buyers appreciate this candor, not only because it lays the groundwork for a loyal relationship from day one, but also because, more than anything, it explains the home-buying process.

ACT LOCALLY

From time to time a buyer will have a relative who is a licensed real estate agent who isn't active in the local community. A buyer's cousin may be an agent who operates more than an hour away, but he or she wants to use Cousin Al for the transaction. It would make sense; he's your cousin, you've known him for a long time, and you trust him. He might even plan to refund you part of his commission, which could very well be enticing. Maybe he is new in the business, and you want to support him. Nine out of 10 times, working with a relative is a bad idea.

If you are serious about purchasing a home in a particular area, it's important to work with a local agent, someone who works the neighborhood, town, or area on a regular basis. These agents have relationships in the local real estate community, understand how business is done, and are familiar with recent home sales, comparables and the inventory. Work with someone who is unfamiliar with the real estate customs of the community, and you could be on the road to making a huge mistake.

Local agents prefer to do business with other local agents. They know the processes, and they have assurance that the agents they are working with are advising buyers appropriately, thereby reducing issues in the transaction. As agents we tend to do business and do it well when it is with people whom we know and trust. Every community will have a market of agents who know one another. Reputations go a long way, too.

I've seen situations where a well-qualified buyer with an out-of-area agent keeps losing out on homes. I've been on both sides of this scenario. A couple was referred to me after working with their aunt for months. Aunt Annie was from Richmond and knew nothing about San Francisco. They mentioned a home that they loved but couldn't understand why they didn't get it after offering so much money and a quick close. With a cursory look in the MLS database, I learned that a well-respected, experienced agent represented the buyers of that home, which sold for $10,000 less than what these buyers had offered through Aunt Annie. When I asked the listing agent why, he confirmed that he had multiple offers and that the folks whose offer was accepted were not the highest bidders. We believe that the sellers and the listing agent didn't want to risk $10,000 on an out-of-town agent whom they didn't know.

Once I received an offer from an out-of-town agent who wrote the offer on a contract not typically used in San Francisco. It wasn't a bad offer, 30 percent down and with a quick close, but I sent the contract and the offer back to the listing agent and asked him to use the local, approved Association of Realtors contract relative to my listing's jurisdiction. This was specific to the rules, laws, and customs of San Francisco. I was not able to accept another contract. It took that agent a day to get back to me and tell me that he didn't have access to that contract and asked me to fax one over. Two days later I received a new offer from that agent on a contract that was riddled with mistakes. He clearly wasn't familiar with it.

I hopped on the phone and went through the contract line by line with the agent. Given that there were so many mistakes in the contract, I didn't want to put these buyers under contract with my sellers. There would likely be more mistakes down the road. This out-of-town

---

🏠 EXPERT   Lockhart Steele, Founder of Curbed

"The story of the real estate in last ten years is there is so much more transparency. Agents controlled everything before the Internet, from comps to days on market, they knew the information and controlled it," Lockhart told me. "I think that's flipped on its head now, whether it is Curbed laying out what really goes on inside neighborhoods, or everything the syndicates, like Zillow and Trulia, are doing. The best brokers have adapted to this realty and have blogs. They write about the local market. You can now find smarter brokers in the age of the Internet really get a sense of an agent and whether they know their stuff or not, based on their blogs. Be open to local blogs and go outside blogs run by brokerages. Chances are you will run into someone with a blog who might be a great resource for you, especially since it's important to stay local."

agent wasn't familiar with this local market, which would tie up the sale for the sellers, who were serious about selling. Two days later I received a new offer. He had reviewed my comments and gone to his manager for help writing the new offer. Unfortunately, there had been a third showing during this weeklong debacle and another offer was made, which is not atypical in real estate markets across the country. These new buyers won out.

If you think that you could save some money by using Cousin Al or that you trust your aunt more than anyone else, think again. I can only imagine that ultimately these buyers either overpaid for a home because they kept getting frustrated or finally gave up and worked with someone local. Obviously you as the buyer have the right to use anyone you want, and a listing agent can't refuse to submit your offer to his or her seller. However, I believe that you are doing yourself a disservice. If you are serious about buying a home today, remember to act locally.

What Can I Really Afford? Building Your Financial House

A woman named Suzanne reached out to me via social media. She was in what she called limbo. She was six months from turning 27 and newly single after she and her college sweetheart decided things weren't working anymore. Living with her parents, Suzanne felt as though she was ready to settle into a home of her own, and she wanted to buy. The economy was finally turning around, and for this woman, whose stagnant adulthood frustrated her, it was now or never.

Suzanne's grandfather had drilled into her head that the magic number for a down payment was 20 percent. However, at the rate she was going, she would never buy because she lived in the suburbs of Boston, where prices were higher. If she could even find a small house, it would probably be upward of $300,000, so she'd have to enter the market with a down payment of $60,000. Frustrated, Suzanne read a post about down payments on my blog and reached out for advice. Surely there had to be a way to do this. She turned to me for my take on what her options were and how to get started. I explained to her that her grandfather was correct. The 20 percent down payment was still the safe and smart approach. However, there were other down payment options that she could qualify for in the next generation of real estate. There were Federal Housing Authority (FHA) loans and programs that she could qualify for with only 3.5 percent down. Shocked, Suzanne listened on.

I shifted the focus of the discussion, asking, "When you were living with your boyfriend, how much rent were you paying?" The reason is that I wanted to get a feel for what she could afford on a monthly basis, and this was precisely something that Suzanne hadn't considered when she was toying with the idea of buying. She was so focused on down payment and purchase price that she didn't quite understand that it wasn't much more money to own a home than it previously was when she rented.

I pointed her to Zillow's breakeven horizon index, statistics that demonstrate how many years of owning it would take to cover the costs of purchasing and be even cheaper than rent. Today, in many places in the country, it takes less than five years. I wanted her to see that, over time, it could be cheaper for her to purchase. (See the chart on page 28.)

What made things even trickier was that Suzanne is a hairdresser, and she was new to the business. Her first year or two was slow as she built up her clientele, but the past year was strong. Suzanne didn't realize that what she pulled in last year would not be the income the bank would use for qualification purposes.

When I asked Suzanne her credit score, things really weren't looking good. She had no idea what it was and didn't know why it mattered. She had rarely missed a payment, and if she was ever late on her cell phone or car insurance, it was at most by two days. Suzanne later learned that she was the one responsible for the electric bill in the apartment that she and her boyfriend lived in together. After she moved out, he missed two payments before she took it out of her name. Guess what? Her credit was affected, and she had no idea. It would most definitely make a difference in whether she got a loan, what kind, and for how much.

Toward the end of their call, Suzanne told me that she felt both hopeful and frustrated at the same time. Although it seemed like buying a home was actually a possibility, it seemed like there was much more to the equation. She had no idea how complicated getting a loan would be. Her next step had to be to speak to a mortgage professional and get prequalified. She needed someone to delve deeply into her finances and appropriately advise her. A real estate agent can only provide so much information, the basics. But only a local mortgage professional could break it down for her.

★

Most would-be buyers have a general good feeling about what they can afford just based on knowing their finances, having some idea of what homes cost in their area, and playing with mortgage calculators online. It's rare that people stay in their home for the entire length of a 30-year mortgage, so they don't think about the total purchase price when they think about financing. Instead, today's buyers are so focused on the monthly payments. If you've been renting currently, then you know how much of your monthly budget goes toward housing. You may believe that you are already at your max and that therefore you have more reason to want to purchase—to get the tax benefit—or you may feel comfortable with what you are currently spending and believe that you could even afford to put more toward it. That is your first indication of what you can afford. Most buyers start out looking at homes and meeting a real estate agent, but if they want to really get serious, they need to run the numbers and be educated on loans. (See the sample mortgage calculator on page 23.)

🏠 EXPERT   Spencer Rascoff, CEO of Zillow

"Buyers should spend more time searching for a mortgage than they typically do," Spencer told me. "People spend more time researching car purchases and vacations than their mortgages—likely the biggest and most important financial transaction of their life. Buyers will mull over the difference between $10,000 in a purchase price and not the difference a half a point can make in interest rates. Mortgage particulars are more important than the price, but too often home buyers act on mortgages as an afterthought."

THE ROLE OF A MORTGAGE PROFESSIONAL

Quick! What's today's rate on a 30-year fixed? If you know the answer to that question, you are a rare bird. Most first-time homebuyers couldn't tell you what the current interest rates are or the kinds of lending options out there, and even if you go online and Google it, there is much more to understand about mortgages in the next generation of real estate. Considering there are likely more than a dozen loan products, helpful tax incentives, constantly changing qualification guidelines, and federally backed loan options, it's enough to overwhelm not just Suzanne, but also you!

There are three main types of mortgage professionals: a mortgage broker, a mortgage banker, and a direct lender. *Broker* and *banker* are terms that people don't really know how to distinguish. *Broker* does not necessarily mean intermediary, which is a common misunderstanding. I've seen buyers who assumed they should cut out the intermediary, the broker, and go directly to the source—the bank. There is no right answer here. It depends on the market you are in, your particular financial situation, and previous bank relationships.

A mortgage banker is simply that, a person who works at a bank. These are the banks that you know and have heard of: Wells Fargo, Bank of America, Chase, or a local or regional credit union. A mortgage broker is someone that facilitates loans between a buyer and any number of wholesale banks.

You can walk into any bank's branches or reach out online to find out about what they have to offer you. On any day, each bank would likely have, say, five loan programs available to you. If you go to the competing bank down the street, it likely has five similar loan programs. When you work with a bank, you get your loan directly from them. You can choose from only one of their loan programs, and you are subject to the underwriting standard and guidelines that they have in place for their institution.

If you have a great relationship with a current bank and have a lot of your savings and a different loan, such as a car loan, with it already, it might be advantageous to work with that bank on a home loan. With some of the big banks, if you keep a certain amount of money with them, they provide all kinds of discounts. These discounts could be in the form of a credit for closing costs or even a better rate on your mortgage. Banks like to reward their good customers and encourage them to keep their business with their bank. If you have a good relationship with a bank, that would be the first place to start. In the past, I have seen clients who had a lot of money, but it was dispersed in various savings, checking, and brokerage accounts with multiple banks. They consolidated their accounts with one bank so that they could get the best possible loan terms.

🏠 EXPERT   Vera Gibbons, Personal Finance Expert

Vera advises new buyers seeking a mortgage to start with a bank they already have a relationship with. "Even if you don't think you want to go with that particular bank at least you have gathered some baseline information with which you can move forward to comparison shop with other lenders," she added.

When you work with a mortgage broker, he or she will likely have all of those same programs that you have access to through the bank branch. But as a broker of bank loans, they are available through those banks' wholesale divisions as well. What's great is that the broker also has access to dozens of other banks that specialize in mortgages only. These types of banks don't offer savings, checking, or credit card accounts. They only sell mortgages, and they sell them wholesale, through brokers, not to the public directly.

There is a third type of lender that you may encounter, and that is a direct lender. Direct lenders are a single loan source, who deal directly with borrowers and loan to them from their own pool of money, as opposed to helping borrowers shop around, which is what brokers do. Many mortgage brokers today are also direct lenders and can provide that option to their clients.

If you are self-employed, like Suzanne, the retail bank up the street just may not have the best program for you, or it can't offer a good rate for self-employed people. However, one of the wholesale banks, accessed only through a broker, may specialize in entrepreneurs and self-employed people. Also, your retail bank may require 20 percent as a down payment, but you have only 10 percent. If you go through a mortgage banker, it's quite possible that you can get two loans: a first loan of 80 percent with bank A and a second loan of 10 percent at bank B. That way you can do the 10 percent down purchase.

Let's say you have a ding on your credit history, and your bank's underwriting guidelines are strict. Your bank won't give you the best rate because of the problem on your credit report. However, maybe you have a huge down payment and lots of money in reserves (sav-

How to Find a Mortgage Professional

The best way to find reliable mortgage brokers or mortgage bankers in the next generation of real estate is actually not very next generation at all. It goes back to what is still the surefire way of doing business—through referrals. As I discussed in the last chapter, real estate is a business based on referrals. Do a great job, and word gets around. Do a terrible job, and word gets around. This is even truer for mortgage professionals.

I believe getting a mortgage referral from your real estate agent is a smart buying strategy. A good local mortgage professional is as valuable and necessary as a good local real estate agent. Like the concept of getting an agent referral through a friend or coworker, the referral from a good agent is valuable because agents are on the front lines. They know when their former clients have gotten the royal treatment, and that includes the best rates, advice, and mortgage programs in the most efficient time frame. Communicative, patient, relentless, hardworking, creative, well connected—these are some of the traits you want to see in a mortgage professional. Your agent will be a great source of truth about the reputation and work experience of mortgage professionals in your community.

ings after you close on your home). A smaller local bank may understand that it was a one-time credit issue, and because you have such a large down payment and have a lot of money to keep in the bank, they see you as less of a credit risk and actually as a new business score for them.

There are so many factors at play in getting a loan. If your financial situation is clean, or you have a deep relationship with a current bank, then working through a bank might be a good option. If you don't have strong ties to any one bank, or your finances are complicated, working with a broker might be a better option. I once saw a very successful mortgage broker quote a rate from a large bank that was actually lower than the rate the actual bank quoted directly to that same buyer. In this case, the broker did a lot of loans with this bank, and he got a better rate on the back end.

It is helpful to note that the market sometimes affects how people best get loans. When loans and credit were easy to get in the mid part of the last decade, mortgage brokers were doing a huge chunk of the business. There were many loans available, and the brokers had access to so many banks and could really get creative when helping a buyer obtain financing. Agents rarely saw buyers coming with preapproval letters from banks directly. It just seemed easier and more efficient to work with a mortgage broker. However, after the real estate market crash and credit crisis of 2008, everything changed. Wholesale mortgage banks were going under or closing up shop, and access to credit was shrinking quickly. Mortgage brokers were having a hard time getting and offering loans. Within one year, we noticed that a majority of loans were going through a mortgage bank and not a broker. Today, direct lenders are starting to take up a good chunk of market share. Being smaller, quicker and more nimble, they've become very competitive and a good option for the next generation buyer. Things vary by region and by the strength of the market. Ask your real estate agent who is doing the most loans and what is going on in your local community. Remember, real estate is local.

NEXT GENERATION REAL ESTATE FACT: ONLINE MORTGAGE BANKING MAY NOT BE THE WAY TO GO

One would assume that in the next generation of real estate, the logical option for getting a mortgage on a purchase would be through an online bank. Websites such as Zillow's Mortgage Marketplace and Lending Tree are name brands to where one would assume the next generation buyer would turn for a loan. I think these places are great for refinancing a current loan or in a slow buyer's real estate market, but in a purchase situation, these options can take up too much time. Unfamiliar with your local market, online lenders are prone to make mistakes that could prove costly or even kill a deal.

I had a client named Doug who was convinced that he would get the best rate from an online lender he found. He had researched early on, and it seemed to have the best possible rates, bar none. I explained to him that, though the rates seemed appealing, many times online lenders just couldn't deliver. I suggested that Doug also get approval through my preferred mortgage broker. Reluctantly, Doug agreed. He was determined to prove me wrong.

Fast-forward two months. Doug got into a contract on a condominium. There was another offer on it, but Doug prevailed. He had 30 days to get his loan approved, which was an eternity in that current market, but I figured I should give this online bank some extra time but still prodded Doug daily for updates. It almost became a battle, albeit a fun one, to see if this could work. One week into the contract, we learned that Doug's application and the purchase contract were sitting on someone's desk in Omaha, Nebraska. Processing hadn't started. The listing agent began calling and asking why the appraiser hadn't yet called to come out and do the appraisal. The pressure was on. Long story short, at nearly three weeks in, Doug received a call from someone in Omaha. The caller had a million questions about the condo he was purchasing. He was clueless and asked the caller to call me directly.

As it turns out, Doug was purchasing a condo in a small four-unit building. One owner owned two of the units. The bank had an issue, because in this case, 50 percent of the units were owned by one person. According to this online lender, this was a risk because if the majority owner defaulted or went bankrupt, the homeowner's association would be in severe jeopardy. Unfortunately for Doug, this bank only had experience lending to condos nationwide in large condo complexes. They looked at this building from that perspective and rejected the loan.

Dozens of local mortgage lenders and brokers were familiar with these smaller condo buildings, which are common throughout California, and regional banks saw them as less risky. Luckily for Doug, once he got into the contract, I alerted my trusted mortgage professional and asked him to start processing the loan. I knew it wouldn't work out with the online bank. Within days, and nearly in time for Doug to sign off on the loan approval for his contract with the seller, my contact had the loan fully approved.

How did this happen? The local mortgage professional did loans like this all day long. He could do it with his eyes closed. Second, he relies on referrals from past clients and agents like me. He wanted to get the deal done in record time.

Do I say *never* use online banks in the next generation of real estate? Absolutely not! They may be able to offer better rates for someone with a basic home purchase and absent a complicated financial situation in a noncompetitive situation. If you are buying a home in a slow buyer's market or refinancing a current loan, both examples of when there is not a time limit to get the loan done, an online bank could be a great option.

WHAT TO EXPECT FROM YOUR MORTGAGE PROFESSIONAL

Entering into a relationship with a mortgage professional is a unique situation because you skip the niceties and go straight into dissecting your most personal financial information. It could catch you off guard and be a little unnerving at first, but a good professional will make you feel comfortable. Be prepared to answer the following:

- What is your annual taxable income?

- How much do you have in savings, money markets, stocks, and so on?

- How much debt do you have?

- What is your credit score?

Based on your situation, a good mortgage professional will provide you with the different types of loan options available for your situation and explain them all to you. Get an explanation of how each program works for your financial situation. What most people are concerned with these days are their monthly expenses. This is the total amount of loan principal, interest, property tax, and homeowner's insurance, also known by the acronym PITI.

Some loans are better for someone who is more conservative and wants a fixed payment for the life of the loan. Other products may provide much lower monthly payments today but could adjust up or down if rates fluctuate in the future. Some people know they want to live in the home for only five to seven years but still want their payments to be fixed. There will be a program for them.

Loan Lexicon

When searching for a loan, you might feel as if you're learning a second or third language. Although the mission is to borrow money, the methods vary greatly. To help you ease into some of the language and loan types you will hear about from your mortgage broker or banker, here is a little sneak peak. No spoilers here, though! For details and advice, head toward the end of the chapter.

- Fixed-rate loan

- Interest-only loan

- Adjustable-rate mortgage

- FHA

THE DIFFERENCES BETWEEN PREQUALIFICATION AND PREAPPROVAL

Getting prequalified indicates that you have spoken to a mortgage professional, disclosed your financial situation, and talked about the different types of loan programs and how to best approach the home-buying process from a lending perspective. Assuming all the information you provided the mortgage professional is accurate, the lender would prequalify you for x amount of money to go toward a home purchase. A prequalification is certainly nice to have because it's helpful to know what you can afford, but in the world of smart buying, it doesn't mean squat.

Once you are serious about moving forward, you'll need to be preapproved for a loan. With preapproval, both your real estate agent and a potential seller will know you are serious and informed about heading deeper into the market.

A preapproval is a full-blown loan approval of your personal financial situation. In this case, the mortgage professional will pull and verify your credit score, ask to review the past three months of bank statements, and see the last couple of years of W-2s or tax returns. He or she may ask you to provide verification of some or all of your assets. This is the information that the bank requires to assess whether it can loan you the money and, if so, with what terms. Looking at your credit, debt, income, and savings levels will allow the mortgage professional to tell you exactly what you can afford in terms of a loan amount and monthly payments based on the best loan

---

EXPERT Greg McBride, Vice President, Senior Financial Analyst, Bankrate.com

"If you want to increase your chances of getting a better interest rate on your loan, pay your bills on time," advises Greg. "Two-thirds of your credit score is measured by paying your bills on time and how well you pay down debt."

programs available at that time. It could be months before you actually buy a home, so the numbers may change because interest rates change. However, it's going to be a pretty accurate assessment of what the bank will lend you. The biggest unknown is the actual property. Is it a house? Is it a condominium? Will you be purchasing a fixer-upper? There are variables on the property side that will affect the type of loan or your rate.

What's most helpful about getting preapproved early is you still have time to get your ducks in a row. You may not have the down payment required to actually make a purchase today, but you may find out that you can receive gift money from a relative. You may notice that your credit is not as stellar as you thought because of something small. This could give you time to fix it. Some banks will require that you have an amount in your savings account that equals a certain number of monthly mortgage payments, in addition to your down payment, so you may need to save for a few more months. If you are newly self-employed, or like Suzanne, coming off your first strong fiscal year, you may need to wait a little while longer before buying a home. Going through the preapproval process is educational and helpful. Doing this helps you build your financial house as well as the team and resources you need to get into the home-buying game.

WHAT DOES YOUR FINANCIAL HOUSE LOOK LIKE?

Often, buyers are motivated to take the plunge and seek preapproval after they see a home that they love, but that's too late. After the preapproval you may have to do any number of things to get the best possible mortgage and rate, and that can take time, sometimes so much time that the house you were excited about is snatched up. I see dozens of instances where buyers find a home first and attempt to get preapproved, only to find out that they really can't make it work at that time.

Not all interest rates are created equal. If today's interest rate is 5 percent, it doesn't mean that getting prequalified means you'll be paying at that low interest rate. Interest rates move up and down with the financial markets. Not everyone will get the same rate for the same home, in the same community, at the same time. Rates are also relative to how strong your financial house is. If you live in a brick financial house, you will be awarded that low interest, but if you live in a straw financial house, get ready for the big, bad wolf to blow a high interest rate your way. Your credit score, debt, income, down payment, and even perceived job security all build your financial house, so the less you have to offer in the bank's view, the more in interest you pay, and vice versa. Also, there are hoops you need to jump through to prove that you deserve the rate you qualify for. Maybe you need to transfer your money out of an account that you share with your business partner and into your own account or provide an old credit card company with proof that you made a payment on time to fix your credit score. You might have received a great chunk of money from Uncle Bob over the holidays. This money may have to season, that is, sit in your account, for up to three months. Obtaining preapproval well in advance will give you time to get your financial house in order.

🏠 EXPERT   Greg McBride, Vice President, Senior Financial Analyst, Bankrate.com

"Getting pre-approved before home shopping is a good idea because it doesn't waste time and it gives buyers an idea of what they should be shopping for," Greg told me. "Once you put in an offer and it's accepted, you're not married to the pre-approval, and you're free to shop around and obtain a quote specific to your situation. Once you get a good faith estimate from each lender you can decide who you are going to partner with."

At the end of the day, when you are ready to make an offer on the home of your dreams, you will want to know that you can get a loan and how much it will cost, without any surprises. You'll want to know what you can afford and what the upward and downward limitations are on your home search.

After Suzanne found a good local real estate agent and got approval from that agent's favorite local mortgage broker, she discovered that, with about 5 percent down, she could afford as much as $350,000. At $300,000, however, she could buy a home and still afford to travel, eat out with friends, and spend money. She wouldn't be totally house poor at the low end, but she could get a lot more bang for her buck at the top. This was for her to evaluate with her real estate agent.

The preapproval helps you be more educated and helps you in the market. You can now take that preapproval and use it to tell a potential seller or listing agent that you've already gone to the bank and that you've removed any doubt about your ability to actually get a loan. You are a far more serious buyer than one who is only prequalified.

I Qualified for How Much?

It is common to see buyer clients who start with a maximum of $425,000 for their budget and get preapproved for up to $500,000. Now, the idea is not to forget about the original budget and head straight for $500,000 homes. However, what I've seen is, knowing that the $425,000 number is achievable; some buyers start snooping around at homes priced closer to $500,000. If they have met with and are now working with an agent and it's a slow market, don't be surprised if the agent sends them to see homes that are priced closer to $525,000 or more, because inevitably, sellers reduce their prices, or a buyer can come in with low offer. More on this in Chapter 8, which covers the search process.

GREAT RATE?

Just like when you get a great deal on a barbeque grill at the end-of-summer blowout sale or a designer bag for a fraction of the cost, you want to brag about the rate you locked in when you buy a house. Cocktail party after cocktail party we hear people comparing and contrasting their rates:

"Oh, Joe just refinanced."

"Oh, yeah? What rate did he get?"

However, as we saw with Suzanne, buying a home is so much

more than the rate, and understanding how you get the rate is important. Your mortgage professional will certainly help you determine the pros and cons of each option he or she brings to you, but here are a few big-picture ideas to help you buy smart with a rate that is truly the best.

For starters, not all rates are created equal. At 25 different mortgage websites, you will see that the numbers are very similar for your loan amount. Maybe one bank is lower by an eighth of point. You immediately assume that's the cheaper rate and head off to call that bank. What you might not realize, at least not until farther down the road, is that you would be required to pay a point, or a percentage of the loan, up front, to achieve that better rate. Also, it could be that this bank offers better rates but charges thousands of dollars in closing costs.

The ultimate rate you end up getting will depend on a variety of variables that the lender uses to assess how risky your entire profile is. This includes your finances, the size of the loan, and the type of home. Remember: The lower the risk, the higher the rate, and vice versa. If Steven, a W-2 union employee, is putting 20 percent down on a single-family home with a 30-year mortgage, you can bet your bottom dollar the bank would think he is less risky than Suzanne, self-employed with a fluctuating income, who is putting 5 percent down on a condominium.

When the time comes to officially lock in your rate and move ahead, you don't want there to be any unknowns or uncertainties. That is why you will inevitably receive both a truth-in-lending statement and a good faith estimate, which outline all of the fees your lender requires. This should happen within days of getting a contract on a home. The last thing you want is to see that what you thought you were getting isn't true. (A sample truth-in-lending statement and a sample good faith estimate appear on the following pages.)

This lender, who seemed to have the best possible rates and was the best deal, actually could be the worst. Now, you are forced, in panic mode, to go find another lender, compare rates, and get back on the train, but since you first started going down the path with this person, interest rates have gone up. Now you will have to lock in your

The Truth-in-Lending Act is aimed at promoting the informed use of consumer credit by requiring disclosures about terms and costs.

SAMPLE TRUTH-IN-LENDING DISCLOSURE STATEMENT
(THIS IS NEITHER A CONTRACT NOR A COMMITMENT TO LEND)

Applicants:
Property Address:
Application No:

Because you may be paying points and other fees, the APR disclosed is often higher than the interest rate on your loan. The APR can be compared to other loans to give you a fair method of comparing prices.

Prepared By:

Date Prepared:

The mortgage amount minus prepaid finance charges (loan origination fees, points, adjusted interest and initial mortgage insurance premium) and any required balance. It represents a net figure to allow you to accurately assess the amount of credit actually provided.

ANNUAL PERCENTAGE RATE	FINANCE CHARGE	AMOUNT FINANCED	TOTAL OF PAYMENTS
The cost of your credit as a yearly rate	The dollar amount the credit will cost you	The amount of credit provided to you or on your behalf	The amount you will have paid after making all payments as scheduled
%	$	$	$

The estimated total amount you will have paid, including principal, interest, pre-paid finance charges and mortgage insurance, if you make minimum payments for the entire loan term.

REQUIRED DEPOSIT: The annual percentage rate does not take into account your required deposit

PAYMENTS: Your payment schedule will be:

Number of Payments	Amount of Payments**	When Payments Are Due	Number of Payments	Amount of Payments**	When Payments Are Due	Number of Payments	Amount of Payments**	When Payments Are Due
		Monthly Beginning:			Monthly Beginning:			Monthly Beginning:

Principal, interest and mortgage insurance if applicable.

The estimated total amount of interest payments for the term of the loan, the amount of interest paid at closing, origination fee and any other charges paid to the lender.

Defines circumstances under which the remaining principal and interest amount of the loan is due and payable on demand.

DEMAND FEATURE: This obligation has a demand feature.

VARIABLE RATE FEATURE: This loan has a variable rate feature. A variable rate disclosure has been provided earlier.

CREDIT LIFE/CREDIT DISABILITY: Credit life insurance and credit disability insurance are not required to obtain credit, and will not be provided unless you sign and agree to pay the additional cost.

Type	Premium	Signature	
Credit Life		I want credit life insurance.	Signature:
Credit Disability		I want credit disability insurance.	Signature:
Credit Life and Disability		I want credit life and disability insurance.	Signature:

INSURANCE: The following insurance is required to obtain credit:

  Credit life insurance   Credit disability   Property insurance   Flood insurance

You may obtain the insurance from anyone you want that is acceptable to creditor

  If you purchase   property   flood insurance from creditor you will pay $ for a one year term.

SECURITY: You are giving a security interest in:

  The goods or property being purchased   Real property you already own

FILING FEES: $ ◄ *An estimate of the cost of recording the legal documents (mortgage or deed of trust) connected with the transaction, which will be charged at closing.*

LATE CHARGE: If a payment is more than   days late, you will be charged   % of the payment

Defines whether a fee will be charged and if you would be eligible for a refund if you wish to repay part or all of the loan in advance of the regular schedule. If you are not entitled to a refund, you will be charged interest for the period of time you used the money loaned to you. Your prepaid finance charges and any interest already paid are generally not refundable. If you pay the loan off early, you should not have to pay the full amount of the finance charges shown on the disclosure.

PREPAYMENT: If you pay off early, you

  may   will not have to pay a penalty.

  may   will not be entitled to a refund of part of the finance charge.

Defines whether or not the loan can be passed on from a seller of a home to another buyer, where the buyer "assumes" all outstanding payments.

ASSUMPTION: Someone buying your property

  may   may, subject to condition   may not assume the remainder of your loan on the original terms.

See your contract documents for any additional information about nonpayment, default, any required repayment in full before the scheduled date and prepayment refunds and penalties.

** NOTE: The Payments shown above include reserve deposits for mortgage insurance (if applicable), but exclude property taxes and insurance.

THE UNDERSIGNED ACKNOWLEDGES RECEIVING A COMPLETED COPY OF THIS DISCLOSURE.

_____
(Applicant)   (Date)

_____
(Lender)   (Date)

Lenders are required by law to provide the information on this statement in a timely manner. Your signature merely indicates that you received this information and does not obligate you or the lender in any way.

The Real Estate Settlement Procedures Act (RESPA) is designed to inform consumers when shopping for a mortgage loan by disclosing the estimated costs associated with obtaining the loan.

SAMPLE GOOD FAITH ESTIMATE

Applicants:
Property Address:
Prepared By:

Application No:
Date Prepared:
Loan Program:

The information provided below reflects estimates of the charges that you are likely to incur at the settlement of your loan. The fees listed are estimates - actual charges may be more or less. Your transaction may not involve a fee for every item listed. The numbers listed beside the estimates generally correspond to the numbered lines contained in the HUD-1 settlement statement, which you will be receiving at settlement. The HUD-1 settlement statement will show you the actual cost for items paid at settlement.

Total Loan Amount $ Interest Rate: %   Term: mths

No.	Item			PFC S F POC
800	**ITEMS PAYABLE IN CONNECTION WITH LOAN:**			PFC S F POC
801	Loan Origination Fee		$	
802	Loan Discount			
803	Appraisal Fee			
804	Credit Report			
805	Lender's Inspection Fee			
808	Mortgage Broker Fee			
809	Tax Related Service Fee			
810	Processing Fee			
811	Underwriting Fee			
812	Wire Transfer Fee			
1100	**TITLE CHARGES:**			PFC S F POC
1101	Closing or Escrow Fee:		$	
1105	Document Preparation Fee			
1106	Notary Fees			
1107	Attorney Fees			
1108	Title Insurance:			
1200	**GOVERNMENT RECORDING & TRANSFER CHARGES:**			PFC S F POC
1201	Recording Fees:		$	
1202	City/County Tax/Stamps:			
1203	State Tax/Stamps:			
1300	**ADDITIONAL SETTLEMENT CHARGES:**			PFC S F POC
1302	Pest Inspection		$	

PFC= Prepaid Finance Charge (fees that affect the APR)
S= Seller Paid
F= FHA Allowable Fees
POC= Paid Outside of Closing

Estimated Closing Costs

No.	Item				PFC S F POC
900	**ITEMS REQUIRED BY LENDER TO BE PAID IN ADVANCE:**				PFC S F POC
901	Interest for days @ $ per day			$	
902	Mortgage Insurance Premium				
903	Hazard Insurance Premium				
904					
905	VA Funding Fee				
1000	**RESERVES DEPOSITED WITH LENDER:**				PFC S F POC
1001	Hazard Insurance Premium	months @ $	per month	$	
1002	Mortgage Ins. Premium Reserves	months @ $	per month		
1003	School Tax	months @ $	per month		
1004	Taxes and Assessment Reserves	months @ $	per month		
1005	Flood Insurance Reserves	months @ $	per month		

Elements of your projected loan payments (interest, taxes and insurance) that must be prepaid to establish the escrow account and the loan schedule.

Estimated Prepaid Items/Reserves

TOTAL ESTIMATED SETTLEMENT CHARGES		
		$

TOTAL ESTIMATED FUNDS NEEDED TO CLOSE:		TOTAL ESTIMATED MONTLY PAYMENT:	
Purchase Price/Payoff (+)		New First Mortgage (-)	Principal & Interest
Loan Amount (-)		Sub Financing (-)	Other Financing (P & I)
Est. Closing Costs (+)		New 2nd Mtg Closing Costs (+)	Hazard Insurance
Est. Prepaid Items/Reserves (+)			Real Estate Taxes
Amount Paid by Seller (-)			Mortgage Insurance
			Homeowner Assn. Dues
			Other
Total Est. Funds needed to close		**Total Monthly Payment**	

These estimates are provided pursuant to the Real Estate Settlement Procedures Act of 1974, as amended (RESPA). Additional information can be found in the HUD Special Information Booklet, which is to be provided to you by your mortgage broker or lender, if your application is to purchase residential real estate property and the lender will take a first lien on the property. The undersigned acknowledges receipt of the booklet "Settlement Costs," and if applicable the Consumer Handbook on ARM Mortgages.

_____ Applicant   _____ Date   _____ Applicant   _____ Date rate somewhere else quickly because the clock on the home purchase is ticking, and you need to move ahead and order your appraisal.

This time you go with a better, more up-front mortgage professional, but your monthly payments have now increased because of the time you wasted with the bank that had those great rates. We know that this almost happened to Doug. Luckily for him, I had already thrown a life raft in the water and gotten Doug an even lower rate.

I've seen too many buyers go through the previously described scenario. You can't really compare and shop around for mortgage rates and programs until you have a real opportunity in front of you: an address, a signed contract, a purchase price, and a type of home. You can look at ballpark rates online or even ask the mortgage banker you interview early on what his rates are, but until you have a contract and a live deal, it's hard to say what your rate will be.

First, mortgage interest rates change all the time. You may see rates online at 4.5 percent, but that may apply only to a certain buyer (W-2 or paycheck employee with perfect credit) getting a certain type of loan (under $417,000), putting down 20 percent, and purchasing a particular type of property (single-family home). You may be self-employed with fluctuating income. You may have perfect credit but only 10 percent down, and you are trying to get a $500,000 loan and want to buy a town house condo, which is not quite the same home as a single family. Your rate will be slightly higher for a few reasons:

1. You are self-employed and therefore subject to variable income;

2. You a have low down payment, which means your loan is larger (a loan for more than $417,000, for instance, is seen as riskier and thus subject to higher rates); and

3. The rules, guidelines, and oversight of a Homeowners Association as well as the uncertainty of other owners and tenants living in the building are considered riskier factors in the eyes of the lender.

It is no longer entering a deal with just an owner and the lender itself. In a loan for a single-family home, it's you and the bank, and that's all.

Meet Your Credit Report

Before the Internet, your credit report and subsequent credit score were these unreachable things that you didn't have direct access to, let alone control. To break it down simply, three credit bureaus exist in the world to monitor consumers' bill-paying habits and the amount of credit taken out at any one time. These three firms—Experian, Equifax, and TransUnion—then sell this profile of you and your credit to companies, including mortgage lenders, credit card companies, and other folks who believe that they need to know about your credit history to decide if they want to provide you a loan. Did you miss a payment to your credit card company at some time? Chances are, these bureaus have picked up on it and added it as a line item to your credit history, a big red flag for lenders.

If you are thinking about buying a house, you should know your credit score or at least have an idea about your credit. You would likely know if there were dings on your report because a missed payment likely would have resulted in communication from your credit card company. However, from time to time, things happen: Letters get lost in the mail, companies don't receive money, or companies allocate payments to the wrong account.

Each of the three bureaus has its own website and offers a service to allow you to track your credit report. The Fair Isaac Corporation (FICO) is a company that provides a service to a majority of the mortgage and other lenders out there. It tracks your credit through each of the credit reporting bureaus and assigns a score between 400 and 850. The higher the score, the less risky of a borrower you are. It offers a consumer service called MyFICO, which allows you to access your FICO score online at any time.

Given all the concerns with identity theft these days, it's helpful to monitor your credit regularly. If you are moving toward becoming a home-buyer in the near future, you should be aware that your FICO score and credit history play a huge part in the lender's decision-making process. Even if you are more than a year away from getting serious about buying, it can't hurt to start cleaning up and monitoring your credit now.

Just keep in mind that rates, closing costs, and any associate fees at any number of banks are all going to be pretty close to one another when it comes down to looking at your profile. Don't drive yourself crazy looking for the absolute best rate. You are ultimately comparing between what amounts to just a few dollars per month.

WHAT'S THE BEST LOAN FOR YOU?

When my parents bought their home 25 years ago, their plan was (and still is) to live there for a long time, until they retire or die. My dad had a local business in place, and they kept with it. They were committing to the area for the long haul. However, we know the next generation of real estate looks very different, and you might ask yourself why you should commit to a 30-year loan when you know you'll be there for only five. This is a good question, which we'll answer using my parents again.

Because they were committing to their home for a lifetime, the only real option, and one that made complete sense for them, was the 30-year fixed loan. The word *fixed* means that every month the payment to the lender would be the same, and as long as the family made the payments each month, the loan would be paid off over the course of 30 years. The good news is that the interest rate and therefore the monthly payments were fixed for the entire term. As opposed to an adjustable rate mortgage, they could anticipate month in and month out for the entire 30 years what their expenses would be. Of course, if they wanted to pay down the principal earlier, they could do that, without penalty. The graph on the following page shows the average rate on a 30-year fixed rate from 1981 until 2013. Rates go up and down with markets. If you were able to lock in a 4.5% loan in 2014, you would be protected if rates increased much higher, like they did in the 1980s.

However, what was good for my folks might not be good for you. There has certainly been a generational shift. The homogenous lifestyle of the 80s family is no longer the standard, a fact that actually comprises the crux of this book. The eclectic lifestyles of the next generation created a market for customizable borrowing options, and

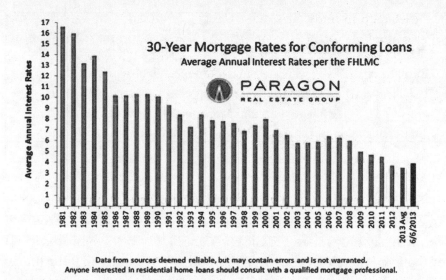

30-Year Mortgage Rates for Conforming Loans
Average Annual Interest Rates per the FHLMC

Data from sources deemed reliable, but may contain errors and is not warranted.
Anyone interested in residential home loans should consult with a qualified mortgage professional.

banks responded by inventing new products to suit these needs. Many people believe that it is this craftiness in lending that led to the housing crisis. However, you will still see these loans out there today, and I need to talk about them. Next generation buyers should be informed on all their options to determine the right one for them.

Interest-Only Loan

For next generation buyers who know they might be moving out of the country for work once that promotion is nailed in a few years, a new loan product—the interest-only loan—emerged about 10 years ago to meet needs such as those. It's helpful to understand that there are two parts to loan payments: principal and interest. Principal is the portion of the payment that goes toward lowering the total balance of the loan amount. The more principal you pay over time, the smaller the loan becomes. Interest is the money that goes to the bank, at the rate they charge. This is how they make their money. In the first few years of any long-term fixed loan, buyers actually pay more interest than they do principal. The more you pay off the principal, the lower the interest payments get because you are now paying down the loan.

> **🏠 EXPERT**   Barbara Corcoran, Real Estate Expert
>
> Barbara says, "Even with the slight increase in interest rates, money is still cheap. In the 1980s mortgage interest rates were typically 18 percent, and in 2000, rates hovered around 8 to 9 percent. Today's rate of around 4 percent is a remarkable value, virtually unheard of prior to 2010."

An interest-only loan is generally a 30-year loan with the option of an entry-level period of either three, five, or seven years over which you will pay only interest to the bank and not pay down the principal of the loan; therefore, you are not building any equity in your home. In a market with historically low interest rates, this can be a very enticing product. Because the monthly payment is going toward interest only, the payments are much lower than they would be with a traditional mortgage. However, once that entry-level period ends, there are two important things to know:

1. The interest rate you have been used to paying will change after the entry-level period.

2. You will now have only 25 years (in the case of a five-year loan) to pay off the loan.

The result: higher monthly payments that you might not have anticipated or be prepared or equipped to make. *These loans were never intended to be long-term options.* Talk to your mortgage professional to run the numbers.

For the mobile professionals, generally in the more expensive urban centers of our country, in the early part of this century, this loan made sense. Home prices are higher and their careers had them moving around all the time, and they couldn't commit to more than just a few years in one place. If that were the case, why would they pay more per month? At the same time, the real estate market was on fire. Homeowners back in 2003 purchased a home and then sold it three years later for a 20 percent (sometimes more) profit. If they could bank on home appreciation at such phenomenal rates, they could see the short-term loan working in their favor.

Because they were not paying any principal, the interest-only loans were cheaper, in those first few years, than a competing 30-year principal and interest loan. Buyers took the savings (the difference between the interest-only payment and the principal and interest payment) and use it to pay down other debt or invest it so that they could get a higher return. If they knew that their income was on the rise, they could keep their monthly payments low and then pay down a big chunk of the principal balance once their income rose and then refinance the loan to a more conservative loan. Or they could just sell for a quick profit. Also, with an interest-only loan, you can pay down any amount of the loan's principal at any one time.

This loan became very popular with people who were savvy when it came to managing money, credit, and investments. If used properly, a smart borrower leveraged these loans and had their money working for them elsewhere. They were knowledgeable not only about the loan but also about how to make it work best for them.

Unfortunately, these loans became mainstream in the early to mid 2000 time frame. Folks were lured in by that same rapid appreciation and low monthly payments. They didn't take into consideration what would happen once the loan adjusted; that their interest rate and their monthly payments would rise significantly. This contributed, in part, to what happened with the housing and credit crisis.

Adjustable-Rate Mortgage

An adjustable-rate mortgage is just what it sounds like. The mortgage payment changes depending on interest rates. These loan products are great in times of low interest rates, but you can't lock anything in, and the rate, along with your monthly payment, will fluctuate with the market and interest rates. There is very little predictability with an adjustable-rate mortgage. However, for someone who is focused on the absolute lowest rate and maybe has a chunk of money coming in the future to pay down the loan amount, this could work. Adjustable-rate mortgage loans are generally cheaper to acquire than the fixed rate, until rates start to rise. From 2003 to 2008, many consumers were sucked into adjustable-rate mortgages because of low rates. However, rates rose after some time, and so did their monthly mortgage payment. These loans are best for those who will have some reason to sell or refinance before rates rise too much. For example, a couple may plan to do some renovations to a home and then refinance afterward to get a higher appraised value and a long-term fixed rate.

FHA Loan

The FHA program has been around since the 1930s, functioning to reduce the risk of homeowners defaulting on their mortgage payments. This is a popular loan choice for many first-time homeowners. The federal government provides insurance on the loan to help mortgage lenders offer accessible and affordable loans.

If you don't have a 20 percent down payment, the FHA loan is an option you might want to consider, because you need a minimum amount down payment of only 3.5 percent. Do you have less-than-stellar credit? FHA can be a bit more forgiving on that point, too, which again makes this loan type a popular one.

However, there are a few downsides to the FHA loan, and if you aren't prepared for them, they could rain on your parade. For instance, because an FHA loan does not have the strict standards of a conventional loan, it requires two kinds of mortgage insurance premiums: One is paid in full up front—or, it can be financed into the mortgage—and the other is a monthly payment. Additionally, the house must meet certain conditions and must be appraised by an FHA-approved appraiser.

I received an e-mail quite recently from a woman named Lara in Oviedo, Florida, who was frustrated by her loan process. She was in a contract on a 20-year-old house and had ordered the inspection. The report came out terrific, better than she expected, given the age of the home. After the FHA appraiser did his job, he noticed an electrical pole that was close to the house. The next day, Lara got a call from her agent saying the loan was not approved. The government thought it was too risky to back a home with a pole so close, despite that it had been there with the current house for at least 20 years. She lost the house, and being that she was set to close on her current home in three weeks, she was now going to have to live in a hotel! This is an extreme example. In fact, many mortgage professionals today say that FHA has eased up in the past ten years.

HOW MORTGAGE LENDING HAS EVOLVED

Pre-2008, loans with low-down payment requirements were widely available. Lending standards were very loose. Anyone with a pulse and an offer on a home could get a loan from a bank. People with horrible credit were getting loans with very little down payment or even no money down. Often, they were getting a first loan and a second or even a third loan and not putting any of their own money into the equation. We all know that these folks were paying a huge premium on interest rates and either were not informed or ignored the fact that their rates could change.

Fast-forward to 2014, and lending practices have changed incredibly. Between the fall of 2008 and up until early 2013, banks were very stringent in their lending practices and often took extra days or weeks to approve a loan. It was common for buyers to be flat out rejected 30 days into their purchase. Lenders double, triple, and quadruple checked every borrower's loan application prior to giving the OK.

Today, less than 20% down loans are common again and standards have eased a little bit. However, only people with jobs, verifiable income, good credit scores, and a history of saving money and paying bills on time are getting qualified for loans. Although some government programs assist buyers with a down payment of as little as 3.5 percent, not everyone can qualify for them. Today's buyers should attempt to make the largest down payment they can, given their financial situation. If you aren't comfortable stretching it, wait to enter the real estate market.

NEXT GENERATION REAL ESTATE ADVICE: GO FOR 30!

The 30-year fixed is still the safest and most conservative loan out there for most people. If you plan on buying a home and being there for a long time, don't think twice. If you don't know how the money markets work, or you aren't sure you have the discipline to save money, you should fix in your monthly payments for 30 years when you make a purchase. As tempting as it may be, don't be seduced by lower monthly payments or affordability of lower or short-term rates. You should live below your means. Properties may not appreciate as they did, at 10 or 20 percent in less than a year, during those boom years before the housing and credit crisis.

Many of the younger homebuyers today, younger than 45 years old, and real estate agents alike don't have the experience or the history to understand what it would be like if interest rates skyrocketed. In the 1980s interest rates were more than 10 percent, as high as 18 percent. If you lock in a 30-year fixed loan now, you'll have nothing to worry about. Your monthly payments will be the same forever, and you can plan your finances with stability.

The next generation buyer will likely come across 15- and 20-year loans. More common when interest rates are lower, you can potentially pay off your entire mortgage in a shorter period of time. What's the catch? Well, if the term of your mortgage is ten or fifteen years shorter, your monthly payments are going to be higher. If you can afford the extra, it makes sense to go for a shorter-term loan. Ultimately you will pay less in interest and you can have your mortgage paid down sooner.

Game On!
Let the Search Begin

You've upped the ante and have decided it's time to buy! But where? What kind of home? When? How long will this take? How big, how small? By now, you have met the right agent, have been preapproved, and have even done a little research on your own through Internet and open house searches. Now, you are teamed up with an agent who has your back; knows your financial, practical, and emotional needs; and is providing you market insight and knowledge that keeps you informed and confident about the search and purchase process.

When doing your own home searching, there are always questions that cause you to scratch your head: *Why is this priced so low? Isn't this priced too high? Are these rooms legal? Why do I get much more for my money just a few miles away?* Now that you've collaborated with a good local agent, not only do you have a resource at your disposal, but you can also offload some of the process onto him or her. However, the agent can't begin until you both have firmly established what it is you are actually looking for, and nobody can decide that but you.

TO HAVE OR HAVE NOT: THE QUESTION OF CRITERIA

You have your list of wishes and requirements. If you are buying with a partner, this list is probably not neat and tidy and could even be a bit contradictory. This is where prioritizing comes in. The following are three of the top priorities in a general real estate search: location, price, and size.

CRITERION 1 Location

Location, location, location. The thing about location is it can't be taken away from you. Once you own a home, you can't pick it up and take it elsewhere. You can add on to a house to enlarge it. You can paint the front of the house. You can landscape the back or add a pool. You can renovate the bathrooms or install a chef's kitchen. All of these things are variable, and they are dynamic. There are financial, practical, and emotional reasons why people want to be in certain neighborhoods or towns. They want to be in convenient neighborhoods, by the best schools, close to public transportation, or near the best commercial districts.

Understanding how valuable location is often leads people to look for fixer-upper homes in great locations. A developer can take a crappy home on a great lot in one of the best school districts and improve that home to add value. That same home in a lousy school district, right by the freeway on-ramp, or on a busy road may sit on the market, even if it has been given a major facelift.

CRITERION 2 Price

What's my price range? This is the main question you'll ask yourself before you really set the other basic criteria, such as number of bedrooms and bathrooms, finishes, size of lot, and parking. Price is the hefty consideration and dictates where you are going to live and what type of home you are going to live in. Likely you and your mortgage professional have come up with a price range that you are comfortable with. It's helpful to now go out, look at homes in your price range, and get a feel for what you get for the money at both the low end and the top end of your budget range.

I encourage buyers to look a little over the top of their budgets. Why? Because I want them to be aware of the amenities or features they can get for a little bit more money so that they can accept what they get in their current range. It also helps to understand the ranges of homes in the general area. What does a starter home cost in one neighborhood versus a larger luxury home? Seeing the difference informs you how location works in your home-buying abilities and lays the foundation of your home-purchasing power.

Additionally, homes that are priced 5 percent above the top of your range either may be negotiable or, after months without any offers, could be reduced down into your range. As a buyer, you should always be aware of what's for sale over your range. This is market intelligence. All of the information is out there. Use it in conjunction with your agent to your advantage.

CRITERION 3 Size and Specs

You need a third bedroom, a finished basement, or a bigger backyard. You want to downsize, don't need that formal dining room, and think two bedrooms is just right. Whatever the situation, most people care about *space*. They either want more or less of it or just a different kind, or there is some specification that is key to their home search. After location and price, the typical buyers then comment on the size and the specifications of their desired home. This is where the buyer says, "We need at least three bedrooms and two full bathrooms and a minimum of 2,000 square feet."

An Important Lesson on Square Footage

It's the one question agents hear nearly every Sunday when standing in at an open house: "What is the square footage?" It's not an easy question to answer because measuring square footage is not an exact science.

Determining the square footage of a home is one of the things real estate appraisers do as a part of the bank's appraisal process (see Chapter 8), but three different appraisers could come up with three different numbers. If an agent tells you that a home is 1,150 square feet, he or she may be getting that number from the town or county tax records or the assessor's office. However, it could very well be that the home was renovated or expanded and that particular assessor's office doesn't cross-reference its numbers with the town building department, from where the building permit was pulled. Often, the tax records are from 40 years ago and don't reflect the correct number.

Other times a seller could have recently refinanced his or her home and needed to have an appraisal done. The appraiser measured some of the rooms in the attic that may not be official rooms. Although those rooms are set up and are used like bedrooms, it's possible that, in the eyes of the city, they are unfinished or unlivable space. The same holds true for basements. You may see the most amazingly finished basement, but because the ceiling height is low or because there aren't enough windows, it may not be legal. In some communities, even though this appears to be great living space, it may not be in the eyes of the jurisdiction.

Every community has its own issues with permitted rooms. Sometimes there is an entire 500-square-foot mother-in-law apartment with full kitchen and bath, but it may not be up to code and therefore not a legal apartment in the eyes of the city. In this case, the size of the home could be considered 500 square feet less, based on the tax records. If you take the seller's number to be true, you will surely be let down when the appraiser for your bank's loan comes back with a square footage that is smaller.

Developers of new constructions, for example, will sometimes submit their engineer's plans to the town as the final plans for entitling and signing off. These plans were made in the office of the engineer and the architect and often use "walls out" measurements. This means that the little bit of space between the living room wall and the actual building exterior is included in those numbers. That little bit of space, over the size of a large home, could end up being a good 100 square feet or more that you should not be paying for.

Thousands of real estate lawsuits have come, gone, and been settled over square-footage issues. It's wise for a listing agent either not to mention any number or to mention it with a disclosure; for example, "It is 1,200 square feet per the appraisal done last year," or, "It is 1,250 square feet according to the county records." This is simply safe real estate practice.

Prepare to Prioritize

You and your agent should determine your home-buying criteria on day one. To start, cast the widest net. Your main search criteria should include the top three priorities outlined earlier: location, price, and size or specs.

Next, add things to the list, such as size of the lot, whether there is a pool, how much lawn maintenance you want or don't want, whether the basement is finished, or the number of parking spaces. Depending on your location, there could be different criteria. In some communities, having a pool is a main requirement. Talk about this from the get-go. The point is, you and your agent should agree on the criteria and know you are both on the lookout for the same things. Be as broad as possible, to see (at least online) as much as possible early on in the process.

Believe it or not, when they first meet with agents, many first-time buyers aren't quite clear on what their search criteria are or what they are willing to sacrifice once they see what the market bears. When they are asked if they know what kind of home they are thinking of, some buyers become quite tongue-tied. To loosen your lips, ask yourself the following questions:

- What are your top priorities in a new home?

- What are your must-haves or nonnegotiables?

- What are your nice-to-haves?

- What would be a total bonus, something you don't need?

- What do you like about your current living situation?

- What do you hate about your current living situation?

- What are your top three locations, and what would be secondary?

- Is there any part of town where you do *not* want to live?

- How big of a home do you need?

- What is the minimum number of bedrooms and bathrooms needed?

- What is the minimum lot size that you need?

- Would you be open to doing some work on a home?

Many times the answers to these questions will be the first time buyers articulate what's on their mind, and their own answers may surprise even them! Hearing themselves aloud often opens the floodgates of ideas, debates, and priorities.

As tempting as it is to buyers, who are sometimes focused on the price per square foot, don't get hung up on square footage. Focus on whether the home feels like the right amount of space for you. Either it works or it does not. Although it's helpful to get some idea of the number, don't count on that number as rock solid. Instead, use it as information to add to your expanding base of knowledge.

An agent friend in California would respond to buyers with the following answer to the question of square footage: "I am not sure of the exact size. Does it seem to fit your needs?" The point he makes is that either the home works or it doesn't. If the home is too small, you will know. Although it's helpful to get an idea of the square footage of a home, don't get hung up on it.

HOW TO STAY THE COURSE DURING YOUR LEARNING CURVE

With the criteria set and your partnership with your agent established, you'd expected calm seas ahead. However, you don't see anything that excites you, and you feel like you've been spending every waking moment either with your agent or in communications with him or her. At best, you're feeling a bit sick and tired of the process. It's not you. Home hunting is not for the faint of heart. It can take some time, and it's normal to get a little worn down in the process. You'll know when this happens. You can spot it. To pick up some wind in your sails, you may need to make some shifts in how you approach the process.

Be Prepared to Compromise

It's rare that buyers get everything on their wish lists. Know your must-haves versus your nice-to-haves early in the process, and be mindful that they could change over time. Once you have been in the market for a while, you will understand what you get for the money and where you need to compromise. If you are searching with a partner or spouse, know where each of you stands on some of the search criteria. Once you've seen enough homes and you've been in the market for some time, it will become evident where and when to compromise.

At their first buyer meeting with me, Nan and Carl were explicit about not being the fixer-upper types. They were busy people and wanted a turnkey home. Carl was a chef and needed a modern, fully loaded kitchen in his home. This was an absolute requirement. After searching for months and realizing that they could only afford a condo in their desired neighborhood, Nan and Carl reevaluated their criteria and decided to settle for less. They were about to enter into a contract for a pink house in a neighborhood they hadn't spent much time in and with a kitchen that hadn't been renovated since the late 1970s.

I said to them, "This is exactly the type of home that you said you didn't want to buy." I went on to quiz them about their decision and brought them back to our original conversation. I wasn't trying to talk Nan and Carl out of the pink house, but it was my role, as their trusted advisor, to ensure they were comfortable with their new approach to the market, review what we had seen together, and hear why this house now made sense to them.

I warned them that the house would take up a lot of time that they didn't have and that the kitchen didn't even have a gas stove, which Carl needed. However, the price was right, and as they thought through it, getting three bedrooms now would make it unlikely that they would need to upgrade in three to five years. Also, because it needed some work, the price was lower than some condos they were looking at, so they could afford to do a quick renovation before moving in.

They bought what they endearingly nicknamed the Pepto Pink Palace. After renovations and a paint job, Nan and Carl love their home and now are raising two boys in it. They're not looking to go anywhere.

The relationship between buyers and their agent can run deep, and Nan and Carl's situation is exemplary of why an agent is helpful in the process. By being informed about the extreme change in plans, Nan and Carl would confirm that, in fact, they were confident with their decision. Working alongside your agent, you will learn the market, and seeing enough things may help move you to be more specific as the process moves along and even to pull a Nan and Carl and find that you go with something that would surprise even you.

What If You're Not Getting What You Want and Not Ready to Compromise?

What you want and need may not match what the market will bear. Time after time buyers enter the market, wanting a Mercedes Benz for the price of a Honda Accord. Buyers spend weeks and months looking at homes in their price range but complain that they want something bigger, more renovated, or on a bigger piece of land. They may even look at listings that are priced higher and make a low offer, only to be rejected. This kind of action signals to the agents, both of the buyers and of the sellers, that you might not be a serious buyer. Agents have a private joke about buyer clients who are perpetual buyers. They've been looking for years or made lots of offers but never come to the table. This happens and you should be aware that you are doing it and consider why. Maybe you are not emotionally ready to buy a home. It's a big commitment, both financially and psychologically. Buying a home means settling down, establishing roots, and making a home. It's not just committing to a physical home, but in some ways, it's also committing to yourself.

Talk with your agent early on about establishing your criteria. It could be that you have multiple searches going. If you think you want to shoot for homes in area A under $500,000 but that you would also be open to a town house in one of three communities, also in area A, talk about this as an option. You and your agent should have a very open discussion about any variations in search criteria and how you will go about looking. Buyers always want to focus on one thing but find themselves opening to new things as the process continues. Don't forget, there is a learning curve to buying a home. You need to see many homes over time to learn the market. Seeing homes you hate will help inform you about homes you like, justify pricing, and solidify your knowledge about your desired market.

If you want to be in neighborhood D, and you want three bedrooms, 2,000 square feet, and at least one acre, great. You are establishing your wants and needs. However, your agent is right there, early on in the process, to tell you how your wants and needs match up to the current real estate market.

If that type of house is just not possible in neighborhood D, you need to know that, consider it, and see if it's something you can compromise on and alter your list of criteria a bit. Your agent may then suggest you look in neighborhood E to get the house style you must have, or if location is your nonnegotiable, then maybe you would be open to a smaller home, a smaller lot, or even a home that is the right size and on the right lot but that needs some renovation. Take this meaningful information and process it. You may need to see and feel the market on your own to understand that what you want just doesn't match what the market will deliver. Buyers who are not emotionally ready to buy will resist and resist and keep on looking for their needle in the haystack. Buyers who are emotionally ready to buy will take these data points from their agent and, after seeing it for themselves, will either quickly move on to neighborhood E or come to terms that, if they want the location, they are going to have to compromise on the type or size of the home. Be on the lookout if you find yourself resisting the market. It may be a sign that buying isn't right for you right now.

Establish Your Communication Style

Your agent will set up your entire search criteria through his or her Multiple Listing Service (MLS) and will receive daily or even hourly e-mails about homes for sale that match your criteria. The agent will be on the lookout for homes that might be sitting on the market because they are overpriced, which could be a good match for you. There are a variety of ways that you and your agent will work successfully in the process. Be up front about your communication preferences.

The majority of next generation buyers today prefer to communicate via e-mail for non-time-sensitive issues. Some forward-thinking agents and their clients are communicating via new software that allows them to collaborate via the web or mobile apps. If it is just about looking at listings, making notes, or receiving market data, these tools might be best. If it is time sensitive, that is, you are waiting for a response on an offer or trying to set up a last-minute showing, phone calls or text messages might be better. Everyone communicates differently, and the home-buying process should be done on your terms. If you do prefer to speak on the phone, tell your agent. Be up front.

The following graph from the California Association of Realtors 2013 home-buyer survey notes how the desired communication of buyers differed from the actual communication with them and their

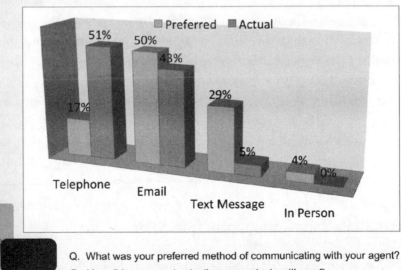

Gap in Phone & Text Communication

Preferred | Actual

- Telephone: 17% / 51%
- Email: 50% / 43%
- Text Message: 29% / 5%
- In Person: 4% / 0%

Q. What was your preferred method of communicating with your agent?
Q. How did your agent actually communicate with you?

www.car.org   CALIFORNIA ASSOCIATION *of* REALTORS®

agents. Could it be that their agent didn't listen or that things happen differently in the throes of a real estate transaction? Either way, communicate with your agent early on.

I have one caveat. Even if you despise in-person meetings and communications, agree to at least one day when you will drive around to look at homes with your agent. (See more on open houses a little later in this chapter.) If your agent isn't open to doing this, push back. I find that this is such a relevant exercise, and it helps set the framework for a successful home search. If you feel that one Sunday is enough, so be it. If you think you would benefit from doing it more than once, ask your agent.

See More, Know More

You should feel free to keep whatever search engine or website search you have going, once you have connected with a local agent, but do so along with your agent's MLS search. Working with the MLS provides your agent with the most up-to-the-minute changes and variations in the market, whereas some of the syndication websites will have delays in status changes. The MLS is your agent's instant messenger about new listings, price reductions, or recent sales. All of this is market intelligence, and your agent should bestow it on you during the home search.

Your agent will now be searching daily and may start sending you e-mails or may set you up to receive automatic e-mails from the MLS. With buyers' approval, I prefer to send them the auto e-mails. Even though I am searching on their behalf and know what their requirements are, I think it is helpful for them to see everything that I am coming across. Buyers are busy and may only proactively search late at night or first thing in the morning. If they have auto e-mails during the week, it's another way to help buyers stay on top of the market.

Even though a buyer doesn't want a home that needs work, it's entirely possible that something that needs work would show up in a three bedroom/two bath search in area A. If an agent doesn't send it to his or her buyers, they wouldn't be aware of it. By being aware of the home that needs work, the buyer will see that the price is a good

20 percent less than everything else that they are seeing. This helps form their working knowledge of this market. If they hadn't seen it, then when they saw the completely renovated home come across days later at a much higher price, they might not have a good reference point as to why the price increased. I always say, "The more you see, the more you know. You have to see a lot of what you don't like to understand and determine what it is that you do like."

You don't know what you don't know, so seeing a lot of homes, with the commentary or feedback from your agent, helps educate you on the market.

Request Showings by Appointment

Did you see a home at an open house on Sunday that you liked? It's common that by late Sunday afternoon good real estate agents' phones will ring or their e-mail and texts will start going wild as they settle into their Sunday evening routine. It might happen this way for you. A new listing hits the market on a Thursday. Your agent points it out to you as a new listing with a little bit of commentary about it, or maybe you see it online first and forward it to your agent for commentary. You check it out on Sunday, and you like it. The next step is to request a private showing.

It's helpful for the buyers and their agent to see a home together. Even if you and your agent have seen it separately, go back together to dissect the home. What is it that you liked? Point it out to your agent. What are your concerns? See if the agent thinks they are valid. This is also the time to check out a home privately, absent 10 other buyers running around. Now you can feel comfortable opening the closets, looking inside the kitchen cabinets, and having private time with the listing agent to ask questions.

If an open house is like peeking through a magazine while waiting in the checkout stand of the grocery store, the private showing is bringing the magazine home and reading it cover to cover. Don't be afraid to poke around and ask lots of questions. Go to the back of the lot and look at the back of the home. Go into the basement. Open windows and doors. This is your chance to get more comfortable in the home, to highlight both the good and the bad. In the absence of other buyers running around, you might see things that you missed. Seeing the home at the open house sparks enough senses to know that it is a possibility. It's what happens at the second showing (or even the third), where you can really let it simmer and consider the home, the area, and the neighbors more and whether you can really see yourself there. You can also feel comfortable asking the listing agent questions about the property, the sellers, or the seller's situation without feeling as though people are listening. Be aware that this is likely the opportunity for good listing agents to start asking you some questions. If they see that you are interested and may be moving toward writing an offer, they will want to do their due diligence. Don't be turned off by it. If you are serious about this home, you won't mind that the sellers have a better understanding of who you are, your interest, and your experience in the market. Just know that whatever you say to the listing agent will likely get back to the sellers. In fact, I'll discuss in the next chapter just how such an instance can actually work in your favor!

Be Patient

You and your agent have the MLS search all set up and are communicating during the week via e-mail and monitoring the market; you've had at least one Sunday of attending open houses together. Now why does it feel as if the home search has gone on a bit of autopilot?

The home-searching process takes time. Having a meeting with your agent early on, getting set up on the MLS, and going out to see places together set the framework for the search process, but you can't expect so much action week in and week out. It's possible that weeks go by without any good listings popping up. It's unlikely that each week you will have six homes to see on a Sunday open house tour with your agent. Sometimes it will feel like feast or famine, and that's normal because in some communities real estate is cyclical.

Don't take this as an indication that your agent has forgotten about you. Just keep looking at listings online and attending open houses on your own. Sometimes, in a market where there is lots of good inventory, agents will send their buyers a list of open houses to see at the end of the week. Know that your agent is looking out for you, watching the market, and setting you up each week. It could be that you know exactly what new listings hit the market in the past seven days, and you know the two that you want to see on Sunday. Maybe your agent points out something that you missed. By remaining focused and communicative with your agent, your home will come. As long as you know what you want and are clear about the process and what's expected of you and your agent, it will come—it always does. Buying a home is not for the weak. If you are able to stay patient, you will emerge strong.

Visit Open Houses with and without Your Agent

In many communities, the Sunday open house is the gold standard in real estate. It's the chance for buyers to test-drive the market, see the new homes for sale, and get in and out of many homes in a short period. Open houses don't require agents to tag along, nor do they deal with getting the seller to allow a showing by appointment.

However, at least in the early stages of your partnership, your agent should take you out on open house tours. The next generation buyer may not want to drive around with an agent week in and week out, but I advocate going and seeing a variety of homes together, which allows your agent to see how you react to certain homes. Going out early in the process, you can point out examples of what you like and don't like. If a particular community tends to have one certain type of home or floor plan, point out to your agent whether you like it or not. In real time you can show him or her features that you absolutely can't stand or tangible examples of features that you love. Going to open houses together will also allow your agent to point out trends and respond to your criticism of homes.

Attending open houses with your agent also makes it possible for you to get up-to-the-minute commentary on a particular home and how it fares in the market. A good agent can walk through a home, read the property's flyer or marketing statement, and instantly know that it is priced too low, too high, or right on. Agents may point out

Buyers Are in the Driver's Seat . . . Literally

My newly married buyers recently hired me to help them find a home. When I told them, for all the reasons mentioned earlier, that I would like to plan a day for them to drive with me to look at properties together, they looked at each other and then looked away. *Why are they so apprehensive?* I wondered. I was just suggesting one Sunday, that's it.

After our meeting, the couple sent an e-mail explaining that they had previously worked with another agent, who insisted on driving them around to see properties, but he was such a poor driver that the wife got carsick sitting in the backseat. Besides telling the agent he was a bad driver, they chose to start fresh with me, and to do so they must be honest in their desire to be the ones who drove. Although the old standard in real estate is that the agent drives the buyers around, the next generation of real estate literally turns the tables and provides the opportunity for the agent to be chauffeured. It's not such a bad gig, in my opinion!

that this is a new listing and that you've been in the home for 25 minutes, and not another soul has walked through. Also, they may point out small flaws or highlights in the home that you wouldn't see on your own.

For example, there may be wall-to-wall carpet, but if it's an older home, your agent will know to ask if there are hardwood floors beneath. The windows may be single pane, old, and not very energy efficient, and your agent will point that out to you. There could be a boiler for heat, but no air-conditioning system. Having seen so many renovations, your agent could tell if one was a good renovation or a cheap one. He or she may have a good relationship with the listing agent, who may share inside knowledge about the sellers or the property that you might not get otherwise.

You will likely attend many open houses without your agent. Also, as the search process goes on, there will be weekends when there is just one home to see. Other times there will be five. How do you approach open houses when you're ready? Here are a couple of open house strategies that I like my buyers to use.

1. Pick the Showing Agent's Brain

The showing agent at an open house may be the agent who represents the seller or another agent standing in for the listing agent. It could be an assistant or another agent from the office who is working hard to meet new clients. Either way, this person is active in the local market and likely knows a lot about the house, the neighborhood, or the state of the market. The agent is there to chat with people. Feel free to ask for his or her opinion about the home, the neighborhood, or the school nearby.

You can learn a lot from other agents. I have a friend from Seattle, whose agent was encouraging her to make an offer at full price on a home that she absolutely loved. Before offering, she went back to see the property at the open house. There, the showing agent told her that the sellers were about to make a price reduction. She was ready to make a full-price offer but now knew she should not. Be on the lookout for these little gems or clues.

Something that you should also know is that, although it may be polite, you don't have to introduce yourself to the agent at the open house, nor should you feel compelled to. You don't have to provide contact information. If you don't wish to give it out, just provide your name and politely decline to offer further details.

2. Watch the People at the Open House

As a buyer who is serious about making a home purchase, go to open houses to determine more about a particular home and the market's response to it. You can even learn something about the seller, the pricing, and the market. Watch the people at the open house. Is buyer after buyer coming in and leaving quickly without much interaction with the showing agent? It could be a sign that there isn't a lot of strong interest. There could be a pricing issue, concern about the condition of the home, concern about the location, or all three.

Are buyers coming in and staying? Do you see husbands and

wives huddling in the corner for long periods? These are likely signs that they are excited by what they see. It could be well priced, or the property may show pristinely, like a model home, or both. Are there buyers engaging the listing or showing agent, asking questions about the property? This is a sign that the home could be competitive and that these buyers are your potential competition. They likely have similar search criteria to you. Watch them. See how they respond. This is real-time market research. You can learn a lot about the current state of the market just by observing the other buyers in the open house. If you are feeling good about a home, you might feel uncomfortable that you are the only one hanging around, when the other buyers seem to be coming and going quickly. Keep this in mind when you are on the open house circuit.

NEXT GENERATION REAL ESTATE FACT: THERE ARE FIVE TYPES OF PEOPLE WHO VISIT OPEN HOUSES

As the name implies, a property is open to just about anyone who learns of the showing in an online or print ad, drives by and sees the agent's A-frame sign, or receives a notification postcard in the mail. However, not everyone who goes to an open house is a potential buyer. Here are five types of people likely to pass through a property during an open house.

1. **Real buyers:** These people are somewhere in the home-buying process. Either they're testing out the market or they're serious and fully qualified, ready to take action. Sellers want them coming through the door.

2. **Nearby neighbors:** These folks have been waiting for years for an excuse to get inside this home for various reasons. Their home may be similar—maybe even designed by the same architect—and they want to compare the properties. There might be other reasons to see it, too: They may have heard late-night music or noise and

want to see what it's all about. An open house might also give a neighbor the chance to see how much privacy they actually have.

For example, at an open house of a property in El Dorado Hills, California, a neighbor came into the house and made a bee-line for the back deck. Meanwhile, in the neighboring home across the backyard, the neighbor's son sat in the window. What followed was a cell phone conversation in which the father instructed his son to move to the right, move to the left, go upstairs, and so on. The father's goal was to determine from exactly which points in his home he and his family were visible to their neighbors. You'll no doubt encounter nosy neighbors, too. They live nearby and just want to satisfy their curiosity about the home—or even about you.

3. **Agents scoping out the place for clients:** Agents constantly check out properties for their buyer clients. The vast majority of the time, they're professional and courteous. There are exceptions, of course. Not long ago, in the living room of a packed Sunday open house, an agent sat on the couch and spoke to her client on the phone. The agent summarized the property loudly and in none-too-complimentary terms.

   "The finishes are cheap, the floor plan is off, and the bathrooms need updating. Don't waste your time coming over here," she said. Obviously, the seller's listing agent—who witnessed the conversation—was flabbergasted. Even some of the buyers touring the property seemed uncomfortable. The listing agent politely asked the other agent to continue her conversation outside.

4. **Agents who lost the listing:** In many cases, a seller interviewed multiple agents before selecting a listing agent. Sometimes agents spend a lot of time working with a potential seller to secure a listing. Obviously, not every agent interviewed will get the listing. When the property lands on the open house circuit, agents who lost the listing may visit. They want to know if the seller took any of their suggestions. Did the seller paint the orange room a more neutral color or renovate the kitchen or bathrooms as suggested? The open house is sometimes the losing agent's chance to run

through the property anonymously because most agents usually won't know with whom they competed for the listing.

5. **Previous owners or their relatives:** Over years of open houses, a busy listing agent will surely run into an old seller or his or her children or grandchildren who grew up in the home. These people come to the open house to see how it looks and to reminisce. Lots of memories happen in a home, and the opportunity to go back in time can be a real treat.

   Usually, there's no harm done. However, you might encounter the former seller's cousin Steve, who tells the listing agent about how the current sellers did a horrible job on their backyard makeover. Even worse, you might get a relative who starts crying on the listing agent's shoulder about her grandmother, a previous owner, who recently died.

Good listing agents will let any and all of this roll off their shoulders, keep a professional game face on, and keep their eye on the ball. They solicit feedback from buyers and make notes of their comments, reactions, and questions.

Can you imagine all of these personalities in one living room at one time? It happens. Just thinking about it sounds like a great big circus. However, regardless of who you are in this list or who you might being sharing space with at open houses, keep it fun by remembering these categories of folks, and if you get nervous or overwhelmed, when all else fails, I say just picture them in their underwear.

THE PSYCHOLOGY OF THE LIST PRICE

Again, although your other search criteria can steer the direction of your home search, I am well aware that nothing can happen unless the price works. How is the list price set, and is it always fair or reflective of the home's value? With the guidance of their listing agent, the sellers ultimately decide on the listing price for their home. When you buy a gallon of milk at the grocery store or purchase a television at Walmart, the prices are set based on inventory levels, regular market

My Agent Keeps Showing Me Crap!

The chief complaint I hear from buyers is that their agent is showing them places that they don't like. I say to buyers up front that they should see as many homes as possible. A good agent should prepare you for this by saying something along the lines of, "From time to time I'll send you an e-mail with something that is not always what you are looking for. But there will always be a reason for doing so. I'll want to point it out for market data or to let you know that it would be a good comparison to something you previously saw that you liked, or there could be something special about that home or its pricing that would be helpful for you, the buyer, to understand." Be open to seeing as much as possible and listening to the feedback of your agent.

Of course, if you think your agent is sending you places that don't provide any value or color to your search, let him or her know that. I sometimes see agents who aren't the best at listening to their clients. They may keep communicating with their client or sending listings just because they haven't communicated recently. Some agents feel the need to stay in touch. The fact of the matter is that if there isn't anything to send to or show a buyer, that's okay. If you feel like your agent is pushing things on you or sending you on wild goose chases, say so.

research, and competitive price intelligence. The seller, a big company, likely has so many of the same products to produce and sell that they can't afford to keep inventory on their shelves. These prices are generally not negotiable. The same holds true for car prices. There is a manufacturer's suggested retail price, which considers all of these. There is a little bit of room for negotiations, but the range is pretty clear.

The thing about real estate is that there is just one seller, and that person has only one home to sell. Although they should be, some sellers aren't interested in what the neighbor's homes are selling for or how many similar homes are for sale on the market. They are laser focused on their home, its amenities, their experience there, and their financial situation, as it relates to the home sale. Sellers hire a real estate agent to help inform them of the value of the home and ulti-mately the list price. This number comes from an analysis of recently sold homes and current homes on the market. Most listing agents give their sellers a price range based on this data.

Selling a home is an emotional decision, and as such, we agents have a phrase we use to describe the pricing strategy (or lack thereof) of an overpriced home. We call it "seller pricing" when sellers won't listen to or take the advice of their agents on list price. Many times sellers overvalue their home, and that can be an emotional response to how connected their history is with the house, how they feel about how it enhanced (or didn't enhance) their lives, and so on. In cases such as this, and many others, including financial issues, such as the sellers need the most money for an important reason, or practical issues, such as they put a lot of money into the house and think that it's practical to expect it back, they don't listen to their agent's input or they ignore the comparable sales data supporting a lower number. It's the sellers' prerogative to do so, and therefore they can ultimately choose to list the home at whatever price they want. For a home that's worth $500,000, can they list it at $750,000? Sure, if they want to. There aren't any rules or laws about pricing that a seller has to fol-low. It's their home, and they can do what they want with the price. It would likely have a negative impact on their ability to sell, but that's their issue.

If the home meets all of your criteria but seems overpriced, don't rule it out. The list price is not always reflective of the market value, and you might not necessarily have to pay the list price if you want to buy a home. Sometimes the number is arbitrary.

Go see the home. If the home is listed for sale, it is an indication that the seller has some motivation to sell. It's not as though you drove by a random home, knocked on the door, and tried to convince a homeowner to sell. If this person has listed it, there should be some reason. If you think it's worth the effort, see if you can make it work. But I also advise not obsessing over it if the seller isn't interested in lowering the price.

In this next generation of real estate, numerous tools are available to the buyer for situations such as this. Previously, you had to take your agent's word that it had been on the market for a long time, or you both agreed it was overpriced. Now you can look up the history, type the address into Zillow, and look at the days on market (DOM) yourself. Has it been on the market for six months? Did you notice that it was previously on the market a year earlier, also for six months, but with another agent? Your next generation agent should call up that former listing agent and try to get a feel for the sellers and how motivated they are. Sometimes the former listing agent will reveal a lot of information. You may see that the home previously was pending or under contract. Find out what the story was on that offer. Why did it fall apart? It is your job as a next generation buyer to use the information to your advantage. Work with your agent and the vast amount of data to try to deduce what the story is with this seller.

If you love a home, and it meets all of your needs, don't let the list price deter you. Often sellers will list high because they expect buyers to come in and negotiate them down. Maybe they just don't believe what their agent tells them, think their home is special, and need to learn a hard lesson on their own. It could take two months of zero showings, dead open houses, and no offers for those sellers to realize that they need to reduce the price.

Work with your agent to make sure the listing agent knows that this home meets many of your needs but that you are hesitant to move ahead because you feel the pricing is off. A good agent will also be able to sense how motivated the seller is. Many times sellers, just as I've discussed with buyers, simply might not be all in. (See more about that in Part III.) It's quite possible that in one month's time, your agent will get a call from the seller's agent to say the sellers are now open to negotiate the price or to give a heads-up that they will be making a price reduction.

NEW CONSTRUCTION: FUNCTION OR DYSFUNCTION?

In many parts of the country, real estate developers and homebuilders are busy buying up building sites and building new homes, condos, and communities. Is a new home right for you? If you have been a lifelong renter and enjoyed knowing that your landlord was just a phone call away when the appliances broke or the roof leaked, then new construction may be right for you, because it is unlikely boilers, heaters, and appliances will be breaking down any time soon. Talk to your agent early about this prospect to determine if new construction is common in your area.

Many homebuilders advertise new communities while they are under construction and even start to sell homes before the community is finished. If you are interested in new construction, you and your agent should begin by isolating some communities that could be of interest. What's important to note is that local homebuilders may not always have their own agent or may not hire a listing agent to sell their homes. Instead, they have their own in-house sales team to market and sell the homes. If this is the case, then these homes may not be listed in the MLS. This doesn't mean that you can't still work with your agent. A good homebuilder knows how important it is to cooperate with (and pay a commission to) a buyer's agents and the local real estate community in general. Some people believe that homebuilders don't need to work with agents, which I say is shortsighted. In slower times, builders know that agents can be a great source of business and will need them to help sell homes. Good builders will welcome working with your agent. If they don't, let your agent know this right away.

New construction is likely found on some of the syndicates' websites because homebuilders can add their own listings manually or advertise on them. No matter how the home is listed, you should get out and see new construction if it appeals to you.

Unlike the typical seller open house, when you go to see new construction, you likely will tour the model home, which houses the sales office. This model home will display the types of floor coverings, bath and kitchen fixtures, and finishes, such as bathroom tiles, cabinetry, and faucets. You can sit in the sales center and review the different types of homes available. In any one new community, there could be five different home floor plans to choose from. In a strong market, it's quite possible that you will make an offer on a home that isn't yet built.

Unlike typical sellers, who have just their one home to sell, homebuilders treat home sales more like business transactions. Sure, you are buying a home, and that will have all kinds of emotional, practical, and financial considerations for you. But for the builders, who are generally people behind the desks of an office somewhere off-site, it's really about the numbers. They've done their homework on the market. They know how to price their homes and where their thresholds and break evens are. In a strong market, they may release only a few homes at a time to determine how the market responds to their product. If they sell 10 homes quickly but have 40 more to build and sell, they may choose to raise the prices on some of the final homes. It's economics: supply and demand. Be prepared for a less personal home-buying experience when buying through a homebuilder's sales office.

Many homebuilders will provide their buyers with finish and fixture options. In this case, buyers can customize or personalize their home by picking out hardwood floors, carpets, or even appliances from a selection the homebuilder offers. This is one of the fun parts of buying new construction. You get to make some personal decisions. However, know that all the trimmings are not of equal value. There will be some higher-end features and some lower-end and some ways to cuts costs, such as plywood cabinetry over oak. It's similar to buying a car. You might love the sedan but can't afford it. Take away the leather and GPS, and then it might wind up in your price range. In the case of a slower real estate market, this is where there might be some negotiation. If it's slow, a builder might throw in an upgrade package or install hardwood floors for free. Always ask your agent if there are any options for negotiating, even in a strong market.

There could be lag time from the time you make your offer until the time you move in, depending on which home you choose and where the builder is in the process. Particularly with the initial home sales, you could lock in a home price a good year before the home is delivered to you. In a strong market, this could result in some added equity at the time of closing.

For example, you may lock in the price of $299,000. But by the time it is built and you close and move it, the home may be worth $312,000. Also, early in the process, know that builders want to get some homes sold quickly. For starters, many builders take out construction loans, and they may need to go back to the bank and pay down some of the loans as soon as possible. They might need to increase their loan amount or apply for new loans to finish the final homes or phases of the community. If they can show their lenders some traction, in the form of sales, it helps their lenders feel secure in loaning more.

Why does this matter to you, the buyer? Because if you are one of the first buyers in a new development, the developer may be more willing to get some sales done quickly. This means there would be more wiggle room in the price or some type of negotiation to get a few deals done.

Be mindful that being the first also comes with some risks. The development hasn't sold any or many, and it hasn't proven itself yet. Some people don't want to be the first or the guinea pig. What if the builders don't sell? What if they are asking for too much? What if the developer goes under? There are always pros, cons, and risks of being the first buyer. Talk about these considerations with your agent.

Putting Your Money Where Your Mouth Is: Formulating and Presenting Your Offer

You've been in the market for a while and now you are close. You can feel it. Once you see a home that you think could really be the one, things start to jell. It's time to take things to the next level, making an offer.

BEFORE YOU MAKE AN OFFER

There are a number of ways you might have come across your new potential home. You may see it via an automatic Multiple Listing Service e-mail. Your agent may call or text you to tell you about a home that he or she previewed on a broker's tour. You may be searching online, playing with some criteria, and a listing just pops up. Because there are so many factors going on when choosing a home, I recommend you not make an offer on a home after seeing it once, no matter how you saw it. If you haven't done so already, go back to the home for a second or third showing. These showings, usually set up between the buyer's agent and listing agent, by appointment, are critical to a buyer because these are opportunities for you to speak more with the listing agent. The next generation buyer knows that listing agents are most likely the only connection to sellers. They are the only person in the transaction who interacts with all parties, and they report back to the sellers on what's happening on the ground.

Good listing agents have a lot of knowledge about the home, who has also viewed it, and how the market is faring. Most important, they have the full trust of the seller. That trusts leads to influence. I recommend you always get in good with the listing agent. Make yourself known if possible. Go to the open house, and make a point to introduce yourself to the agent. If you are in an area where there are homes for sale only by lockbox (for which only the agent can unlock to retrieve the key to the home), ask your agent if it would be possible to do a showing with the listing agent present. Good listing agents, knowing that they have a serious buyer in front of them, will want to meet you so that they can best present your offer to the seller. Going this extra mile with the listing agent is not only about you and making a good impression but about showing a serious interest in the home for sale. Your actions communicate that you are committed, and in the case of a strong market, a seller may be face two, three, or even 23 offers. In cases such as this, sellers don't necessarily believe the highest price wins the bid. Although preapproval and opening offers are certainly important considerations, there are numerous considerations sellers make that play into what can win you the house you want. They might ask themselves:

- Who are the buyers?

- Do they know the neighborhood?

- How long have they been looking?

- Why do they like our house?

- How much are they offering?

- What's their down payment?

- Are they using a local mortgage professional?

- How long until they have their inspections and appraisal?

- How many times have they seen our home?

- Do they have a good local agent?

- What was the agent's impression when he or she met them?

In the event all offers are considered equal, the sellers might look to the listing agent for help in breaking the tie and choosing the winner, and many times the listing agent will recommend the person he or she has met. A little elbow rubbing can go a long way.

All Things Considered

Diana and Brent were sellers, frustrated by the slow market, until they saw the light at the end of the tunnel: two offers around the same time. Although the offers came in well under asking price and were close in terms, I was still encouraged for my clients. An agent I didn't know presented one set of buyers to me, and they seemed very interested, very serious, and even a bit zealous to get the house. At one point the buyers even called me directly to ask some questions and made themselves known. The second offer came from a very successful and well-respected agent, someone I knew very well, but the buyer was unknown.

In the end, after a little negotiation, Diana and Brent accepted the offer the first buyers submitted. The buyers signed the contract and, before they even had the inspection, broke the contract. They found another home that they liked. I called the other agent, the one with the mystery buyer. He was still on board to buy. They signed the contract and moved forward with the home sale.

There are two morals of the story:

Moral 1: Making yourself known and forging relationships with the listing agent goes a long way when you are ready to make an offer. Had this mystery buyer introduced himself, just once, at the open house or had a private showing, I may have advised the sellers to go with his offer.

Moral 2: It is so important to be represented by a good local agent. Against my (normal) better judgment, I advised the sellers to go with the buyers who were represented by someone I didn't know. A good local agent might have been able to gauge that this couple was still apprehensive and could have advised them not to even bid on the house.

NEXT GENERATION REAL ESTATE FACT: CONDUCT RECONNAISSANCE THROUGH THE LISTING AGENT

Because listing agents know the seller, they are your access to the mind of the seller. Knowing as much as you can about the sellers and their situations will help you make the best offer possible. Think of it this way: The sellers have something you want. To give the sellers exactly what they want, you need to ask questions. You need to do your homework and figure out as much as you can about who the sellers are, what their current situation is, and what their motivations are. Sure, you know that they've listed the home at a certain price, and common sense says that if you just give them that price, you would get the home. However, what if it's overpriced, or what if you are competing against other interested parties?

It is rarely cut-and-dry when getting an offer accepted on a home. Most of the time you should be prepared for some negotiating. Knowing as much as you can about the seller will give you the edge in the negotiations. Ask the listing agent some of the following questions. Even if you know the answers to the questions, allow the listing agent to answer, and listen well. Sometimes the agent will say too much or will say things that can be revealing. Think of it as real estate reconnaissance.

1. Why are the sellers selling?
2. How long have they lived here?
3. By when are they looking to close?
4. Where are they moving?
5. How open would the sellers be to negotiating the price?
6. Have they already bought or found a new place?
7. How long has this home been on the market?
8. How do you know the sellers?
9. Have there been prior offers?
10. Why weren't any previous offers accepted?

If the answer to the first question is that the sellers are divorcing, you may quickly realize that this could go nowhere fast, and if you don't, your agent should have the sense to simply warn you. Generally in the case of a divorce sale, one party isn't accepting of the divorce, so resistance to the home sale for as long as it's possible might be on the mind of one of the sellers. On some listings, you will see seller's pricing in the case of a divorce because one party wants to list it higher than market value to resist a sale or impede the sale. *Seller's pricing* indicates to other agents and buyers that the sellers have gone against the advice of their listing agent, in terms of setting a comparable price. In this case, I would recommend you not become attached or spin your wheels.

On the other hand, if the agent says that the sellers got a job transfer, that they've already moved, that they are about to move, or that they bought or rented another home already, you know that you are dealing with some seriously motivated sellers. You may have some additional negotiating power.

Many times you will get listing agents who are eager to close the deal. This could be because they are savvy enough to recognize you are a serious buyer. They also know they have a serious seller, so why not just get going? They know how to make deals work.

By asking the listing agent if there have been any other offers presented, he or she might reveal what the magic number is or that they've had certain offers at *x* price ranges and turned them down flat. This kind of information provokes smarter buying because, along with the input of your agent, you can put an initial offer together that will show you are committed.

Real Estate Reconnaissance through the Internet

Reconnaissance entails more than just asking good questions. We have technological tools today that we can use to find out as much about the seller as possible. Zillow is a good place to begin your mission, particularly by using a tool called Make Me Move. Much like eBay's Buy It Now feature, homeowners can log in and set a price for their home that they would sell for. In doing so, owners can update their home's listing and make changes, additions, and upgrades. For instance, if Zillow's other online tool, Zestimate, lists the house as having two bedrooms, one bath, and 1,000 square feet but the sellers had done a renovation and added a bedroom, a bathroom, and 500 square feet, they can include it to update the home and therefore adjust the Zestimate or their Make Me Move price. Below is a sample screen shot of listings from Zillow.com. In this instance, I looked at homes in the Sacramento area that have "Make Me Move" prices.

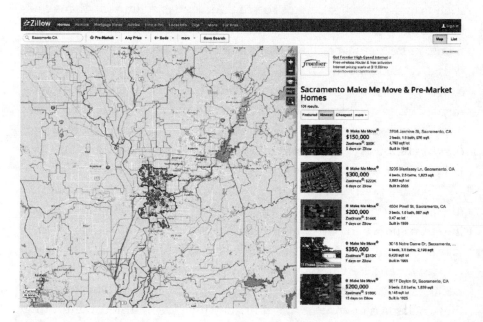

Why is it helpful to see this? If owners took time to sign up for a Zillow account, find their home, claim it, and add in their renovations, they clearly are well-informed sellers. They are knowledgeable about the value of their home and the comparable homes, independent of their agent. They may, in fact, be a next generation seller (see Part III). Absent this, sellers could simply be relying on their agent for value assessment.

When I get into Part III, which is geared toward the next generation seller, don't be surprised when I flip the following story and throw daggers and balls of fire at the sellers to deter them from using social media poorly. But for now, for the next generation buyer, I would be remiss if I didn't include how to read between the lines in social media and take advantage of some of the verbal vomiting that goes on, on the part of some sellers. Combined with talking to the listing agent, social media reveals a lot about sellers and their situations. If you are a serious buyer, you need to use all the tools available at your disposal to paint the best picture of the seller and to make the smartest offer.

I noticed that my seller client, Alex, posted on Facebook for all his friends and friends of friends to see that he was selling his home and having an open house. This could only result in more exposure for the home, more buyers coming through the door, and more interest in the property. Later in the day many subsequent Facebook notifications came in: Sally, Suzy, and Johnny liked the post, someone had commented, someone else had commented, and so on. I thought it was brilliant, more exposure for the listing. Social media works. We held our first open house that same day. It was not as busy as we would have hoped, but it was not the end of the world. These things take time.

I checked out Facebook the next day, clicked the notification button, and noticed all the comments. I couldn't believe what I was reading: In response to one person wishing Alex "Good luck today," Alex went on to tell pretty much anyone who has access how slow the open house was and how nervous he was that he wouldn't sell it. Okay, you know the type. They reveal all on Facebook. We are fine hearing about that great glass of wine or that little Joey took his first steps, but listing agents definitely do not want their sellers to reveal that they are anxious about the sale of their home on Facebook. I called Alex and told him to delete the post.

Now, if you were a serious buyer, you could take this information, call your buyer's agent immediately, make an appointment to see the house, and know that you have the upper hand here in negotiations. You might be able to see that Alex was getting married in June and in five months would be moving out of state. He needed to unload his home.

In reality, the reason why reconnaissance works is that financial aspects are not all that go into the buying and selling of a home. There are practical and emotional considerations, for example, that Alex is moving and that he's nervous, which can help you leverage your position and make a smart offer. When it comes to making the offer, let's get down to it.

🏠 EXPERT   Barbara Corcoran, Real Estate Expert

Barbara says, "Buyers today typically lose two homes before they finally close on a third. Not having the needed financing in hand, low opening bids, and overbidding in an inventory-short market get in the way."

PREPARING THE OFFER

Here's the gist of an offer: price and terms. Price always seems to be the most important, and, for the most part, it is. But the terms matter, too. Keep reading. You and your agent will likely have discussions about the listing price, and you'll formulate your opinion about what you think the house is worth. Your agent will likely provide you with some recent comparable home sales to consider. If you have been in the market for a while, in this particular area, you may know the last few comparables, because you saw them in person. This is why it helps to spend some time looking before making an offer. It could be that a home you loved, but weren't ready to make an offer on two months ago, closed for much more or much less than this home is listed for. These experiences inform you and will help guide you in coming up with a price to offer.

By the time you are making an offer, you or your agent has gotten some insight from the listing agent as to the motivations of the seller. If it seems like the seller is serious and motivated, this is the time to act like a serious and motivated buyer. Pricing is never an exact science. As I stated in Chapter 6, there is a market value, a list price, and sometimes a psychology behind pricing. The comparable houses in the area, or as we say in the business, the comps, are never exact, and the ultimate value of the home is what a buyer and seller are willing to agree on. Some buyers are more confident crunching the numbers and less willing to see some of the more subjective reasons to go higher or lower in their offer. They need to see the numbers to assess how best to reach the right price.

I've sat across from investment bankers and certified public accountants who try to make it into a numbers game, analyzing price per square feet or putting values or exact numbers on renovations. When it comes down to making an offer and negotiating the sale, there is so much more to it than that. It becomes personal—an emotional act and less of a business transaction. You need a home to live in. You want to imagine yourself in this home. You want to make memories here. You like the home, and you want to be in this neighborhood. You know that you and the seller are in the range.

At some point, you will put your guard and Excel spreadsheet down and realize that you are very close to making a large personal decision, a decision that will affect the next stage of your life. You'll realize that there is more to this than those last few thousand dollars. I'm not advocating that you throw all of your money at the seller and overpay on a home, but I do know there is much more in play here than the price negotiations. Making an offer can be emotional. Be aware of this early on, and be open to making adjustments fast.

RIGHT PRICE OR BAD OFFER?

It's common for buyers to make a few offers on other homes before actually coming to terms and locking in their home. It takes time. Even if you've been looking online for three months and then with your agent for another two or more, you still need some experience in the market. This means getting excited about a home, doing some research on it, running the numbers, and making an offer. The point at which you make the offer is a major decision. Nobody takes it lightly and nearly everyone hesitates. This is human nature. Go with your gut. Do not be pressured by your real estate agent, by the real estate market, or by all your friends who seem to be buying their own homes.

It's common for buyers who make their first offer to make a very low one. The sellers come down, but buyers just say no again. Something stops these buyers, and most often they are aware of their behavior. The second time they make an offer, they're getting a little bit more comfortable. They bid lower on a home that is clearly over-priced, and—What do you know?—it still doesn't pan out. It was probably a safe offer because clearly the seller wasn't serious.

The third offer could be on a home that is well priced for the market as well as a new listing. However, the buyers again lowball, offering 5 percent less than the asking price, against their agent's advice, in a market where two other buyers offered more than the asking price.

🏠 EXPERT   Barbara Corcoran, Real Estate Expert

Barbara's advice is that when you've found the right home, don't mess around. She says, "Buyers who want to get their dream home need to put their best foot forward from the start. It's silly to shop without your financing in hand, and low-ball offers are a waste of time. The deals that get made are going to buyers that minimize contingencies and are flexible on closing dates."

By all means, I am the biggest advocate of getting in the market and making offers. I know of a couple who made 11 offers before closing on their home. But if you continue to make offers that aren't panning out, then you should raise a red flag. This could mean that you are resisting the home purchase. You just aren't psychologically or emotionally ready to do it. Are you really ready for this? You may absolutely think that you are a real buyer and that you are ready to buy, but there could be that littlest bit of doubt in the back of your mind about your financial, practical, or emotional situation that is holding you back. Consider this, and ask yourself the following questions.

Are you wasting your agent's time and your own? This sounds like a horrible thing to ask. Agents are in the service business and agents should be at a buyer's disposal, right? Don't forget, most agents are self-employed and earn a commission only when a buyer buys or a seller sells. Be mindful of your relationship with your agent and his or her time spent with you. We've all had a buyer who takes a long time to buy. That is par for the course, a reality of the business. As agents, we talk about it among ourselves and with our managers. But just know that presenting offers, doing negotiations, and requesting second, third, and fourth showings do take time. Some agents don't have enough time or capacity to work with a buyer who is hesitant about buying. This is the reason some buyer-agent relationships end. Many other agents are patient and prefer to stay the course with these buyers. If you are slow to go or sense that you are resisting, be mindful of your agent's time.

How to Break Up with Your Real Estate Agent

The road to buying a home is often a long one. Along the way, you may discover that your relationship with your real estate agent just isn't working anymore. Maybe the agent is moving faster than you'd like. Or they're not as available as you need them to be. Maybe they just don't get you. Now what? Is it okay to break up with your real estate agent? And if so, how can you gracefully end it?

Real estate agents earn their commissions from sellers, which are split between seller's and buyer's agents. As a general rule, as a buyer, you won't be asked to enter into a contractual or financial agreement with a real estate agent. This means that you can end the relationship whenever you want to. Though there are some agents who ask buyers to sign an exclusivity agreement, in which the buyer agrees not to work with another real estate agent, this isn't the norm.

Instead, a buyer makes a handshake agreement with the real estate agent. You're basically agreeing to exclusively rely upon that agent. And that's fair: Agents often work hard and spend a lot of time engaging with buyers, watching the market, writing contracts, showing properties, reviewing disclosures, and so on. Imagine how they'd feel after spending months working with a client, only to be informed that another agent found them the home they want?

If you're not quite ready to be tied down to a particular agent, it's better not to engage one until you *are* ready. That said, it's OK to look for agents even if you're, say, a year away from making a serious move into the market. Some buyers need data and advice as they tip their toes into the market. Just be honest. A good real estate agent will read your situation well and provide the appropriate amount of attention. They'll act as a resource and be available when you need them. A big turn off for buyers is an agent who puts on the full court press, when they are not nearly ready to buy.

Make sure you've picked the most compatible agent you can find. Also, my biggest piece of advice is to start slow and feel out the relationship. It is harder to break up with your agent if you have too deeply engaged them.

As time goes on, you may find that the relationship just isn't working. If that's the case, just be honest and upfront before too much more time passes. Offer the agent constructive feedback about why it's not working for you, and give them examples. It's possible that, after an open dialogue, the agent will do a better job for you. If not, at the minimum, you'll have given the agent important feedback, which will help them do a better job for the next client (in theory, at least). And you won't be hitting the agent out of left field with the sudden announcement that you're buying a house through another agent.

YES, YOU'RE REALLY DOING THIS: SUBMITTING THE OFFER

Submitting an offer to the sellers is their first impression of you. Put your best foot forward. Ask your agent to submit a letter of introduction. Get a mortgage preapproval letter from your mortgage professional with the address of the property. Put your offer forward to the seller, ensuring all the information is accurate. After all, would you present a résumé that has typos or leaves out an important fact about your experience? Most offers are presented to a seller with an earnest money deposit. This is an amount of money, anywhere from 1 percent to 3 percent (sometimes as much as 10 percent) of the purchase price, depending on where you live. This money doesn't actually go to the seller when you present your offer. Instead, after you get an accepted offer and come to terms, it is deposited into a third-party account. Known as an escrow, this is an account of a neutral third party who takes instructions from both buyer and seller with regard to taking and dispersing money based on the terms of the contract. This is somewhat like a deposit on a hotel room or vacation rental. It shows that you are serious. You are putting your money where your mouth is. Also, this check is refundable, should something happen during your due diligence period, which I will discuss further in Chapter 8. Ask your agent what is common and what is the most that a buyer should put up. If you are serious, go to the maximum.

Put yourself in the sellers' shoes. Imagine that they've lived in this house for years, raised a family, and made some memories. Ask your real estate agent if it would be appropriate to include a personal letter to the seller. At the minimum, your agent should include a letter of introduction. You do this simply to let the seller know more about you. Highlight the terms and conditions of your offer. Remember you don't get a second chance to make a first impression, so if your offer isn't airtight, you can actually do yourself a disservice. I can't tell you how many times I've received a sloppy contract, or an offer without a preapproval letter, or a three-line e-mail from a buyer's agent as the buyer's offer. If you are serious about this property, give it your best shot, and don't hesitate to ask your real estate agent to do the same. Appearances matter, and in the case of a home purchase or sale, they matter even more.

WHY TERMS MATTER

Asking about the situation of the sellers can help frame the terms of your offer. If you find out that they are relocating for a job and that they've already moved, likely a quick closing would really matter to them. It may matter so much that they would be willing to leave money on the table. Make sure your mortgage file is complete, and ask your mortgage professional how quickly he or she can get the loan approved. If you can speed it up, do it.

You may find out the opposite, that the sellers haven't found a place to move yet or that they don't close on their new home or can't move into their new rental for some period. In this case, present them with a long closing option or offer them a quick closing but with the opportunity to rent the home back from you after closing. Known as a rent back agreement, the sellers can be assured that the sale has gone through, but they won't be under the gun to move out. If you don't need to be in the home right after the closing, this could be a win-win and a critical differentiator to the sellers. There are dozens of ways to structure your offer to meet the sellers' needs head-on. If you do it in such a way that you save yourself some money, that's even better. Be open to different ways to make the deal work. Ask a lot of questions and have an open mind.

When markets face low inventory and strong demand from buyers, competitive situations begin to surface. In the face of competition, structuring your offer and your presentation in a competitive way will give you a leg up on the other offers. Consider some of the following:

- **Order a property inspection before you make an offer.** The normal course of business is that you make an offer, get it accepted, or sign a contract contingent upon property inspections. The property inspection always tends to necessitate a second round of negotiations, or it presents enough issues with the property that the deal falls apart. I tell my buyers (and sellers) that the deal isn't really done until the inspection has been done, and all terms renegotiated, if necessary. If you have a property inspection before you make your offer, you can eliminate that uncertainty with the seller. You base your offer on the results of the inspection. In the case where there are some issues with the home, you are laying all of your cards on the table right then. The seller can be sure that this is a done deal and that there won't be further negotiations. In the case of a clean inspection, the seller knows that you are not going to walk away. Most important, having an inspection up front shows the seller that you are serious and committed to the property. It will cost you a few hundred dollars and a few hours of your day to inspect a home for sale, but you can be sure that your commitment is relayed to the seller clearly.

- **Negotiations are very stressful. Get ready for nail biting.** Once you've made your offer, it's in the hands of the sellers. They have three choices: accept your offer, reject your offer, or counter your offer. Realize that it is rare that a seller will simply accept your offer right out of the gate. Expect some back and forth and some give and take. Some buyers will purposely start with a lower offer, expecting some sort of negotiation back and forth. It seems like it's human nature not to simply put your best number out there. A home sale negotiation can go on for two hours, two days, or even two weeks.

   There are both financial and emotional considerations when negotiating the terms of a sale, for both the buyer and the seller. If the sellers are particularly attached to the home, things could drag out a little longer, or they may hold back on negotiations because they aren't quite ready yet. If you really want to have this house, you may find yourself caving in early to the sellers' counteroffer. The sellers may really need every penny out of the sale because they are in a financial hardship. This could result in their not being willing to come down in price or not being realistic. Know up front what the value range of this home is for you. Get a feel for the most you would be willing to pay. When it comes down to the last few thousand dollars, someone usually caves in. It could be you, or it could be the seller.

   Know that all of this uncertainty and on-the-fly decision making can be very stressful, but knowing the reality is that it is rare to "get a deal" can provide some solace. It is not as if you are buying a widget from the store. This is your future home. It's likely the most expensive transaction of your life. Do your best not to let your emotions get the best of you. Be practical, and know your limits. It could be that you can afford the sellers' latest counteroffer, but you or your agent isn't certain that it's really worth the money. Talk about it. There are times when a buyer just goes the extra mile to get the deal done. Be up front with your intentions and motivations.

- **Make a last call before signing.** If you think you are about to cave and are about to agree to the final purchase price last thrown into your court by the seller, announce last call to yourself. Before you shake on the deal, know that the negotiations end there. Ask yourself if you really can live with the price and the terms, are comfortable with the compromise, and are excited about the prospect of owning that home. Although it is common that the results of an inspection could open some new negotiable issues, you can't always be guaranteed that option.

HOW TO KNOW WHEN TO WALK AWAY FROM A NEGOTIATION

I've established that a home purchase is based on emotional, practical, and financial aspects of your life, and the practical ones get you to the negotiation table. The location, space, and size of the home work for your needs. But once you are going back and forth on the final purchase price, there are serious emotional and financial implications and reactions. If things are dragging on, and you and the seller seem to be at a standstill, don't be afraid to walk away or step back. The negotiation does not have to happen instantly. Sometimes a few days away from the bargaining table can be just what the doctor ordered. You need to remove yourself from the situation to think clearly. After a day away you may realize that this isn't the best home for you for the amount of money the seller wants; or you may realize that the fear of not getting it or of losing it has taken over, and your instincts tell you to go for it. Conversely, a few days away may scare the sellers into thinking they've lost you. They may come back and accept your last counteroffer. The first rule of smart negotiating is to be willing to walk away. In doing so, you clear your mind, validate your concerns, or inspire the seller to come down to more realistic expectations.

Although it could take longer than you expected, the right house for you will always come at the right time. You finally came to terms with the seller? Congratulations! You now have an accepted offer or a signed contract, likely with some contingencies. It is done differently in different parts of the country. Next stop: due diligence before closing on the home.

Ready for Action!
The Anatomy of the
Real Estate Transaction

Your offer has been made, your nails have been sufficiently chewed, and after a few nerve-wracking games of telephone tag, the sellers have accepted your offer! But this is not the end. In fact, it's just the beginning. A real estate transaction is a multilayered process, which is why it is the time in your search when you begin to invite a slew of people onto your team. Your agent will no longer be the only professional assisting you. Now, with referrals and recommendations from your agent, your team will include at least five professionals. The real estate transaction varies by state and, in some instances, by different counties in the same state. Ask your agent who will be involved in the real estate transaction and what their roles are.

REAL ESTATE ROLL CALL

Before I break down the anatomy of the real estate transaction, let's meet the players who usually help you get it done:

- **Real estate agent:** Your agent is on the front line, navigating the waters and deflecting issues, if necessary. Ever have a question or need to know what to expect next? Your agent is your ally.

- **Real estate attorney:** The role of the attorney in a real estate transaction varies by state. In many states, attorneys aren't involved at all, whereas in others, the attorney is an integral part of the contract negotiations and closing.

- **Mortgage broker or banker:** Mortgage professionals step up their game the day you have an accepted offer or a signed contract. They will likely be in touch with you in those first few days, as much as your agent was in the days leading up to the negotiations with the seller.

- **Inspector:** Property inspectors, licensed by the state, swoop in for just a short period. They are there to do just that: inspect the property top to bottom and issue a written report on their findings.

- **Appraiser:** The appraiser is hired by the bank (but paid for by you) to physically review the property and issue a written report with an opinion of value so that the bank feels justified before it agrees to lend.

- **Title officer:** When you purchase a home, you receive a title to the home with your name, the owner, on it. A title that is in your name means that you are the sole person who has legal claim to the home. Nobody else has claim to it. Title officers are usually background players in the game, but their role is important. Just like buying insurance on a car, you are required to purchase title insurance for your property. However, this kind of insurance is unique because it ensures you that unknown past issues can't come back to bite you, such as a disgruntled ex or long-lost cousins claiming Grandma's waterfront property is theirs. Title insurance also ensures that there are no other liens or clouds on the property and that the home is cleared to be purchased.

- **Escrow officer:** In states where a title and escrow company handles the closing, the escrow officer is responsible for facilitating the transaction, in particular the disbursement of funds. You simply don't want your bank to send a wire or a cashier's check to the seller directly, without some confirmation that the sellers agree that you are the new owner.

You will rely on each member of your team to understand the specificities of his or her individual specialties. The goal is to surround yourself with people you trust so that you can let them do their thing and turn your focus toward your function throughout the steps of the transaction. Every real estate community and local market does things a little differently, and you should ask your agent how the process works in your community. For the most part, however, the anatomy of the transaction encompasses these seven steps: writing an offer and contract, disclosure review and due diligence, property inspection, appraisal, loan approval or commitment, walk-through, and closing.

MAKE AN OFFER AND WRITE UP A CONTRACT

When you love a place and think it could be your future home, it's time to take a serious and legally binding step toward purchasing it. This means writing up a purchase offer and signing a real estate contract. Yes, at this early stage of the game, you need to sign a legally binding contract. By signing on the bottom line, you're committing to moving forward with the seller on the purchase. In some states, agents write the contract; in other states, they step aside and a real estate attorney steps in. In states such as Texas, there aren't any real estate attorneys involved in any aspect of a real estate transaction. Your agent will write up the contract and explain all of the terms and conditions to you.

There are contingencies, or opt outs, written into many real estate contracts. Most contracts will be contingent upon inspections, disclosure review, loan approval, appraisal, or other matters. These contingencies are ways to exit the contract in the event of something unanticipated. For example, in an offer to purchase that is contingent upon an inspection, if the inspection doesn't go in your favor, you can cancel the contract.

Once you sign a contact, you will be required to put up some kind of earnest money deposit into an unbiased third-party escrow account. Much like a deposit on some other large purchase, you want the seller to know that you are serious and that you have some skin in the game. Depending on the market, this money can vary from $1,000 to 3 percent of the purchase price. The money you've set aside for escrow, or earnest money, is refundable only if you exit the contract via one of your contingencies. Otherwise, it goes toward your eventual down payment. Once deposited, the earnest money can be released only upon written approval from both the buyer and seller based on the terms of the contract.

In Texas, buyers can offer to pay an option fee to the seller. Instead of having an individual contingency for due diligence or an inspection, they have the option to cancel the agreement for a certain number of days. If they're serious about a property and want to make a good impression, buyers can raise their option fee to $500. If a seller receives an offer from someone who never even saw the property, with a $50 option fee, chances are that buyer isn't very serious. Why would the seller want to tie up the property with someone who could walk away with the risk of losing only $50?

DISCLOSURE REVIEW

It's standard practice in real estate to give a home a fresh coat of paint before putting it on the market. Nine out of 10 times, the intention is to show the property at its best, but every so often, the seller paints the house in hopes of covering something up. That's why I always triple check the disclosure documents of newly painted houses to ensure there were no recent leaks or other damage. It's the seller's obligation to disclose known defects of the property that would affect either its value or habitability. Disclosures are meant to protect the buyer and to put it all out there. Before closing on the new home, it's the buyer's responsibility to know as much as they can about the property. Once they own it, there's no returning it.

Therefore, the first few days after getting your offer accepted are meant for you to start to familiarize yourself with the property, its history, the seller's experience living there, and how the township, town, or county sees your property. During this time, you may learn the zoning district you're in, if there are past permits pulled on the property, if there are any easements, if there has been any crime in the neighborhood, or if there are any flaws in the home, such as a broken septic tank, a leaky roof, or an unpermitted sunroom. A formal review of this documentation is serious business and should be done with your real estate agent or real estate attorney. He or she should be able to guide you through what to look for and what the red flags are.

Disclosure Review Should Go Hand in Hand with the Property Inspection

A disclosure document is something given to the buyer by the seller documenting his or her knowledge of the property. It is not the same thing as an inspection because there are things the seller may not be aware of that an inspection brings to light. For example, if the sellers know that the plumbing under the kitchen sink has a history of leaking, they should disclose it, but they may not know that their roof is near the end of its useful life and needs replacement. The kitchen sink leak may not be present at the time of the inspection, but the inspector will surely comment on the condition of the roof.

This is why the buyer should always have the property inspected. The inspector will check the property out from top to bottom, many times verifying what the seller has disclosed but sometimes bringing to light new issues. Sometimes, a next generation seller will hire a property inspector *before* going on the market. It seems backward, but this is the seller's opportunity to hire an independent party to inspect the property in case they missed or were not aware of something. In fact, as I'll discuss in Part III, "Faster Selling," I encourage sellers to have an inspection done before going on the market.

In some markets, disclosure documents are provided to buyers once the sellers have accepted their offer. In addition to their inspections or loan contingency, the buyer has an opportunity to review the sellers' disclosures. If buyers discover something negative about the property through disclosure, they can usually back out of the offer without losing their escrow deposit. Next generation sellers provide these disclosures to the buyers even before they receive an offer. Some sellers prefer to have buyers know everything they need to know up

The Risky Business of Disclosures

After they moved into their new home, and after the first rainstorm of the season, Mira and Stan called. I was their agent for the purchase. The windows in the master bedroom were leaking, and they wanted to see if I remembered anything about this from when they bought. Upon review of the disclosures, no leak was documented, and the property inspection report at the time of escrow made no mention of it either.

I suggested to Mira and Stan that this could be the result of something that was building up over time or that just never showed up for the sellers or at the time of the inspection. The buyers hired a window and siding contractor to inspect the area around the leak. The next-door neighbor happened to be doing work on his lawn and checked in to see what was going on. He went on to say that the previous sellers had had the same leaky window a year earlier. They had asked him for a referral for a good window contractor.

Given this new information, it was clear the previous seller had not properly disclosed. The buyers did more investigation, got bids on repairs, and determined exactly what the issue was. Armed with the knowledge of the neighbor and the approximate costs, they went back to the seller through his seller's agent. It did not turn into a lawsuit; the seller took responsibility and the situation was resolved quickly and fairly.

But too often, the lack of proper disclosure can result in a lawsuit. I know of a story in which a buyer bought a house, with the seller disclosing that a kitchen renovation was done without permits. A few years later, that second owner went to sell the property but didn't disclose that the previous owner had renovated the kitchen without a permit. The third owner wanted to do some electrical work with a permit. The city inspector discovered that some things had not been done to code and, upon digging deeper, said that much of the kitchen renovation (both plumbing and electrical) was not to code. The third owner was on the hook for ripping out the kitchen and doing it over. A lawsuit arose between the third owner and the second seller for not disclosing. The original sellers had covered themselves by disclosing these facts, but the second seller had not. Because of the lawsuit, the second seller was responsible and ended up having to pay the third owner for damages.

front. This is better for buyers as well. If the home has some major issues, the buyers can decide whether they want to engage too much. Disclosures before the fact save everyone time, hassle, and expense by preventing deals from falling apart once they're in escrow. Again, I prefer to encourage my sellers to do this. For more on that, check out Part III.

Buyers must sign off on disclosure documents and reports, so it's important to review them carefully and ask questions if you need to. Once you own the home, you won't have much recourse if defects were disclosed. One time, a homeowner in Rhinebeck, New York, reached out to me for advice on a home he had bought a year earlier and signed off on the disclosure documents, acknowledging an illegal living space over the garage. His agent explained to him that many homes in the area had these illegal living spaces. The buyer was buying the property for a good deal, so he didn't think it was much of a risk.

Fast-forward 15 months. The new owner decided to renovate the main house. To do so, the city building department took a good look at the entire property. It questioned this space over the garage and realized it was not permitted. This new owner was now responsible for abating (or removing) this space. It was costly. If you aren't sure of something in the disclosures or uncertain as to how it could affect you, ask. Sometimes, little things don't seem like a big deal, or in the rush to own a home, you let things slide. Just know that there are repercussions.

What Do Sellers Typically Disclose to Potential Buyers?

The work and upgrades sellers have done to their property are a common disclosure, especially whether they did the work with or without permits. If done with permits, buyers are advised to crosscheck the seller's disclosure with the town building permit report. Doing work without the town signing off with a permit is a key disclosure. If the town did not approve the work, it may not have been performed to code and may cause a fire or health hazard. Buyers should independently investigate any unpermitted work that sellers did.

Other common disclosures include the existence of pets, termite problems, neighborhood nuisances, any history of property-line disputes, and defects or malfunctions with major systems or appliances. Disclosure documents often ask sellers if they are involved in bankruptcy proceedings, if there any liens on the property, and so on. Failure to disclose can result in a messy conflict with the buyer after the sale.

Some disclosure documents are very detailed. For instance, among the questions the California Association of Realtors disclosure statement poses is whether the seller is aware of any of the following:

- Substances, materials, or products which may be an environmental hazard, including asbestos, formaldehyde, fuel, lead-based paint, mold, radon gas, or chemical storage tanks, and contaminated water or soil on the property;

- Additions, structural modifications, or other alterations or repairs done without permits;

- Any settling or sliding, slippage, or other soil problems;

- Problems with flooding, drainage, or grading;

- Major damage to any of the structures or the property from natural disasters;

- Problems with noise or other nuisances in the neighborhood; or

- Any common area (facilities, including tennis courts, pools, and walkways, or other areas co-owned with others).

Aside from the boilerplate documents sellers must complete, if there is any written (or sometimes verbal) communication regarding something negative about the property, they should disclose it to the buyer. For example, there was a property for sale with a dispute over a tree on the property line and whose responsibility it was. The neighbor faxed a letter to the seller's real estate agent, documenting the dispute. This immediately became a disclosure item that both the seller and buyer needed to sign off on.

DUE DILIGENCE NEXT GENERATION STYLE

If you are in a part of the country where there are few or no disclosures, you need to take disclosures into your own hands. In the age of Google, social media, and the Internet, here are my tips for breezing through escrow and disclosures.

- **Google the address of the home.** You will likely see the syndicator's websites and the local listings of your potential home when you put the address of the home into the search engine, but what else could come up could surprise you. Once when a client did this, the address was published in an online version of the local community's monthly newsletter. Right there in the police blotter was a record of a bike stolen from the front of the house. Simply putting the address into a search box takes little to no time and could help you uncover a lot.

- **Use Google Street View.** Using Google Street View could be one of the smartest things you do. Google Street View is like a snapshot in time. It's a look at the house at some point in the recent past. Why is this relevant? Keep reading to see how it nearly killed a deal. Google Street View allows you to not only look at the house but also zoom in, see if there was a previous paint color, or view details that may not be there anymore. What's more, you can use it to look up and down a block, revealing things about the neighborhood or potential neighbors that you may not have seen in just two or three showings.

  I once took a listing in San Francisco on the ground floor of a three-story building. The windows were right at the sidewalk, and they had bars on them from years earlier. In addition to giving the building a good paint job, the seller and I decided to build out a small garden on the sidewalk next to the home to create a buffer between people walking on the sidewalk and the home. It would also look pretty. It made perfect sense. Unbeknownst to us, a serious buyer Googled the address and looked on Street View. There was the same home, with a bad paint job and bars on the windows. It looked like a different home altogether.

Seeing the windows with bars on them in Google Street View raised questions for the buyer: *Is the neighborhood unsafe? Is there a history of crime in the neighborhood or on the property? Are the street-level windows safe?*

Upon further research, the buyer concluded that for her, the house was just too close to an unsafe area. Even though the seller didn't disclose any issues regarding crime, seeing that the bars were there simply spooked her away from moving ahead on this property.

- **Use Google Earth's satellite view.** Type in your address and see the top of your home and your backyard from space using Google Earth's satellite view. I've never heard of any major disclosure arising out of someone looking at a home with Google Earth's satellite view, but I can imagine that there have to be some interesting things, if not to just fulfill your curiosity. See it as an additional resource for you.

- **Check building records.** Before the Internet made data easy to access, a lot of the details and information about a home were on microfiche somewhere in a cold and dark room in the basement of town hall. Sure, nearly all city property records, including building permits, tax records, and applications, have always been available to the public. It was just challenging to get the records 20 years ago. You would likely have to take some time off work to go to each city department and uncover as much as you could about the property and the city's records. Today, nearly every town in the country has consolidated its databases and put everything up online for public consumption. This pool of online information inspires real estate blogs to conceive story ideas and enables the syndicator websites to offer data, statistics, and information to their visitors.

- **Search the address in the Kids Live Safe database.** According to PR Newswire, as quoted on the website "Kids Live Safe" at Kidslive safe.com, the number of registered sex offenders increased by 23 percent from 2006 to 2011. Buyers with children will certainly find this tool an essential one when thinking about buying a property.

- **Read the police blotter from the past six months.** During the disclosure period, sellers are likely asked to complete some disclosures about their knowledge of crime in the home or in the neighborhood. Although the sellers may not have experienced crime themselves, it is impossible to know about all crime nearby. You might assume that it's a safe neighborhood because you are in new turf, but it's possible there could have been some crime nearby. The only way to be sure is to read police blotters from the past six months. This could be reassuring for buyers, especially those who are new to an area.

Getting Your Loan All Teed Up

Among the very first things you and your mortgage professional should talk about are timing and interest rates. Are rates fluctuating much or will they be stagnant for a while? How long do you need to do the closing? You may have had some general discussions when you first reached out. But that could have been months ago, and now it's time to get more serious. Within a few days or maybe a week of reach-

---

EXPERT   Greg McBride, Vice President, Senior Financial Analyst, Bankrate.com

"People who have good credit, proof of income, and money for down payment will ultimately get a loan," Greg told me. "The question then becomes, will they get the best possible loan? If you are in an orderly financial situation, you will have a real incentive to shop around because bank fees and interest rates vary. On Bankrate.com, lenders' rates and fees are listed, and consumers can put in applications with multiple lenders at the same time with no penalty. In fact, doing a triple comparison is a good idea, but it should be done at the same time or else you will lose a side-by-side comparison. This way, when a lender comes back and says they are going to charge you $4^5/_8$, and the other bank quotes 4.5 percent, you know the rates are based on the same market conditions."

ing a deal with the seller, you should nail down the type of loan that you want to do and lock in an interest rate. Locking in your rate means exactly what it sounds like: Once you have a contract, you see what the rates are for the type of loan you want and for the type of home you are borrowing, and you lock in on these rates going forward.

Once you let them know that you have a deal, some mortgage folks may advise waiting a few days because rates may fall, or they may advise locking in a rate immediately because rates may be on the rise. If you are seriously considering making an offer on a home, you should be in constant contact with your mortgage professional. You'd hate to miss a lower rate because your mortgage professional didn't know that you were making an offer, let alone that you came to terms with a seller. The most likely scenario is that you reconnect with your mortgage person before you make an offer to get a breakdown of monthly payments, based on current interest rates. By doing this, you can reconnect and show that you are active in the market. The mortgage professional may advise you about rates and program options and will likely give you some feedback on what your monthly payments would look like.

Be aware that so much can change in the course of a day, let alone a week or a few months, from the time you got preapproved. It's possible that you got preapproved in February, but you finally have a deal in July. Originally, the approval could have been for a single-family home with 20 percent down. Now, you may have found a condo that you love, at a lower price, and you want to put down 25 percent. These small changes will affect your loan. Stay connected with your mortgage person at every step of the way. The lender will require lots of documentation and backup in the process. This could be very paperwork intensive and stressful in the first few weeks—prepare for the worst.

APPRAISAL

While you are busily doing your due diligence on the home you are about to buy, your bank is doing its due diligence in the form of an appraisal. An appraisal is the financial institution's way of making sure the contract price is the right price. Most buyers will put a certain amount of money down toward the purchase price, and the balance comes in the form of a loan the bank gives. However, the bank isn't going to hand over that money unless it has written proof verifying the home's value and validating the contract price.

At the buyer's cost, the bank sends an unbiased third-party appraiser to the home, mainly to confirm that the contract price is in line with the neighborhood's comparable sales. The appraiser does this by doing a physical inspection of the home, reporting on the most recent comparable sales, and commenting on the condition, location, and value of the home. If there are issues, the bank can deny the loan or change the terms. For many years, appraisals were pretty cut-and-dry parts of the real estate transaction. They happened in the background, and the buyer didn't know much about them. The appraiser came out, took measurements, looked around, and reviewed comparable sales nearby. He or she then submitted the documentation to the lender for final review.

However, in the years leading up the mortgage meltdown and housing crisis, lenders started giving out loans to anyone with a pulse. They also allowed homes to be financed with zero money down. This is when the appraisal business started going sideways. During that time, there were situations in which the appraisers and mortgage folks (as well as real estate agents and buyers or sellers) were working in cahoots to get a property to appraise at a high number just to get a deal done. Because they were being guaranteed appraisal orders from their favorite mortgage or real estate agent, home appraisers were signing off on home prices that weren't worth what buyers were offering. Some mortgage professionals sometimes turned a blind eye to get a loan through and make a commission.

In response to this practice, in May 2009, the Home Valuation Code of Conduct (HVCC) was implemented. The HVCC was meant to reduce the potential for the type of inflated property appraisals that often occurred during the last real estate market boom, which some believe contributed to the subsequent bust. The goal of the HVCC was to put a distance between the appraiser and the bank or broker to get a truly independent appraisal of the property.

Since HVCC's passing, the lender—instead of selecting its preferred, locally experienced appraiser—must order an appraisal through a third-party appraisal management company, also known as an AMC. The AMC is a neutral buffer between the appraiser and the

---

🏠 EXPERT Jonathan Miller, CEO, Miller Samuel Appraisers

"The role of the appraiser has changed from Trusted Advisor of the Bank to Deal Enabler to Deal Killer," Jonathan said. "Before HVCC came on the scene, appraisers were hired by a bank, which was comfortable with its network of appraisers, trusted their experience, and worked with them to analyze a deal. After HVCC, the ability of the bank or mortgage brokers to hire from their pool of appraisers was taken away and replaced by the hiring of unknown appraisers, who most of the time do not have local market knowledge. With little information on the home, appraisers come in often too low on their reports, which can wind up killing the deal for everyone involved."

Jonathan also says that the biggest misperception on the part of buyers regarding the appraisal is that they think the appraiser works for them. After all, the appraiser is only necessary because the buyers are the ones borrowing money. Couple that with the fact that the buyers pay for the appraisal, it's easy to misunderstand. Jonathan says, "Regardless of who pays for the appraiser, from the appraisers' standpoint, they work for the party that engages the appraisal—the bank. While the borrowers pay the bank the appraisal fee, it's the bank that flows the money through and pays the appraiser. Ultimately, the bank is the party that requires the valuation of the property to determine whether it will lend. To be completely accurate, the appraiser actually works for the AMC, who, in turn, works for the bank. The appraiser is one step removed so there is no influence. The buyer's agent and the buyer don't have any interaction with the appraiser. Buyers need to work closely with their agent, who needs to work closely with the listing agent, since they are the ones who accompany the appraiser on the walkthrough."

banks. In theory, it is a good idea. If the agent or mortgage person couldn't call an appraisal buddy to appraise properties, banks would get true appraisals, without any funny business. However, it's very important to understand that today, many believe that, because of this law and the implementation of HVCC, legitimate purchases are being steamrolled, sometimes making it impossible for sellers to sell, buyers to buy, or homeowners to refinance.

How Appraisals Can Trip You Up— and What to Do about It

Imagine that you've found a home you really love. You and the seller have come to terms on a fair market value. You've had the property inspected from top to bottom and reviewed all of the seller's disclosures. You've submitted every last piece of financial data to your mortgage broker, and you're already picking out new paint colors because you think it's a done deal.

Then, you get an unexpected call from your mortgage professional, saying the property didn't appraise at or even near the contract price. This turn of events could easily scare a first-time buyer from going through with the purchase. For a more experienced buyer or seller, it becomes, at a minimum, a major kink in the process. Unfortunately, this scenario is happening now more than ever and in all markets throughout the country. Here's why.

Some Unintended Consequences of the AMC

There aren't set fees for an appraisal. A good local appraiser might charge $500. However, someone new and inexperienced or from a less expensive market might charge $350. The AMC, in turn, may hire the least expensive appraiser, who may be someone from outside the area. Many times, the out-of-town appraiser isn't a member of the local Multiple Listing Service (MLS), nor is he or she familiar with the area. This can result in appraisals that are considerably off the mark from a property's true market value.

One of my buyers, in 2010, made an offer on a town house condo for the seller's asking price the day it went on the market. There had been a foreclosure in the complex six months earlier. However, there were lots of other recent comparable sales nearby, but outside of the complex, to support this newly renovated home's asking price. Even so, the appraiser the AMC hired focused on the foreclosure as well as other distressed sales a few miles away that weren't comparable. In fact, she appraised the property for $35,000 less than the asking price. All the other people involved in the deal knew the appraiser was off, but we were stuck. We wound up going through the bank's appraisal dispute process, supplying other comparable sales, and still their efforts failed. The loan was denied. The deal, as it stood, was off.

Within a few hours, another buyer came in with an offer. The property ended up selling for the full asking price. Although the original buyer had agreed to pay the seller's list price and felt that it was worth it, in his mind the appraiser was a third-party objective person not tied to the outcome of the deal. If the appraiser, through her report, was saying he would've paid too much, that didn't sit well, but what he didn't realize was that the appraiser wasn't qualified to appraise this home. She didn't have experience in the area. Some could read this as my advocating for overpaying or not taking the role of the appraiser seriously. That's not the case. I've seen firsthand some appraisers walk in and out of a home in fewer than 15 minutes or use comparable sales in their report that really aren't comparable. It's my belief that the fair market value of any home is the price that an able and willing buyer and able and willing seller agree on.

I once listed a large single-family home in San Francisco with a small, legal studio in-law unit below. The home was owner occupied. The owners used the studio for guests and family members. Also, the home had beautiful views. The AMC-hired appraiser, who said he'd never been in this neighborhood before the day of the appraisal, appraised the house by comparing the property to two-unit, tenant-occupied, investment-type properties with low rents. Not surprisingly, the appraisal was off by $100,000.

Had the appraiser been local, he would have understood that there was a trend in the area for larger homes with legal in-law units. He would have looked for comps in the single-family homes category, and he would have found direct comps priced higher than the contract price. Also, he would have understood that San Francisco has strict rent control laws, which brings down the value of tenant-occupied homes. Finally, he'd have understood that homes with views tend to sell for upward of 10 percent more than homes without views in the area.

Another unintended consequence of the AMC is now there are too many cooks in the kitchen. Bringing in another party adds one more step to the already arduous process, taking up more time. In strong markets, the AMC can slow down the deal. Buyers and sellers might agree to set the closing in 30 days, but if the AMC is not responding, it can blow that time. The way to get around this is follow up, follow up, follow up. Be the best pest you can be.

NEXT GENERATION REAL ESTATE FACT: DISPUTE A BAD APPRAISAL

It is important to point out that this practice is really in response to today's appraisals going in the opposite direction of the appraisals before the mortgage meltdown. It's absolutely necessary to have a third-party representative of the bank verify and independently sign off on the purchase price. Both the banks and the buyers deserve it.

Most banks have a process by which you can dispute a bad appraisal. This generally requires the buyers or their agent to supply other comparable sales and explanations as to why they think the appraiser's value is off. The review takes some time and can go either way. If it fails, you still have options to keep the deal together.

If both parties still want to move ahead, the best plan is to extend the loan and closing times and switch to a new lender. If you are working with a mortgage broker, this is easy. It can simply present your file to another bank. If you are working with a bank, you'll need to start over with a new one. Another option is to reduce the purchase price, if both parties agree. The final option, depending on the deal, is for the buyer to bring more cash to the closing. Sometimes the buyer and seller agree to a small reduction in purchase price, and the buyer makes up the difference with a larger down payment.

For example, if the offer was $250,000 with 10 percent down, and the appraiser valued it at $240,000, the seller and buyer could agree to $245,000, with the buyer bringing in the extra $5,000 in addition to their 10 percent down payment. If the seller is serious about selling and the buyer serious about buying, it makes the most sense for all parties to work together to keep the deal in play. In a strong seller's market, the sellers may be less willing to work with the buyer. In a strong buyer's market, they may have to work hard to keep their buyer.

The trick is to avoid getting into this situation to begin with. Check with both your real estate agent and your mortgage professional early on in the process about their recent experiences with property appraisals. If appraisals can be problematic in your market, you can do some things in advance. The biggest thing that your agent can do is to raise the concern about appraisals with the listing agent and, in turn, with the seller. Track the schedule, and ask your agent when the appraiser called. If the seller's agent gets a call from an appraiser with an out-of-town area code to set up the appraisal appointment, it might be the first red flag. In turn, working with your agent, the seller's agent can notify all parties that oversight should be heightened. The listing agent can ask the appraiser on the phone about familiarity with the area, membership in the local MLS, and number of appraisals done in the area in the past six months. If concerned that the appraiser isn't experienced, the listing agent can ask for another.

Also, although buyers don't normally go to the appraisal, they can ask to be present. The listing agent should show up prepared with knowledge of recent comparable sales and be ready to shed light on certain comparable sales for the appraiser. The listing agent and the seller have likely been physically inside all of the most recent sales, whereas the appraiser has not. The listing agent might point out that one comp didn't have a finished basement, that the kitchen for another comp wasn't renovated, that a third comp was in a superior location or had an unbelievable deck off the kitchen, or that comp number four was a distressed sale (see Chapter 9 for more on distressed sales).

Most appraisers will appreciate the data, although some will not,

> 🏠 **EXPERT**   Jonathan Miller, CEO, Miller Samuel Appraisers
>
> "Every home as a story that should be told. Since financial reform HVCC was born 3 out of 4 appraisers that come to a home do not have local market knowledge. This disconnection changes the volatility and role of appraiser from form filler to deal killer," says Jonathan. "If buyers and sellers are concerned that the appraiser will not have an accurate picture of the home and/or the neighborhood, my advice is to tell the story of the home. So many people hide behind the comps, but it must be considered that there are circumstances behind the data of those comps. A home's value can be determined by circumstantial things. For instance, a husband and wife may have been looking for a home for four months with nothing in their price range, which is why when a home was suddenly listed in their range, they offered the list price for fear they would lose it. Or, one of the comps might have a lower selling price, but the fact is the buyers were paying all cash and the sellers preferred a lower sale price with no contingencies than a higher one with contingencies. Knowing such stories are important to the appraiser and should be included or attached to the one-sheet the listing agent hands to the appraiser along with the comps the agent pulled."

depending on how the agent delivers the information. Pushing them around with comps or seemingly treating them disrespectfully will only alienate them and hurt your deal. I say treat the appraiser not as an enemy but as a member of your team.

LOAN APPROVALS OR COMMITMENT

In addition to making certain the property is appraised at no less than the contract price, the bank will want to fully approve your credit, debt, and income history. It will also want to approve the property's preliminary title report to make sure there aren't any liens recorded against the property that might affect its value. The bank can take up to a month, sometimes two, depending on your market, to do its full review, which should result in a loan commitment or full loan approval. Once that's completed to the bank's satisfaction, you're guaranteed a loan, and you're one step closer to closing. Depending on your local market or customs, you may have to sign off on this physically.

EXPERT Greg McBride, Vice President, Senior Financial Analyst, Bankrate.com

Greg told me, "One of the biggest changes in the real estate market has occurred in how people obtain loans. Today, there is so much more paperwork and hoops to jump through than buyers are used to seeing. This is because if they have a loan application that doesn't have its I's dotted and T's crossed, lenders are increasingly on the hook."

INSPECTION

The general property inspection is one of the most important parts of the real estate transaction. You should plan well in advance for it. Block out a few hours on the day of the inspection, depending on the size of the home. Your agent and the listing agent should be present, and these few hours can be critical.

As the buyer, you hire the property inspector, who should be licensed by the state. You sign an agreement with and pay the inspector out of your own pocket. Depending on your local market and the size of the home, it could be $100 to $500, likely somewhere in the middle. Most buyers get a referral for an inspector from their real estate agent. In any given market, it's likely that there are a handful of local inspectors who focus on home property inspections.

This is your one chance to approve the property from top to bottom. If issues arise, you might go back to the seller and negotiate some sort of fix or credit. If something major arises, and the property is just not what you signed up for, you can exit the contract via your inspection contingency.

The Misconceptions of Inspections

The property inspection is a great way to familiarize yourself with the home, and you should look at it as another aspect of your due diligence. Now that you have an accepted offer or a signed contract, dig deeper. This is an important and expensive purchase, and you should be there, in person and paying attention. However, I have to set the record straight. The inspection is not the buyer's chance to tear the home apart, find things wrong with it, and go back to the seller with a list of demands.

I once had a buyer finally agree on the price, and they moved forward to the inspection phase, which went very well. However, the buyer wanted to go back to the sellers and ask for credits off small things that came up in the inspection. It was a competitive market, and the sellers had other people very interested in making an offer. The buyer revealed that he had only agreed on the purchase price at the negotiation table because he expected there to be more negotiations down the road. Here he was, in the face of a home that had a nearly perfect inspection, with an agreement on a price that he really didn't want to pay. He ended up walking away from the home.

He felt that he was overpaying. He agreed on that price only because he figured he'd get the seller to come down in price later on. In this case, the buyer wasn't ready to buy. Had he just held firm on his lower offer up front, he would have saved time, money, and emotional energy on property inspections and becoming attached to the home. Sure, there are lots of times when you can renegotiate a sale after the offer is accepted, and some sellers will accept that. But you should always be confident and happy with your final accepted price.

I always ask my buyers when they are about to come to terms, "Are you sure this is the right price for you? Do you have any concerns? If the inspection comes back perfect, are you still fine to move ahead?" Remember from Chapter 7 that this is the last call! Try to approach it this way: If you get the home for your price, and it just so happens that you can negotiate more down the road, great news. This is the exception, not the rule. If there really are serious issues that come up because of the inspection, surely you and the seller will work in good faith to renegotiate the price, or you will ask the sellers to remedy. But when you come to terms on price, you must assume that the inspection will turn out spotless.

Good inspectors will encourage you to follow them around during the process, and you should do it. The inspection should be your first introduction to how your home works. Once you own it, you will be responsible for upkeep. Your inspector will walk the house inch by inch, and while following along, you can learn about the systems of your home, where they are, how they work, and how they are connected. Whenever possible, go where the inspector goes. Get on the roof, go into the basement, and venture into the crawlspace. It will be helpful for the inspector to point things out to you in real time and demonstrate where the systems are and how they work. Also, although you will get a comprehensive written report after the inspection, some things are understood better in person than read about in a report later. Once the purchase is complete, you'll know where everything is and have short- and long-term plans for maintenance. The goal here is not to become a home specialist but to begin becoming a specialist of your own home.

What to Inspect When You're Inspecting

Unless you're Tim the Tool Man, you might not consider the inspection the most riveting experience of your life. There might be moments when you zone out or you are caught contemplating what wall the couch should sit on. After all, you get another good hour or two to poke around the house, and this time around, you are one step closer to being the owner. At the very least, here are the main features of the inspection that you, your agent, and the listing agent will want to stay awake for:

❑ **Roof:** Find out how old the roof is. A new roof today should last 15 to 20 years. Also, is the roof all the same? Once in a while a seller will have a leak and simply have part of the roof replaced or even patch over the part where the leak was. Ideally, you want the same materials on the entire roof. Seeing a patch should be an alert to go back to the seller and find out if there were previous issues. Go into the top floor or the attic to see if there are any interior stains; this can also indicate a past or present roof leak.

❏ **Furnace or Boiler:** A furnace or boiler can lasts up to 50 years. Again, find out how old the current one is. The inspector should be able to give you an estimate as to the life of it based on looking at it. Make sure the filter of the furnace is clean, and find out if the furnace is energy efficient. Furnaces from the 1980s likely wouldn't meet today's green standards. If it's a boiler, find out how many zones and how the water boils.

❏ **Plumbing:** Galvanized pipes (often found in older homes) collect calcium deposits, which can negatively affect water pressure. Find out what kind of pipes the property has (copper is the standard now), and check hot and cold water pressure throughout the home.

Why Your Uncle Al *Also* Has No Business at the Inspection

I say not to use family as agents, and I haven't changed my tune when it comes to family and friends as inspectors. Oh, I've heard the song before. Uncle Al is really handy; your brother the state trooper just got a side gig as an inspector; your cousin Mike's sister-in-law's brother, Matty, is an awesome contractor and will give you a good break on the fee. Whether they are licensed or not, I do not recommend you get involved with friends or relatives when it comes to the inspection.

Although it may seem logical to bring a relative or friend who is a contractor, be mindful that these people aren't licensed property inspectors. Licensed inspectors are liable for what they write on their inspection reports. If they miss something, you may have recourse with them legally. In cases where a friend or relative is a licensed inspector, he or she could end up causing harmful consequences. Your brother the state trooper may think it's important to point out as many negative things as possible, just to seem helpful. He's far from impartial, however, and you run the risk of raising red flags that don't need to be. Contractor Matty may be a kitchen and bath contractor and has only limited knowledge about roofs, structural systems, or plumbing. A qualified and licensed local property inspector is the best person for the job.

Some people have been living with poor pressure for years, and it is just the way it is. If you are used to good pressure, it would be helpful to identify poor pressure and understand why it's poor.

❑ **Electrical:** Make sure the property has plenty of juice—100 amps or more—coming in to power your computers, flat-screen TVs, and so on. Many older homes were not built to accommodate today's electrical requirements.

❑ **Hot water heater:** Most models last 10 to 15 years, so find out the age. Also, is it energy efficient? How many gallons does the tank hold? If there is currently only one person living in the home, and you will be a family of four who all plan to shower at the same time each day, you may want to consider getting a larger hot water heater.

❑ **Oil tank:** In parts of the country where oil is used as a heating mechanism, oil tanks were once buried below ground. Although this practice is no longer allowed today, many underground oil storage tanks still exist. As a buyer, you need to identify if there is a tank and if there is a leak. Once you become the owner of the property, the tank and the responsibility of the leak become yours. A leaky oil tank can cause damage to the soil and the groundwater. In some communities, by law, the real estate transaction marks the occasion that an underground oil storage tank needs to be inspected for leaks.

❑ **Foundation and structural issues:** This is about the integrity of your home. You want to make sure that there aren't any cracks or breaks and that the home is properly attached to the foundation. The inspector will look at the foundation walls and the floor joists and look for evidence of structural issues, such as sloping floors or cracked plaster.

❑ **Draining and grading issues:** Many times a home on a hillside will have issues with water piling up next to the home, or drains that were meant to collect and divert water are not working as they should. Sitting water will move to an open space, and water can become your worst enemy.

❑ **Previous renovations done poorly:** Especially in an older home, the seller or a previous seller may have undertaken any number of renovations. The inspector is there to make sure that they were done properly and that they would match today's building codes.

WALK-THROUGH

A day or so before closing, you'll walk back through the property to make sure it's in the condition it was when you last saw it. You want to be certain that the seller didn't remove any fixtures, make modifications, or leave behind garbage or debris. You also want to make sure any fixes you negotiated with the seller were indeed fixed.

Final Walk-through Checklist

Here's what you need to know for your final walk-through:

1. A final walk-through isn't a home inspection. You've already done that by now (or you should have).

2. Take your contract with you. You might need to refer to it while on site.

3. In many markets, the buyers and sellers never actually meet in person, but if everyone is agreeable to the idea, perform the final walk-through in the seller's presence. He or she knows the home better than anyone else and should be able to answer your questions and provide some more history of the home.

4. If the home is vacant, it's even more important to do a final walk-through. Since your last visit, for instance, someone might have left a faucet dripping, inadvertently causing water damage.

5. Take along a checklist of things to do during the final walk-through, including the following tasks:

   ❑ Check the exterior of the home, especially if there have been strong windstorms or rainstorms since your last visit.

   ❑ Turn all light fixtures on and off.

❑ Make sure the seller hasn't removed any fixtures, such as chandeliers, that he or she agreed to leave behind.

❑ Check all major appliances.

❑ Turn heat or air-conditioning on and off.

❑ Turn on water faucets; check for leaks under sinks.

❑ Test the garage door openers.

❑ Flush all toilets.

❑ Open and close all windows and doors.

❑ Do a visual spot check of ceilings, walls, and floors.

❑ Turn on the garbage disposal and exhaust fans.

❑ Check the status of any agreed-upon repairs.

❑ Check screens and storm windows. If they've been stored, make sure you know where they are and that they're in good shape.

❑ Look in storage areas to make sure no trash or unwanted items remain. Sellers often leave old paint cans or hazardous materials behind.

❑ Do a quick check of the grounds. Some sellers have dug up and taken plants (even small trees or bushes) with them.

Taking an hour for one last sweep is a good investment in your time. After all, you don't want to spend the first weeks in your new home cleaning up or making unexpected repairs.

THE CLOSING

Depending on the market, the closing may happen at an attorney's office or with an escrow officer at a title and escrow company's office. In some jurisdictions, the buyer and seller don't ever meet. Each goes in to sign the closing papers separately, and the property closes in the background. In others, the buyers and sellers sign the closing documents together.

Regardless of how a closing happens, if you're a buyer and getting a loan, plan on signing dozens of documents. You'll have to show up to the closing with photo ID because your signature will be notarized. Before the closing, your real estate agent, attorney, or escrow officer should send over a closing or settlement statement to review (see the sample settlement statement on the following pages). This will spell out your final closing numbers and what money you need to bring to closing. You can wire in the funds or pay with a cashier's check on closing day. Be sure to ask for the statement early so that there aren't any last-minute surprises.

Three Ways to Protect Your Escrow Deposit

1. Get to know the property during inspection.

2. Get written notice that your loan has been approved, and make sure the property doesn't appraise for less than the purchase price.

3. Review the property disclosures carefully.

The anatomy of the transaction in the next generation of real estate doesn't have to be a ball of twine. If you align with all the right professionals, each of the seven parts of the transaction could unravel neatly and pleasantly. What I have just discussed are the most typical ways to go about buying a home, but as you know, there is nothing typical about the next generation. For my last chapter for you, the next generation buyer, let's turn to a hot and complex topic: distressed sales.

OMB Approval No. 2502-0265

A. **Settlement Statement (HUD-1)**

B. Type of Loan

1. ☐ FHA	2. ☐ RHS	3. ☐ Conv. Unins.	6. File Number:	7. Loan Number:	8. Mortgage Insurance Case Number:
4. ☐ VA	5. ☐ Conv. Ins.				

C. Note: This form is furnished to give you a statement of actual settlement costs. Amounts paid to and by the settlement agent are shown. Items marked "(p.o.c.)" were paid outside the closing; they are shown here for informational purposes and are not included in the totals.

D. Name & Address of Borrower:	E. Name & Address of Seller:	F. Name & Address of Lender:

G. Property Location:	H. Settlement Agent:	I. Settlement Date:
	Place of Settlement:	

J. Summary of Borrower's Transaction		**K. Summary of Seller's Transaction**	
100. Gross Amount Due from Borrower		**400. Gross Amount Due to Seller**	
101. Contract sales price		401. Contract sales price	
102. Personal property		402. Personal property	
103. Settlement charges to borrower (line 1400)		403.	
104.		404.	
105.		405.	
Adjustment for items paid by seller in advance		**Adjustment for items paid by seller in advance**	
106. City/town taxes to		406. City/town taxes to	
107. County taxes to		407. County taxes to	
108. Assessments to		408. Assessments to	
109.		409.	
110.		410.	
111.		411.	
112.		412.	
120. Gross Amount Due from Borrower		**420. Gross Amount Due to Seller**	
200. Amount Paid by or in Behalf of Borrower		**500. Reductions In Amount Due to seller**	
201. Deposit or earnest money		501. Excess deposit (see instructions)	
202. Principal amount of new loan(s)		502. Settlement charges to seller (line 1400)	
203. Existing loan(s) taken subject to		503. Existing loan(s) taken subject to	
204.		504. Payoff of first mortgage loan	
205.		505. Payoff of second mortgage loan	
206.		506.	
207.		507.	
208.		508.	
209.		509.	
Adjustments for items unpaid by seller		**Adjustments for items unpaid by seller**	
210. City/town taxes to		510. City/town taxes to	
211. County taxes to		511. County taxes to	
212. Assessments to		512. Assessments to	
213.		513.	
214.		514.	
215.		515.	
216.		516.	
217.		517.	
218.		518.	
219.		519.	
220. Total Paid by/for Borrower		**520. Total Reduction Amount Due Seller**	
300. Cash at Settlement from/to Borrower		**600. Cash at Settlement to/from Seller**	
301. Gross amount due from borrower (line 120)		601. Gross amount due to seller (line 420)	
302. Less amounts paid by/for borrower (line 220)	( )	602. Less reductions in amounts due seller (line 520)	( )
303. Cash ☐ From ☐ To Borrower		**603. Cash** ☐ To ☐ From Seller	

The Public Reporting Burden for this collection of information is estimated at 35 minutes per response for collecting, reviewing, and reporting the data. This agency may not collect this information, and you are not required to complete this form, unless it displays a currently valid OMB control number. No confidentiality is assured; this disclosure is mandatory. This is designed to provide the parties to a RESPA covered transaction with information during the settlement process.

L. Settlement Charges

700. Total Real Estate Broker Fees		Paid From Borrower's Funds at Settlement	Paid From Seller's Funds at Settlement
Division of commission (line 700) as follows :			
701. $ to			
702. $ to			
703. Commission paid at settlement			
704.			

800. Items Payable in Connection with Loan			
801. Our origination charge	$ (from GFE #1)		
802. Your credit or charge (points) for the specific interest rate chosen	$ (from GFE #2)		
803. Your adjusted origination charges	(from GFE #A)		
804. Appraisal fee to	(from GFE #3)		
805. Credit report to	(from GFE #3)		
806. Tax service to	(from GFE #3)		
807. Flood certification to	(from GFE #3)		
808.			
809.			
810.			
811.			

900. Items Required by Lender to be Paid in Advance			
901. Daily interest charges from to @ $ /day	(from GFE #10)		
902. Mortgage insurance premium for months to	(from GFE #3)		
903. Homeowner's insurance for years to	(from GFE #11)		
904.			

1000. Reserves Deposited with Lender			
1001. Initial deposit for your escrow account	(from GFE #9)		
1002. Homeowner's insurance months @ $ per month $			
1003. Mortgage insurance months @ $ per month $			
1004. Property Taxes months @ $ per month $			
1005. months @ $ per month $			
1006. months @ $ per month $			
1007. Aggregate Adjustment -$			

1100. Title Charges			
1101. Title services and lender's title insurance	(from GFE #4)		
1102. Settlement or closing fee	$		
1103. Owner's title insurance	(from GFE #5)		
1104. Lender's title insurance	$		
1105. Lender's title policy limit $			
1106. Owner's title policy limit $			
1107. Agent's portion of the total title insurance premium to	$		
1108. Underwriter's portion of the total title insurance premium to	$		
1109.			
1110.			
1111.			

1200. Government Recording and Transfer Charges			
1201. Government recording charges	(from GFE #7)		
1202. Deed $ Mortgage $ Release $			
1203. Transfer taxes	(from GFE #8)		
1204. City/County tax/stamps Deed $ Mortgage $			
1205. State tax/stamps Deed $ Mortgage $			
1206.			

1300. Additional Settlement Charges			
1301. Required services that you can shop for	(from GFE #6)		
1302.	$		
1303.	$		
1304.			
1305.			

1400. Total Settlement Charges (enter on lines 103, Section J and 502, Section K)			

L. Settlement Charges		

700. Total Real Estate Broker Fees	Paid From Borrower's Funds at Settlement	Paid From Seller's Funds at Settlement
Division of commission (line 700) as follows :		
701. $ to		
702. $ to		
703. Commission paid at settlement		
704.		

800. Items Payable in Connection with Loan			
801. Our origination charge	$	(from GFE #1)	
802. Your credit or charge (points) for the specific interest rate chosen	$	(from GFE #2)	
803. Your adjusted origination charges		(from GFE #A)	
804. Appraisal fee to		(from GFE #3)	
805. Credit report to		(from GFE #3)	
806. Tax service to		(from GFE #3)	
807. Flood certification to		(from GFE #3)	
808.			
809.			
810.			
811.			

900. Items Required by Lender to be Paid in Advance		
901. Daily interest charges from to @ $ /day	(from GFE #10)	
902. Mortgage insurance premium for months to	(from GFE #3)	
903. Homeowner's insurance for years to	(from GFE #11)	
904.		

1000. Reserves Deposited with Lender		
1001. Initial deposit for your escrow account	(from GFE #9)	
1002. Homeowner's insurance months @ $ per month $		
1003. Mortgage insurance months @ $ per month $		
1004. Property Taxes months @ $ per month $		
1005. months @ $ per month $		
1006. months @ $ per month $		
1007. Aggregate Adjustment -$		

1100. Title Charges		
1101. Title services and lender's title insurance	(from GFE #4)	
1102. Settlement or closing fee $		
1103. Owner's title insurance	(from GFE #5)	
1104. Lender's title insurance $		
1105. Lender's title policy limit $		
1106. Owner's title policy limit $		
1107. Agent's portion of the total title insurance premium to $		
1108. Underwriter's portion of the total title insurance premium to $		
1109.		
1110.		
1111.		

1200. Government Recording and Transfer Charges		
1201. Government recording charges	(from GFE #7)	
1202. Deed $ Mortgage $ Release $		
1203. Transfer taxes	(from GFE #8)	
1204. City/County tax/stamps Deed $ Mortgage $		
1205. State tax/stamps Deed $ Mortgage $		
1206.		

1300. Additional Settlement Charges		
1301. Required services that you can shop for	(from GFE #6)	
1302. $		
1303. $		
1304.		
1305.		

1400. Total Settlement Charges (enter on lines 103, Section J and 502, Section K)		

Diamonds in the Rough:
What You Need to Know
When Thinking about Buying
a Distressed Sale

The next generation of real estate and distressed sales are interconnected in a way that buyers and sellers haven't been since the 1930s. *Distressed* is a general word used to describe short sales, foreclosure sales, and real estate owned (REO sales). In the face of a housing recovery, we will continue to see distressed sales for years to come, and they can present a new set of options for today's homebuyer that didn't exist two or three decades ago as abundantly as they do today. This chapter aims to help buyers think carefully about buying a distressed sale, consider the upsides and the downsides, and consider the potential risks that come along with purchasing one of these homes. If done the right way, a distressed sale can present a great opportunity for the right person who is looking for a way to create value in the home purchase, or as some people say, get a deal. But often deals come with much uncertainty. My goal for this chapter is to help you turn that uncertainty into opportunity.

SHORT SALES

A short sale is a homeowner's attempt to sell his or her home for less than the amount owed to the bank, for example, if the homeowner owes $350,000 on the house but the current market value is $300,000. In this case, the owner is shorting the bank by $50,000. There are two reasons why people would sell as a short sale, and they both have to do with hardships.

First, someone simply can't afford to live there anymore. This was common either when interest rates rose or adjusted or when people were laid off because of the economic crisis. In either case, they were in financial hardship and couldn't afford to make the payments, so they tried to sell their homes to get out from under the financial strain. However, the market had imploded so badly that the value was now below the original loan amount.

Second, and what confuses most people, are situations where the owner just can't stay in the home anymore. The person got a job transfer, had a divorce, or had some other life change. The homeowner wants to sell, but again the values are so far down. Normally, he or she would simply have to come up with the difference between the loan amount and the value. However, prices came down so much in some areas that many people couldn't afford to write a check for 30 percent or even 10 percent of the home's value to the bank, so they had to ask the bank for permission to sell short.

Selling a home as a short sale is cooperating with the bank instead of just walking away. In this scenario, the seller works with the bank to control the process. It's important to know that not all short-sale sellers are behind on their payments or irresponsible. Instead their appropriate life change or event has come at a bad time. Many short-sale sellers use the short sale as the absolute last resort. I've known owners who commuted two hours each way to work because they couldn't sell their home and couldn't afford to take such a huge loss. They eventually went the short-sale route.

FORECLOSURES: SALES ON THE COURTHOUSE STEPS

In a foreclosure sale, the bank tries to sell the home in a public auction, often on the courthouse steps. It is the last step of the larger process known as foreclosure. A foreclosure is not a type of home but is the process by which a bank tries to sell the home out from under sellers who haven't paid their mortgage. The conditions vary by state, but it's helpful to know the general process by which it happens. More than anything, knowing the process is helpful to understand the terms. The foreclosure process could take as little as six months, but I have seen it take up to three years in some cases in the past few years. If owners (borrowers) fall behind on their mortgage payment for three months, the first action the bank will take is to file a notice of default (NOD) against the borrower. This is generally recorded with the town or county assessor's office. Once the NOD is filed, the bank can begin the foreclosure process.

After another three months, the bank will file a notice of intent to sell. This means that it has tried to work with the homeowners, but they still haven't paid. At this point the bank needs to sell the home out from under the homeowner, in other words, foreclose on them. The bank works with the town or county clerk to sell the home publicly, many times on the town hall or courthouse steps. Anyone can show up to purchase the home from the bank at this foreclosure auction, for the amount of the unpaid mortgage plus any property taxes, interest, or fees. If nobody buys the home that day, generally because the mortgage amount is higher than the fair market value, the bank then formally takes the property back from the homeowners, and the transfer of ownership from the homeowner to the bank takes place. Then the home becomes an REO.

REO

REO stands for *real estate owned*, and is often confused with foreclosures, when, in fact, they are not the same. This is the term banks use for a home that a bank owns. Banks have entire REO departments that manage the sales of these homes. Once the bank takes the property back, it needs to hire a real estate agent, figure out the list price, and get it on the market and off their books. Banks were never in the business of owning real estate. They make loans. It is their preference to do what it takes to get these homes off their books while losing as little money as possible.

WHAT TO KNOW WHEN YOU WANT TO BUY A SHORT SALE

Because short-sale sellers still own their homes, you will be negotiating the price directly with the sellers, just as in a regular transaction. The sellers set the price and agree on the final terms with you. They sign the contract. However, once they do this, they need to take that contract and the potential sales terms to the bank for its approval. A buyer's contract with a short-sale seller is not binding and should always be subject to the bank's approval of the sale. As a part of this approval, the bank will want to do its own appraisal of the home and decide whether the seller has a serious enough hardship to allow the sale to happen. The bank isn't simply going to take a loss. However, sometimes banks are backlogged and these approvals drag on and on.

I have seen dozens of situations where buyers fall in love with a home that is being sold as a short sale, only to be disappointed months down the road. They make their offer and the seller accepts. They're ecstatic. Now all that is necessary is for the bank to sign off. I always advise buyers of short-sale homes that it's never that simple. Don't get your heart set on the home and keep looking at other homes. Why? Because the process can take up to a year! It's not a done deal until the bank approves the sale, and until that time, it is completely out of the buyer's and their agent's control. All the while, dozens of new homes could come on the market while the potential buyer waits and waits.

Jenn and Matt are buyers that waited months, only to have the bank reject their offer on a short sale they loved. Then the bank countered the price and simultaneously went back to ask the seller to throw in some additional money to make the deal work. The seller said no and chose to stop making payments. Jenn and Matt walked away from it. You can walk away at any time before the bank approves, but the result can often be a lot of lost time that you might not have. After all was said and done, Jenn and Matt didn't find a new home until 18 months after they seriously started their search. They lost nine months waiting for the whole short-sale scenario to sort itself out.

EXPERT Greg McBride, Vice President, Senior Financial Analyst, Bankrate.com

"If you're in the market for a distressed sale, you might notice inventory is lower than it was a few years ago; therefore, the distressed market is more competitive," says Greg. "When prices are rising, there isn't a lot of financial incentive for lenders to put their distressed sales on the market. The result is not only limited inventory on the market, but limits on how deep the discounts are.

"You could also anticipate that either you'll be beaten out by 'all-cash' buyers, because banks find this scenario a lot easier to deal with, or that distressed properties are not move-in ready, which means you could be looking at tens of thousands of dollars of repairs before you move in."

Where Are the Deals with Short Sales?

Because these approvals can take so long, there is a stigma attached to short sales. Some buyers just don't want to deal with waiting or the uncertainties that come with a short-sale situation. Invariably, short-sale listings lose market share. A big percentage of the market doesn't want to become caught up in the process. Also, although there are some sellers who have realistic hardships, the common assumption is that short-sale sellers are desperate, reckless, or somehow dishonest. If they are selling as a short sale, there is a negative stigma attached to them and the home, and buyers don't want to be a part of it.

For these reasons, short sales will sometimes sell for less than the market value. To attract buyers to make offers, the seller and agent price the home lower. From time to time, you will see desperate sellers who just want out, so they price it well far below market value. In the mind of those sellers, they are already in a bad position, and it's not their money to lose at this point. The bank may, in fact, approve a price even lower than market value if it thinks that this is its only chance to sell the home. The bank ultimately does not want to foreclose. It's costly, and the bank doesn't want to be in the business of owning homes. If the seller's case for hardship is strong enough and the market is slow, the bank will take a low offer and sell.

Finally, in the face of a changing real estate market and a slow approval process, by the time the short sale is approved and sells, the value could have gone up. I tell buyers not to overlook short sales. There is no harm putting in your offer and waiting it out. Nothing commits you to the home, and you have nothing to lose because you won't miss other homes that come for sale. It's buyers who put all their eggs in the basket of this one home who ultimately miss out because they've stopped looking at other options. For an investor or someone who has no emotional attachment to a particular home, waiting it out could spell opportunity in the form of scooping up a home below market value.

WHAT TO KNOW ABOUT AUCTIONS ON THE COURTHOUSE STEPS

Buying a home on the courthouse steps isn't for the average buyer. People hear *foreclosure* or *courthouse sale,* and they think of deals and opportunities. For the right buyer and the right home, there can be lots of opportunity, but there is a tremendous amount of risk. The banks usually require cashier's checks for 10 percent at the time of the auction. No buyer, unless an experienced investor, should ever attempt to purchase a home from the bank in this manner. I've attended home sales on the courthouse steps; they are like a scene from a reality television show. Savvy investors pull up in their town cars just as the auctioneer starts reading off the list of homes for sale. The homes sell much like at an auction, with bidders raising bids in increments of $5,000.

These investors are experienced in real estate, have cash to pay, and are looking for opportunities in these sales. Before the day of the sale, they know exactly which homes to bid on and how much to pay. When the notice of intent to sell paperwork is filed and the courthouse sale is inevitable, these folks pore through the listings and look for the homes that are below value. If they are serious about them, they will go to the homes and look around, but because they are locked up, some guesswork and risk are involved. Some investors break into the homes to look around. If they buy a home on the courthouse steps, it's an as-is sale, so if they don't know what's inside, they could be buying a house that has water damage, mold, cracked foundations, and a host of other costly and serious problems. Therefore, they want to do as much due diligence as possible before putting their money down.

WHAT TO KNOW WHEN YOU WANT TO BUY AN REO

Once an REO hits the market, it's not that much different from any other home for sale. It is listed with a local real estate firm, generally with an agent who is experienced in working with banks on these types of sales. The agent may take pictures of the home, put up a for sale sign, and list it in the Multiple Listing Service. That agent will even have a series of open houses and broker tours. The only difference is that the seller is the bank.

Banks, as opposed to an owner, have never lived in the home, have no experience with the home, and have no knowledge of the home's (recent) history. The person who is responsible for selling the home with the bank sits behind a desk, in some office park, in another state some 2,000 miles away. This asset manager, as he or she is called, is the person in charge of working with the real estate listing agents to get REOs off the bank's books. The banks, as stated earlier, do not want to be in the business of owning real estate. This is not their core competency, and owning real estate brings out all kinds of responsibilities and therefore presents dozens of risks.

The asset manager is tasked with getting each asset (home) sold as quickly as possible and for as much money as the market will bear. He or she has no emotional or practical attachment to these homes. The home you may have fallen in love with is simply a cell within a large spreadsheet lying on the asset manager's desk. It's a numbers game to the bank. The bank knows what it's lost, what the loan amount was, approximately what the market will bear, and what it can sell the home for. It doesn't care about you—at all.

If you are a buyer and find yourself faced with a seller that happens to be a bank, don't get attached to it in any way. Although I've established that home buying is such an emotional purchase, in addition to being financial and practical, in the case of a bank-owned home, you need to check your emotions at the door. The bank won't care who you are, where you live, or how well you know or love the home. It is chiefly concerned with how much you are offering, how quickly you will close, and how much money you have to put down. The higher your down payment, the more likely the bank will deal with you, even if someone has made a higher offer on the home. The banks want certainty and predictability when it comes to off-loading these homes. It's the one time (except for new development sometimes) when all the traditional rules for home buying and selling don't necessarily apply.

Because the seller of the home is not a person and has never lived there, it is not able to, and won't, disclose anything about the property. Banks don't know about a previously leaky roof, the water heater that is busted, or the neighbor's fence that's impeding the property line. There is no way for banks to disclose potential hazards or provide any knowledge of the history of the home. When you purchase a home from the bank, there are no disclosure items whatsoever, and this is why such homes generally are priced lower than a fair market value home, where the seller is responsible for disclosing. Don't forget, it is a bank, potentially a large one and without any ties to your local community. When it comes time to sign a contract, it will definitely be an as-is sale with lots of documents releasing the bank from any responsibility or liability. It's a buyer beware purchase. There may not be any contingencies, but you should always have the home inspected before moving forward. Once you close on the home, that's that. If something is broken, toxic, or decrepit, it's on you now.

Banks may verbally tell you that you have an offer, but don't take it for truth. I have seen situations where banks will spend weeks working a buyer, trying to get more offers, and going to a best and final offer. They want to work every buyer for every penny. It's highly impersonal, which is why, even in the case of the REO sales, experienced investors tend to be the ones to make a play. It's more of a numbers game to them as well and less emotional.

Because so much risk is associated with REO sales, they tend to be priced considerably below market value. Of course, if you are the average and active buyer looking for a three-bedroom, two-bath home for sale anywhere in the United States, the home that comes on the market for 20 percent less than the other homes you've recently seen will make your eyes light up. You'll surely take notice.

With any type of risk, there comes reward. Buying an REO home comes with considerable risk. If you are not a risk taker, I advise against setting your sights on an REO. They are not for the faint of heart and require considerable due diligence, not to mention time and emotional energy. If your local real estate agent is not familiar with the inner workings of a bank-owned property, you could be at a disadvantage if you are not yourself a risk taker or comfortable with the uncertainty that comes with the transaction. If you truly believe you are built to last through the process of a distressed sale, be sure you work with an agent and attorney well versed in the process.

Three Fast Facts about REOs

1. **Prepare to see some homes stripped to the bone.** Some homeowners may have struggled to keep the property or even attempted to sell as a short sale, but the bank wouldn't cooperate. Homeowners often have hard feelings toward the bank and therefore might feel justified in damaging the property before leaving. One of my clients bought a home from the bank whose previous owner, whom the bank foreclosed on, took every appliance out of the kitchen as well as every fixture and faucet from the home. Vandalism such as this hurts the home's value, and you, as the buyer, will be responsible for repairs and replacements.

2. **The bank will not give you credits or fix things.** I mentioned earlier that the sale of the home is "as is," which means that after an inspection, the bank is not interested in negotiating with you. Your offer, and the likely discounted list price (discounted from similar

comps nearby), should already account for the risk you're taking on an as-is property or for the condition of the property. This is why I always insist my clients get a home inspection. Know what you're getting. Once you own this home, there isn't any turning back. It is your obligation to inspect this home top to bottom. If you have an inspection once you have an agreement with a bank, don't count on further negotiation. *As is* also means that the price is the price. There are no more credits after an inspection.

3. **The bank will have its own processes.** The bank usually won't use the local contract from the board of Realtors, nor will the bank follow any of the normal processes or mores that are standard in the local real estate community. The bank instead has its own contract that protects its interests. This contract includes pages and pages of verbiage protecting the bank from future lawsuits; referring to the sale as, as is; and putting nearly all the burden on you, the buyer. Unless you do it this way, the bank will not transfer the ownership.

NEXT GENERATION REAL ESTATE FACT: FORGET FACE VALUE; DO YOUR DUE DILIGENCE

I cannot stress enough that when dealing with sellers who might not disclose, banks who know nothing about the properties they are selling, or auctions on the courthouse steps, this is buyer beware territory. Double due diligence is in order. Here are a few additional things you can do to make sure you've covered all the bases.

- **Meet your potential neighbors.** They are likely to know something about the house or the neighborhood you don't. Remember, the seller isn't there to disclose the crime from last year or the loud music down the block. Ask the neighbors a series of questions:

  - *How long did the previous owners live there?*
  - *Did you know them well?*

- *Are there any issues with the home that you are aware of?*
- *Are there any issues with any of the other neighbors?*
- *Do you know of any major development plans nearby?*
- *Is there anything that you would want to know if you were in my shoes?*

- **Review the preliminary title.** Make sure there aren't any past liens or owners still on title. Also, be assured the bank has paid all taxes and delinquencies before you close escrow. In a condominium, make sure there aren't back homeowners' association dues. Once you close, those liens and unpaid taxes and delinquencies can potentially become your problem.

- **Visit the local building or planning department.** This is one place that buyers don't think to go. Ideally buyers for all properties should review the property's building permit history. You want to be sure that there aren't outstanding permits on the house. If it looks like there was a recent renovation, be sure that it was done legally and that the town has signed off on it. If the city hasn't signed off, and there's a problem with the renovation, the city can cite you. This could result in thousands of dollars in unexpected renovations or fixes. Once you own the home, it's your responsibility.

  Also, check on the neighboring homes. It's all public record. You would want to know if any neighbors have submitted plans to build a mega house or demolish a house nearby. The seller would normally know and disclose any nearby plans or work, but not always, in the case of a foreclosure or short sale.

- **Know the tenants' rights.** If you're buying a property a tenant occupies, you need copies of any leases, knowledge of deposits, and knowledge of length of tenancy. Ask for a tenant estoppel or questionnaire from the tenant. Once the property sells, the tenant becomes your responsibility. You'll have to adhere to the terms of any outstanding leases. Check your local rent board, if there is one, because there are some instances where the tenants may have more rights than you think.

I say don't completely rule out a home just because it is listed as a short sale or as bank owned. I've seen too many buyers walk away from one of these types of sales just because they don't want to deal with the hassle, become caught up in some long and drawn-out process, or deal with some bank across the country. However, if you pull the shades open and have an open mind, there could be an opportunity. If you have a good agent, leverage him or her. Take small steps and tread cautiously. If things are not working out, are taking too long, or pose too much of a risk, don't move ahead. I'd hate for buyers to miss their perfect home just because they assumed the worst. In the next generation of real estate, distressed sales will be out there and, as a buyer, your dream home may actually be one of them.

PART III

FASTER SELLING

Does Selling Make Sense for Me Right Now?

You've been spying that home down the block that has had a for sale sign up for nearly a year. Or, what's worse, you've seen two different agencies' signs on the front lawn over the course of 18 months. You assume it's still a buyer's market because inventory doesn't seem to be moving, despite reports you've heard and read that the economy is coming back. Next generation sellers don't believe everything they see; in fact, there is much more to rely on in terms of information than a static old sign. Head to the Internet, and track most any home for sale in your community, in your town, in your state, or even across the country, and you'll be able to see the bigger picture, an informed one that can provide you valuable data before you decide to go on the market yourself. What kind of data? Multiple surveys among would-be homebuyers, years after the housing market collapse and credit crisis, concludes that homebuyers still believe that a home is a good place to put their money. In 2013, news abounded about buyers coming off the sidelines wanting to take advantage of low interest rates.

A home that sits on the market for too long is the home of an unmotivated seller or one who is not serious. My goal in this chapter is to help you assess whether you are indeed ready to sell. The ultimate goal, of course, is faster selling. I'll share with you some new rules for the next generation of real estate so that you know when you go live on the market it will be on your terms. You'll also learn how to implement some innovative and forward-thinking strategies that will help you wow the buyers who come through.

As a real estate agent who has also bought and sold my own homes, I know that the decision to sell could conjure up just as many emotional, practical, and financial issues as when you bought your home, probably even more. Before you launch that virtual tour and put that "For Sale" sign in the yard, this chapter will help you think seriously about the implications of selling and help you confidently answer the question, "Does selling make sense for me right now?"

The good news is, you've been here before, well . . . sort of. When you bought your home, you might have done so for the first time or have upgraded or downgraded. Maybe it was a marriage, a divorce, a new baby, or a new job; whatever it was, a life change probably happened that prompted you to buy. Now that you are thinking about selling, all those memories and reasons for buying in the first place can come back either to give you pause or compel you to move forward. The one thing you should remember now that you are on the other side of the table is the principles of buying do not hold true when you are a seller. It's a different game with a new set of rules. I don't have to tell you what happens when you play a game without knowing how to, so let's start with considering some of the things you need to know about selling then and now as well as the smartest questions you can ask yourself to be certain that you are ready to sell when you go to sell.

THE DIFFERENCE BETWEEN A SELLER AND A BUYER

This might seem like an odd subject. Obviously there is an understood difference between sellers and buyers because they are on opposite ends of the deal. However, there are different financial, practical, and emotional factors at stake. You own your home, likely your biggest asset and a long-term investment. For folks who've owned their home for decades, the sale not only frees up a huge amount of equity but also comes riddled with emotions. For others, particularly someone who bought before, during, or just after the credit crisis, the home sale could mean finally getting out from under a huge burden, a stress relief. Either way, it's likely an important, let alone very big transaction. You should not take it lightly, nor should you rush into it.

When you were buying a home, you could sway in and out of the market over the course of a few months or even years. Some buyers searched for a home on and off for up to three years. If they weren't quite ready to buy, they could slow the pace down. You were the buyer and each time you made an offer, there wasn't any sort of record of how long you had been in the market, how many offers you had written, or how many real estate agents you had worked with. You simply made an offer when the time seemed right to you.

And even after you had an offer accepted or even got into a contract on a home, you could still walk away via an inspection contingency or some issue with a disclosure you were not previously aware of. Then you could simply go on to look at another house. In fact, in Part II of this book, I encourage buyers to feel out the market, to see many listings, to go to many open houses, and even to make a few offers. I advise buyers to get in the game. They have nothing to lose. That means getting really excited about a home for sale, making a couple of offers (sometimes four or five), and missing a great home or two and dealing with some disappointment. All the while this buyer is getting hands-on market knowledge and getting educated about the process. Being in the game enables buyers to draw upon past mistakes and find the right house at the right time.

As a seller, being in the game at the wrong time or for the wrong amount of time at the wrong price can leave an indelible mark on your listing. Once your home is live on the public market for the entire world to see, the days on market (DOM) start tracking. In the next generation of real estate, they're what every single agent and buyer use to judge how well a home is priced, how the property fares on the open market, and how motivated a seller is. How do they know this? The Internet. When your listing agent includes your home in the local Multiple Listing Service (MLS), the number of bedrooms, number of bathrooms, lot size, and square footage, among other things, are indicated, but what also happens is that the clock starts ticking because listings are now tracked by dates. Before the days of the Internet, it was possible that only an agent knew exactly how long a home had been on the market. Today, that information is for public consumption. Why does this matter to you?

If a home stays on the market for too long, it's human nature for people to think there's something wrong with it. The longer your home sits on the market, the less money you will get for it, period. The biggest mistake you can make is to list your home for sale when you are not seriously ready to sell it. If you have the littlest doubt about selling, stop, consider all things, and keep reading on. You don't want to jeopardize what could be the biggest transaction of your life.

Before you take the plunge, seriously consider whether you are ready to sell. In the next generation of real estate, you have only one chance to make a good impression. If you mess it up the first time around, you could be risking thousands of dollars, if not more, so think long and hard about if selling makes sense to you now.

My friend's parents, Maggie and Don, were thinking of moving to Florida from Indiana permanently. After Don's cancer went into remission, they realized how much the inclement weather was affecting them now that they were getting older. The grandchildren were busy, and Maggie found it difficult to keep up with the large ranch house with five bedrooms. Don, too, was tired of lawn maintenance on his 100 x 150 lot. Maggie decided they should take up full-time residence in the small Palm Beach condo they bought 15 years ago, but Don wasn't quite sure. Would he miss his family, the T-ball games with the kids, or the friends he had made in his cancer support group? Maggie convinced him just to test the market. If they got $500,000 for the house, they would sell and put their plan in motion. Don thought if that's what they got, he'd go.

Their agent told them there was no way they could get that high a price when the comps were going for $50,000 less. Maggie didn't believe her. She loved the house and knew that the interior was worlds better than the insides of houses in the neighborhood, and because she assumed buyers would negotiate her asking price down, she told the agent to place the listing price at $545,000. Despite the fact that the agent told her it was real estate suicide, that's what they put the price up at. Meanwhile Don didn't want a for sale sign on the house. He didn't want the nosy neighbors to know what they were doing. Again, their agent asked Don how serious he was about selling, because the high price coupled with the fact that he didn't want sidewalk marketing was a giant red flag to her.

After six months and few showings, Maggie fired the agent, and the agent was quite relieved. After all, it was clear Maggie and Don had wasted their own time and energy as well as their agent's time and energy.

Recently, my friend called to tell me that her parents had gone back on the market and had received two lowball offers that were both at least $100,000 less than their new $500,000 asking price. Two things are at play here: (1) The buyers and their agent know the comps and are most likely offering market value, and (2) the selling history will forever mark them as high priced and unrealistic. Now that they are back on the market, buyers might think they can get a deal or might consider them still unmotivated and not go see the house at all. Looks like Maggie and Don will have another long, cold winter in Indiana.

Clearly Maggie and Don are not next generation sellers, which brings us to Part III's first next generation fact.

NEXT GENERATION REAL ESTATE FACT: SELLERS ARE SELLERS WHO SELL

A former manager of mine used to use the mantra, "Sellers are sellers who sell." I never really understood what this meant until years later. After seeing so many homes listed for sale, I realized that just because you listed your home didn't mean you were ready to sell your home. Some real estate agents who specialize in working with sellers will joke that they don't list homes; they sell homes. Avoid shooting yourself in the foot by recognizing the signs that you are not so serious about selling, especially because you can bet buyers and their agents are looking out for these telltale signs as well.

If buyers think you are overpriced or just not serious, they won't make an offer and in some cases will not even go to see your home. As your home sits on the market without any activity, the DOM start ticking away. The longer it sits on the market, the less likely a buyer will offer you the asking price. If you have to do a series of reductions over time, to get it closer to the right price, the buyers will notice that. Once you get to the right price, buyers will either wait to see if you reduce again or come in with a lower number than what you would have gotten if you'd priced it right to begin with. The perception is that you are unmotivated or uninformed. Buyers will punish you.

TWO REASONS A HOME SITS ON THE MARKET

You've read it earlier in this book, and it's the mantra that agents have been saying forever: If it a home is *priced right* and *shows well* in x market, it should sell within y time. Therefore, there are two reasons why a home sits on the market.

Priced Wrong

Look, there aren't any rules that say you as sellers have to price your home at the current day's market value. It's your home. You own it, and you can do whatever you want with it, including overpricing it when it's time to sell, just as Maggie and Don did. Best Buy or Walmart price their goods at tried and tested prices based on inventory levels, the current market, and competitive analysis. They do this because they have a business to operate and need to make money. If they price too high, they will be stuck with excess inventory and employees to pay. A home seller isn't necessarily in the same situation. Sure, your home isn't a business, and you have only one home to sell. But a serious seller should absolutely look at inventory levels or check out the competition, but the fact of the matter is many do not.

If the comparable homes nearby show a value of around $300,000, a serious and motivated seller will work closely with his or her agent to determine the best list price strategy based on the recent comparable sales and inventory levels in the local market. The list price would be close to $300,000. A seller such as Don, who is not motivated, may attempt to list it for $350,000. I can tell you right now, without even knowing you or your home, it won't sell for $350,000. If you find yourself resisting multiple agents' pricing recommendations, do not list your home for sale!

Shows Poorly

A home could be priced absolutely on the spot, but if the condition of the home doesn't reflect the price, you will see your DOM add up quickly. When it's time to sell, you have to put your best foot forward. This means de-cluttering, organizing, and getting rid of a lot of your stuff. This may even mean painting some rooms or doing clever, little, affordable, last-minute upgrades that will help your home pop. Unfortunately, this means taking that deer head off the wall in your living room or changing out the shag carpet from the 1970s. If you are a serious seller, you will understand that you need to present your home in the best possible light. A home with a presentation that doesn't support the market value for the home risks not getting top dollar. Who wants that?

TWO COMMON SELLER SCREW-UPS DUE TO EMOTIONAL ATTACHMENT

Disgruntled Soon-to-Be Ex

Divorces and breakups happen all the time and usually result in the sale of a home. There is always one person who is unhappy (or at least less happy) about the divorce. Because it takes two to agree to sell a home, one spouse can really make things difficult. I've seen instances through the years where a husband was so upset about the divorce that he made the house difficult to show or the wife wanted a high list price as a way of stalling or avoiding the inevitable. In such instances, the DOM go on, and on, and on. Finally, in the face of serious legal or financial hardship or just over the negative energy, one party gives in.

Tip: If you are in a divorce situation and need to sell a home, talk about it with the attorneys early on. If it's clear that one spouse can't buy out the other, agree to work with an agent who is objective, someone that neither of you know. Find the neighborhood specialist, and bring him or her in for a meeting. If you can't agree on the correct list price or selling strategy, bring it to the attorneys. This is a tough one because emotions get the best of people, and it ultimately has a negative effect on the home sale.

Been in the Home a Long Time

Are your parents elderly and has your home been in your family for decades? Do your folks still live there and have they resisted moving on to a retirement community or home? These are some of the hardest sales ever. Moving is hard for people who rent for one year. Can you imagine living in a home for 50 years? This can be one of the most challenging situations. Many times it is an older sibling or a group of siblings who get together to discuss and plan with the parent. I can't tell you the number of grandma homes I've seen on the market that sat and sat and grew to be old and stale listings. The owner priced the house way too high or didn't take the agent's suggestions about presentation as a way to resist actually making this huge life change. Can you blame them? After all, it's their home! I understand, but this is an emotional reaction and one that could affect your bottom line.

The hardest part of moving out and moving on from a home that's been with someone for a long time is when you are packing up your stuff, taking things off the wall, and de-cluttering. Instantly, 50 years of memories come in front of them. It's emotional, and it takes a toll on everyone involved. I advise these sellers, if they can afford it, to list the home after everyone is out. This way they can mourn the loss of their home privately and even make changes that will make the home more appealing to buyers (see more on home staging later in this chapter). Once they've done so, they can approach the actual listing and sale of their property in the right frame of mind. They'll start to see it more as a financial transaction and less as a childhood home. This is smarter selling.

AM I RESISTING MY SALE?

There are financial, emotional, and practical reasons for selling, just as there are to buying. Is there anything that you might be doing or thinking that is sending a message that the time to sell is just not right now? Ask yourself, *Why do I want to sell?* Is it a job transfer? Is the home too big? Do you need more space? Have you lost your job? Are you retiring? Has a life event, such as a death or divorce, happened that forces a sale? These are all good reasons why people seek to sell their home. Some of them, such as a job transfer, require immediate action on the part of the owner. Others don't have timelines attached to or associated with them.

Many times it's the sellers whose reason falls into the latter category who ultimately end up putting their home on the market too soon and risk losing money. It sounds obvious, and everyone should know why he or she is selling, of course. But understand this so that you can hold back for now. There is no rush to sell your home. You have to do it in your time, when you are ready, and when you have emotionally come to the point of being ready to sell. How do you recognize this time? This is the million-dollar question, but knowing your situation and being aware of your circumstances is the best start.

When I sit down with homeowners, I never assume they are selling right away. Most sellers assume that when the agent shows up, he or she will walk around the home, either praise or criticize their home, and name the price, right on the spot. Instead, an agent should find out why the homeowners contacted him or her and what their situation is. As a seller, you should ask yourself the same questions. As crazy as it sounds, over the years, agents actually turned listings away. Presented with a seller who doesn't listen to the agent's pricing or presentation recommendations, he or she faces weeks, months, and sometimes years holding a listing that doesn't sell. Agents spend money on marketing and invest time in the listing and the owner. After a while, a home whose DOM is approaching 200 becomes negative energy both for the agent and the seller.

It's common in every market for some homes to be listed two or three times by a different agent or company. These sellers are not

The High Price Unmotivated Sellers Pay

I once was called in to meet with Dave, a seller of a home that was being marketed with another agent. I had already been inside the home and knew about the listing. The price was too high, and the home didn't show well. I asked Dave, "Why are you selling?"

Dave explained that he and his wife had just had their third child and wanted to move back to the Midwest to be near his wife's parents.

I asked, "How long have you lived in this area?"

"Twelve years."

"When do you want to be moved back to the Midwest?"

"We haven't nailed that down just yet," Dave answered.

These folks had been in this area for a while. This was where they slept on their wedding night. They brought home all three kids to this home. Moving out of it *and* uprooting thousands of miles away was a big deal. It isn't something that happens overnight.

Not only does it take some serious planning, but it also brings up all kinds of feelings, sadness for one. Some time went by and we met again. Dave felt that, because it was now February, they really needed to get serious because their oldest kid would be starting first grade in September. They wanted to be back home by then. They needed a plan.

The family knew the move east was inevitable, and the wife was pushing to make it happen sooner than later. But Dave wasn't quite ready to let the house go, pack things up, and end life as he knew it in San Francisco. He listed the home too high and didn't listen to any of the first agent's recommendations for presentation, including removing the poker table from the dining room, clearing out all of the kids' toys, and removing all of the family photos throughout the home. In one sense, he thought he was moving ahead. He was taking the first step, listing the house for sale. Surely he was doing the right thing. He'd even had an offer, and at a good price, but he'd rejected it.

Dave eventually withdrew the home from the market and relisted it with me in mid-May, when his wife and the kids were planning to be back in the

Midwest to look for rentals and get things set up there. Absent the three kids, Dave was able to go in and make some changes to the way the home showed. He removed all of the personal items, de-cluttered all of the rooms, and even replaced some of the furniture with smaller furniture. Also, he replaced the poker table with a nice dining table. He and his wife dropped the price nearly 10 percent. They had to. It was still priced too high, and they had to send a message to the market that they were now serious about selling. This wasn't easy for Dave. He knew what he had to do to get it sold. His wife was off in St. Louis, about to sign a lease, so he needed to sell. How much was the offer they ultimately accepted and closed on? Less than the offer he rejected months earlier.

ready to sell. In addition to ignoring their agent's recommendations about pricing and presentation, they think that if they change agents, it will sell. Agents can spot this from a mile away. What do you think they are going to tell their buyer clients who might express an interest in your home? "That seller is crazy. They've been on the market forever. It's overpriced and they are not serious about selling. I would suggest looking at another home." This is how things go down. It's certainly how it went down for Maggie and Don.

CAN I AFFORD TO SELL MY HOME NOW?

In this next generation of real estate, so many sellers simply don't have the luxury of selling when they want or need to sell. For instance, you might sit down with a real estate agent and confirm that your home's value just isn't there. It's not where you need it to be. For that reason, selling just isn't a real option, but you are conflicted. You are ready to sell, and you want to sell. Also you know where you want to move and when. But if the market value doesn't match what you need or want to achieve, you are not going to be able to sell. You may have paid $295,000 and put down 10 percent, $30,000. The value now, after the market rose and fell, is only about $275,000. If you sold at this price, after real estate commission and sales costs, you would lose your down payment money. Who can afford to do that? So you wait it out. You can try to sell your home at $350,000 and even reduce it to $325,000. But either you don't get any offers, or someone comes in with an offer at $275,000. Financially, you just can't pull it off.

Particularly in the years following the housing downturn and credit crisis, I've seen countless homes go on the market only to sit and sit and sit. The seller needs a certain number to be able to let the property go, but the market isn't giving it to him or her.

Maybe you'll need bigger proceeds from the home to buy another or make that big move. Maybe you risk losing all of your down payment money. This is your hard-earned money that you saved and that you anticipated having and not throwing in the garbage; or worse, you, like millions of Americans today, are underwater. Finally, can you afford to keep your home? Some people lost their jobs during the credit crisis and were unemployed for a while; therefore, they dipped into their rainy-day fund. In many cases, when they got new jobs, they paid less than their old jobs, and they were struggling to make the payments. In these times, if you can't sell your home for the number you need, sellers need to have a Plan B, and luckily there are several Plan Bs.

PLAN B: ACCIDENTAL LANDLORD

Do you need to move out of your home because of a job transfer, an absolutely horrible commute, a fourth kid on the way, or some other reason that makes it simply impractical to stay in the home? Is your value too low, and you can't afford to lose your down payment money? Plan B for you would be to rent the home out. This buys you time for the market to pick back up. Hopefully this plan will cover most of your current costs. It depends on how much money you put down, what your interest rate is, and how the rental market looks. For some people, this means losing just a little bit of money per month, when they factor in a new place to rent that is more practical for them. For others, even though they can't sell the home for a gain, they can cover the costs or even make a few dollars, so it's worth it to them to wait it out.

Renting your home brings a whole set of concerns, questions, and uncertainties. Here's how to sell your house while renting it to someone else:

1. **Consult your tax professional.** Talk to your accountant long before you plan a sale because there could be negative or positive tax implications based on when you purchased, when you sell, and when you last lived there. For example, it might be that selling your home will result in a loss, which could help your taxes, but you want that loss to happen in the next tax year.

2. **Utilize your agent.** A good agent could even help you find new tenants, come to the aid of your current tenant, or act as the intermediary between you and your tenant. If you are not an experienced landlord, you likely don't know what to look for in a tenant, how to market the property, or where to get the lease paperwork. Your agent should be there for you. If not, he or she likely can provide a good referral to a rental agent. A good real estate agent will want to continue to provide great service to you as a past and future client.

3. **Choose the right tenant.** Make it clear to the prospective tenant that it is not your intention to keep this as a rental property forever. A family who wants to get its kids into the school system and to settle might be bummed to have to move out in two years. If you communicate with them up front, there won't be any surprise when it comes time to sell the home. Plus, you want a tenant who won't give you any problems. I always advocate for taking less in rent in exchange for a hassle-free tenant. You don't want the phone ringing 10 times per month because of high-maintenance tenants who feel that they are paying top dollar.

4. **Go to the property.** Walk through the property months in advance before selling, if possible. While there, meet face-to-face with the tenant and notify him or her of your desire to sell. Assess whether the home needs work. If so, meet with the necessary painters, carpenters, or stagers. Identify exactly what needs work and get bids. Interview agents if you don't have one already. If you already have

an agent, meet with him or her, preferably at your property. Introduce your agent to your tenant, too, if possible.

5. **Treat your tenant well.** As stressful as it is for you to sell a home, your tenant is under stress, too. The last thing you want is to scare the tenant away while you are in the selling process. Giving tenants enough notice will benefit them and you. If the property shows well, incentivize your tenant (provided he or she is a good tenant) to stay in the property during the marketing period by offering to reduce the rent. By reducing the rent, you can also ask the tenant to cooperate with showings, open houses, or inspections.

    If they aren't great tenants or the home doesn't show well with their stuff there, give them enough advance notice to move out so that you can do any necessary work. Be sure that their lease has officially ended, that they receive their security deposit back, and that there aren't any loose ends.

PLAN B: NEGOTIATE WITH YOUR BANK

If you can't afford to stay in your home, put a plan in place sooner than later. Call your bank and see if you can refinance the loan or do some sort of loan modification. Most banks will want to work with you to keep your mortgage current and keep you in your home. Call the 800 number on your mortgage statement, and ask for the mortgage modification department. Ask what your options are. In some cases, a bank will lower your monthly payments for a length of time or lower your interest rate. Banks are not in the business of owning homes. They don't want to see you default on your loan and ultimately foreclose. In fact, some smaller banks or local credit unions don't even want to see you go the way of a short sale if they can't modify your loan. Call your bank first.

PLAN B: THE SHORT SALE

For some people who are so far underwater or financially not in a strong situation, it's impractical for them to stay in the home, and

The Home Affordability Refinance Program (HARP)

There is a federal program called the Home Affordability Refinance Program (HARP), which the Federal Housing Finance Agency backs. According to the website harpprogram.org, the program "is designed to assist homeowners in refinancing their mortgages—even if they owe more than the home's current value." If you are current on your mortgage, with or without equity, then you are eligible for the HARP; however, 9 of 10 eligible homeowners fail to take advantage of this government program.

The government provides this program to prevent additional short sales and foreclosures. There are so many people stuck with a $250,000 mortgage at a 6 percent interest rate and a home value at $225,000. The HARP allows them to refinance that 6 percent rate to a better one. This lowers their monthly payment and helps make the home more affordable.

renting it out is not a financially feasible option either. If you don't qualify for the HARP, listing your home as a short sale might be your next alternative.

What Is a Short Sale?

Simply defined, a short sale is listing your home for sale when its market value is less than your loan amount. Barry bought his home at the top of the market and with only 5 percent down. After the housing and credit crisis, the value of his home had gone down nearly 25 percent. Barry had lost his job and needed to save money. He needed to move back home to live with his parents.

To sell the home short, Barry needed his bank's approval. If he was selling the home for less than the loan amount, then the bank was going to lose money. To approve this short sale, the bank wanted to do its own due diligence on him and the property. Many banks have built entire short sale departments in recent years to deal with the influx of short sale applications they receive. Although the process can be bureaucratic and requires all kinds of paperwork and proof of hardship, it's ultimately a much better way to go than just walking away and being foreclosed on. Banks prefer short sales to foreclosures as well, and I believe that this is a much more noble and honest way of exiting the property. Working with the bank early on, and often, are always my recommendations.

The decision is a struggle that will occupy your mind and stress you out for months on end. Some people feel that going the route of a short sale is an embarrassment or that they should be ashamed. They don't want their neighbors to know. They don't want their families to know. I am here to tell you that bad things happen to very good people.

If you are unable to afford your home and you are behind on your payments, the clock will start ticking on the foreclosure process. Work closely with your mortgage lender. Find out what it needs and what the process is. Find a local listing agent who is experienced with short sales. You can do this by asking for a referral or looking online.

I can't stress how important it is to hire an agent who is experienced with short sales. The process can be confusing and arduous. One wrong move by your agent in processing the short sale, and you could lose weeks, if not months, on the approval process. This could lead to the bank moving forward on the foreclosure. Note: Even if you are working with the short sale department of your bank, the foreclosure department at many banks is run independently and not in conjunction with the short sale department. I've seen people lose out on a solid offer on their short sales because the foreclosure department sprinted ahead.

Although it is a negative situation, the short sale is a more collaborative process than a foreclosure. You can have a good deal of control of the situation and timing of the sale. If you work with the bank and do a short sale, you could ultimately net a higher price and owe much less after the sale. Or, in some instances, a bank, as a part of the short-sale negotiation, will agree to waive a deficiency judgment. This means that you would not owe the bank the amount of money lost. Every bank is different; so when it gets down to negotiating a short sale, make sure you completely understand the terms and conditions.

You don't want to be stuck with a collections company coming after you for the difference six months later.

PLAN B: ROLL THE DICE

With the housing market turning around in many parts of the country, you may be in a situation where the number you need to sell could be possible. You may know that the comps support a lower number, but you want to try to list it for sale anyway at the higher price. This was the case with many sellers in 2009 through 2011. They really wanted to move, and they didn't want to take no (or as I say, *low*) for an answer. In some cases the numbers were so far off that there wasn't a chance. In others, it was close, but still no cigar. Either way, you as a seller might just need to see it to believe it. You may need to literally go through the experience to get a feel for how the process works, or doesn't, at the price or showing you put out there.

Warning: Only try this for a certain period, maybe a month or two, depending on your market. Give it enough to see how the market responds. If you aren't getting any calls for showings and your open houses are empty, you should put the listing out of its misery, stop the clock, and take your home off the market. Otherwise, you risk the DOM ticking, creating ghosts in your closet, such as negative history or a super failed listing. I support folks who are trying their best. Your Plan B could be simply to make the best of it and wait it out a little while longer. When your time comes, turn the page.

The Price Is Right!
Four Steps for Understanding &
Maximizing Your Home's Worth

You might think that because you were once a buyer, you have a leg up on how the real estate transaction works. Certainly you are not as blind as you might have once been; however, you need to shift your mind-set a bit to get in the mode of the seller, which means getting your home ready to sell, researching the costs involved, and learning what to expect from the factors that determine your home's value.

Now that I've drilled into your head the number-one way to botch up a sale—poor pricing—let's turn to the four stages of selling in the next generation of real estate that can create a terrific scenario: conduct initial research, understand pricing, engage an agent, and gather some more nuts and sit on them. Going through these four stages can help you determine your own home's worth and work with professionals who will help you achieve your goals for faster selling.

STEP 1   CONDUCT INITIAL RESEARCH— UNDERSTAND THE MARKET

Knowing your home's value is inherent to being a homeowner, but it's never an exact science. It's possible that a refinance appraisal value from two years ago still sticks in your head, or you know that your good friends and neighbors down the block recently sold their similar house for x dollars. Over the years, you've likely received dozens of "Just Listed" or "Just Sold" postcards in the mail from local real estate agents. Although all of these are legitimate factors to consider when thinking about setting your list price, they should not be the only factors.

You should start to become mindful of what's happing locally in your community and in your real estate market. Is it a buyer's market or a seller's market? It's difficult to define what makes a market truly a buyer's market. Is it the amount of time a home sits on the market or how much negotiation goes on? It ultimately comes back to a supply-and-demand issue. If there is not enough demand from buyers to meet the supply of sellers, then it's more of a buyer's market. If there is simply not enough supply and a lot of demand, it's more of a seller's market. Whatever market you are about to get in, don't put too much emphasis on it at this stage in the game. Stay focused and engaged in your research.

Use Real Estate Syndicators

It could be likely that as a next generation seller, the last time you bought a home, there weren't many online options, especially what have now become known as syndicator websites, including Zillow .com, Trulia.com, and Realtor.com. As a homeowner, you are likely familiar with these websites, which have built hugely successful businesses pulling listings from agencies and Multiple Listing Services (MLS) around the country and making them available from their user-friendly websites and smartphone and tablet apps.

These companies' websites serve as portals for all things real estate. Thinking about selling and want some advice? Head over to one of their blog pages. Need to find a good local real estate agent? You can read reviews of agents from past clients. These websites and their apps have become the one-stop shop for buyers, sellers, renters, and homeowners entering the real estate market in some way, shape, or form. They are loaded with content, features, and advice on all things regarding homeownership, buying, and selling. Zillow recently launched Zillow Digs, a marketplace for homeowners to get ideas for home renovation and design.

One of the most interesting tools is Zillow's Zestimate. Launched when Zillow went live in 2006, a Zestimate is a type of automated valuation model (AVM). It is an automated price estimate that Zillow comes up with for the value of your home. To arrive at the Zestimate, Zillow compiles public data, such as tax records and recent comparable home sales, and gives each home a home value or a range of value based on computer modeling.

What is controversial about the Zestimate and these AVMs is that many people feel the estimate is not accurate. I can tell you that generally it is not. In fact, I have seen instances where these AVMs are off by up to 20 percent in either direction. However, they can serve as a starting ground from which sellers begin to get a feel for their home's value. Some real estate companies incorporate Zestimates into their marketing as a talking point or way to facilitate a discussion with both buyers and sellers about pricing. Nearly every home will be listed with a Zestimate on Zillow. Put in your home's address and you'll likely see something like this screen shot below.

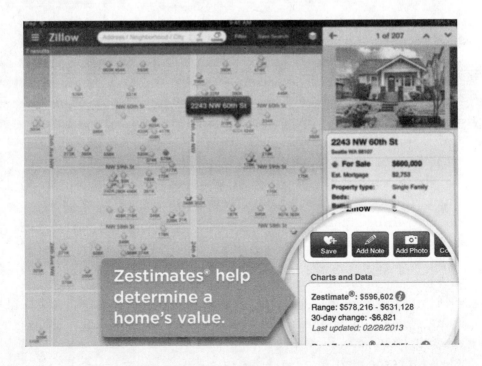

As part of your research stage, go online to Zillow and input your address into its Zestimate feature. Does the Zestimate for your home appear to be too low? Zillow allows homeowners to claim their home. This allows you to make changes or adjustments. One of my clients had added a bathroom and updated the kitchen years earlier, but Zillow hadn't picked that information up. The homeowner let the automated system know this, and it recalculated the renovations into their Zestimate.

The important takeaway is that these AVMs are just that—automated. They haven't been inside your home, they are unfamiliar your floor plan, and they lack a comprehensive knowledge of your neighborhood and the most recent comparable sales. It's simply impossible for them to provide you with an exact value. But it's a great starting

EXPERT   Richard Florida, Senior Editor at *The Atlantic*

Part of the information-gathering process should include knowing who today's buyers is, what they want, and how they operate, particularly when it comes to the real estate search process. According to Richard, the driving forces of the economy and real estate today is, what he calls, the Creative Class. "The Creative Class includes 40 million American workers, about a third of the workforce," he told me. "It includes scientists and techies, innovators and entrepreneurs, artists, designers, and media types as well as knowledge workers in business, management, healthcare, education, and law. The Creative Class people have a wide range of personality traits, but psychologists find the most highly creative people tend to be high in openness-to-experience, and this partly explains the tendency of highly creative people to cluster in exciting urban areas. Likewise, it explains why the Creative Class now demands neighborhoods and communities that are open, diverse, and thick with amenities (a vibrant arts scene, good restaurants, a safe community, etc.). As you can imagine, the rise of the Creative Class and its economy power and interests have a significant impact on the market for both buyers and sellers."

point because, without having to leave your home, you can get a value range of your home, based on recently sold homes and property tax records, all pulled together for you.

Here's something else to take note of: When buyers research the syndicators, they like to see that home they are interested in was actually listed two years ago, but at a much higher price. As a seller, being aware of this type of buyer reconnaissance should teach you to tread carefully when it comes to going live on the market before you are ready.

Visit Open Houses

Data and information collection in your first stage of selling should include open houses. Before the Internet and the seemingly endless amount of information about home values, the best way to get a feel for your home's value was to go to open houses. This strategy absolutely holds true for next generation real estate, and if you are considering selling your home in the near future, going to open houses in your neighborhood is a smart exercise because location matters first when it comes to comparable pricing. See a home similar to yours advertising an open house? Check it out. See how that home's characteristics, floor plan, fixtures, and finishes differ from yours. By walking through another home, you will compare it to your own. You will know intuitively if yours is bigger, better, or more desirable in some way.

Some homeowners enjoy visiting open houses for fun throughout their time as owners. Others pick up the pace when they are considering selling. Going to open houses is also a great way to meet your future listing agent. In many communities, agents specialize in neighborhoods and have experience selling in the area. For many sellers, working with an agent who has sold a lot in the neighborhood is important. Learn more strategies for choosing the right agent in Chapter 12.

If you are in the early stages of the selling process or just curious to get a feel for value for financial or practical reasons, there are many resources to help you gather the information. It's not locked up with someone else holding the key anymore. Using online tools in conjunction with visiting open houses should provide you with enough data to get a feel for what your home is worth. Many times, sellers who are early in the sales process want to research independently and hold off on contacting an agent until they are more serious about selling. I appreciate that.

STEP 2   UNDERSTAND PRICING

The chief concern of nearly every homeowner I meet is how much he or she can get for the home. Of course, they want to know what their home is worth. The market value of your home is ultimately the number that an able and willing buyer is willing to pay on the open market. You won't know this number until you have a buyer, but you need to know the price well in advance of that. Because there are so many unknowns and variables regarding price, I thought it would be helpful to acknowledge a few things regarding that number-one concern.

Appraised Value versus Market Value

Many homeowners refinance their home during the course of their homeownership. A refinance triggers an appraisal. An appraisal is required for the bank to do its due diligence on your home and offer you the right loan terms. Seeing an appraisal is another good indicator of your home's value. Often, when I meet with sellers to discuss potentially selling their home, they will tell me that they recently had an appraisal and that it came in at x. Much to their surprise, I repeatedly report that their home could actually fare better in the open market than it did in the bank's appraisal.

Many homeowners are surprised to know that the appraised value of a home generally comes in lower than what the open market would bear. What's most exciting for me is when sellers are surprised by how high a recent appraisal was, only to find out from me that I believe the market could top the appraised value. This is generally the case, and it's helpful to be aware of it.

As I said, the market value is the price that an active, willing, and able buyer will pay on the open market. A real, live buyer will often pay more than what an appraisal would value the home at, absent a negotiation. The appraiser takes a more conservative approach, and there isn't that emotional connection to a home that can sometimes motivate buyers to offer sellers the list price or pay close to it, if not more than it, in a strong market. In the case of a refinance, absent a contract price, the appraiser comes up with a random number based on recent comparable sales nearby. In the case of a purchase, a real, live buyer is coming to the table with a seller having already named his or her price. If buyers want the home badly enough, and the price is in the ballpark, they will pay for it.

List Price versus Sale Price

Particularly when it comes to home pricing, every real estate market and location works differently. I've communicated with real estate agents in dozens of states and hundreds of communities across the country. What works for agents and their seller clients in Westchester County, New York, simply won't apply to agents and sellers in Houston, Texas. In some parts of the country, especially in strong seller's markets, where inventory is limited, sellers may price a home low purposely to attract multiple buyers and spark a bidding war. Therefore, if you go to an open house and the price seems low, know that the sale price could go higher. Conversely, in a slower or falling real estate market, it could take a few months to sell a home. You may see it in January priced at $325,000, but it ultimately sells in July for $265,000. If you are out at an open house or see a home similar to yours listed online, you should be aware that the home's actual value is not necessarily the price that you see listed. It could sell for 5 percent more or, after a series of price reductions, 15 percent less than the list price you see on any given day. Ultimately, if you work with a local real estate agent, he or she will have the inside track on sales prices of comparable homes. Good agents, as members of their local board of Realtors, will have access to up-to-the-minute MLS data. They also may be able to get insight as to the sale price before a home closes. This real-time data can change on a whim, and this, as you will read in Chapter 15 is precisely the reason we say you shouldn't set the final list price until right before you go live on the market.

Comparative Marketing Analysis

The comparative marketing analysis (CMA) is one real estate agent's assessment of the value of your home. A good local agent can provide you some deep insight into how your home would fare on the open market. Unlike the AVMs, such as Zestimate, real estate agents are actual human beings who tour homes in your neighborhood, are familiar with local trends, and study the market regularly because, after all, it's their job. But what's most important is that they work with willing and able buyers who are regularly making offers and can speak to the health of the market at any one time.

Many would-be sellers reach out to real estate agents early on in the home-selling process to get their opinions. You can play with AVMs online and even see open houses on your own, but having a local agent over can provide you with some context. A CMA is exactly what it sounds like—an analysis of similar homes to yours that have recently sold, are pending, or are listed. An agent should take up to 10 homes and show you, one by one, how each compares to your home. A recently sold comp is the absolute best way to understand your home's value because it's a recent data point, a snapshot in time.

STEP 3   ENGAGE AN AGENT

If you are serious about selling, at some point you will want to engage a local real estate agent. I devote all of Chapter 12 to finding a listing agent, but for now, inviting an agent over to give an opinion of value will allow you to synthesize all the data you've been gathering with open houses and online searching. Good local agents will recognize you as a potential seller and will gladly work to provide you with a CMA. This is their chance to make a good impression or plant the seed for building a relationship later down the road.

Agents live their local real estate market day in and day out. They know the comparable homes and study the listings. Although the information is out there for you to learn on your own, agents bring market knowledge to the table. They know what active buyers are offering on homes and what serious sellers are taking. See a home online that seems fairly priced, but the DOM is growing close to 100? It's likely your agent would know the backstory. If there a new listing down the block priced 15 percent higher than what you assumed your home is worth, without an agent you may simply believe that you could match it. Your agent would be the first to point out that the other lot is extra large and that the owners just finished a new basement.

Having your agent in your home will not only help them in determining your home's value but also he or she look at your home objectively and give you some feedback on how it looks. Agents aren't there to tear your house apart or criticize you. But agents know what sells, what buyers want, and which properties move quickest. Get their opinion of your home. They may tell you that it would need a lot of work, that it is museum quality, or that it is something in between. You may not be excited about or even ready to hear their feedback at this time, but get it. Often sellers have some amount of work that they need to do before listing the home. A good local agent can make you a laundry list of items that they would suggest doing and leave you with resources for painters, stagers, designers, and any number of professionals you can utilize.

Preemption

My former clients Matt and Lucy met with me nearly a year before they sold. They wanted to move to a town with better schools and simply needed more space. After learning their neighbor was doing some landscaping, an unforeseen property line dispute arose; a fence would have to be removed or replaced to resolve the issue. No seller wants to go on the market having to disclose or point out an issue such as this. What made the situation more complex was that fact that it wasn't as if Matt and Lucy or their next-door neighbor were responsible for making these changes. It had been this way for years.

I suggested that Matt and Lucy put a plan in place to work this out with the neighbor and get the fence work completed *before* listing the home for sale. They decided that both parties would benefit from correcting the issue, so they split the costs and got the work done in three months.

STEP 4   GATHER SOME MORE NUTS AND SIT ON THEM

Most would-be sellers simply need to do this market due diligence with an agent early on. You need to take your current housing or personal situation and understand how that would match up in the real estate market. Knowing your finances and what would be expected of you and your home on the market should be included data. Pieces of data are the nuts mentioned in this step.

If, based on the meeting with their agent, sellers believe that a sale is in their future, it would make sense to start gathering more information. Others, after meeting with an agent, understanding value, and hearing about how the home would fare in the market, decide to take a step back, wait a year, or simply do nothing. This is common. People need to know the information inside and out. Without this information it isn't possible to make an informed decision. You should never feel obligated to list your home with an agent just because he or she visited and did the CMA. A good agent knows that you could be a seller at some point down the road.

If a sale is in your future, then you now have some more data to uncover as well as questions to ask yourself as you start to map out a next step:

- Where will you move to?

- Can you afford to buy before you sell?

- Will you rent for a while?

- What work do you need to do before you can go on the market?

- What are your top three tasks?

- How much would it cost to rent a storage unit locally to start removing items from your home?

- Has it been years since you actually fit your car into your garage? If so, what's the plan to clean it out?

- If your home needs any painting or cosmetic work, how much will it cost? How long will it take?

After meeting with an agent, there could be any number of next steps that a serious seller would need to take. I advise taking a step back, and letting this information settle in. If you are overwhelmed, stop. Do not move ahead. If you find yourself resisting the ideas of making changes to your home or taking on these important tasks, these could be important signs that you may not be emotionally ready to let the home go or move on to the next stage of your life.

NEXT GENERATION REAL ESTATE FACT: WHEN SETTING THE PRICE, SLOW AND STEADY WINS THE RACE

Don't forget that if you are serious about selling in this next generation of real estate, you should get it right the first time. It is better to hold off than to rush forward and make mistakes that could cost you money. If there is some outside personal or financial pressure on a sale, such as a new job or divorce, be aware of the emotional baggage attached to a home sale, and set a period for selling. Don't ignore the feelings, though. Most people simply gather this information only to sit with it, to know what will be involved when the time comes. Knowing what lies ahead and having some sort of timeline for it is part of the process.

★

Now you are taking the plunge and executing a plan. Next generation sellers realize they have only one shot at this and should do it right. If you've planned far enough in advance, this shouldn't be a total shock. In fact, I've found that sellers who have planned enough in advance actually have fun with this process and by now are excited for their next adventure, to move ahead, and to close this chapter.

The Gist before You List:
Choosing the Right Agent

When you bought your home, you likely had a buyer's agent working on your behalf. That agent showed you properties and acted as the lead in the home-purchase process. You may have reached out to him or her early in the process and had a little bit of interaction here and there. But as things got more serious and your hunt for a home reached new heights, your relationship deepened. You spoke to your agent regularly, sometimes taking his or her call over one from your parents . . . or your boss.

Good agents will maintain contact with their clients, even after the purchase is completed. If you had a good relationship, you will likely call your buyer's agent first in the home-selling process. If you bought your home a long time ago or didn't benefit from a relationship with a good local buyer's agent, that's okay. Finding a real estate agent in the next generation of real estate is easier than ever, and it's one of the first things you will want to do as you get serious about moving toward listing your home for sale.

CHANGING THE HAT YOU WEAR

It's important to know this time around that there are two major differences in the relationship between seller and agent and between buyer and agent. First, when you were a buyer, you did not have to pay your agent a penny. The seller of the home you bought paid the real estate commission at the closing of your home purchase. The second major difference is that your relationship with your buyer's agent likely was not bound by a formal written agreement or a contract. Most buyers and their agents work in good faith with one another, agreeing to work exclusively, but informally, to find a home for sale.

When it comes time to sell your home, circumstances are a lot more formal. This time around you will be the one paying the real estate commission, and you will be bound by the terms and conditions of an exclusive listing agreement. That means you go with one agent. You sign with that person, and if the agent sells your home, he or she is due a commission. For these reasons, it's more important to choose the right agent when you go to sell your home.

The dynamics are a little bit different, too. The agreement you sign will be with your agent's real estate brokerage, not with your agent personally. Almost 100 percent of all of your communication will be solely with your agent. However, technically you aren't hiring your real estate agent but rather the brokerage firm. In exchange for a real estate commission, the brokerage and your agent will represent your interests in presenting your home to the market, market your home for sale, and negotiate the sale. Brokerages bring a brand name and history to your listing. Maybe you see their signs all over the homes in your part of town. They pour marketing dollars into building their websites and advertising online and in local newspapers and magazines. Many brokerages bring a certain level of prestige to a listing or lend some credibility to the agent.

Some homeowners believe that the right brokerage matters when listing their home. I am here to tell you that it does matter, but that it is not the only factor. Ultimately, it's your agent whom you will call if there is a problem. Your agent will call you with the requests for showings, and your agent will be the one to present you with an offer. The brokerage provides the framework for the agent to do business. It has a name brand that people recognize. It could be a national brand, such as RE/Max, or something more local for a firm that specializes and operates in one town or neighborhood. Ultimately, I say that it is the agent you are choosing, not the broker. You are, in fact, a customer of the agent, and the agent is really a customer of his or her brokerage. I have a list and base of clients from my 12 years in the business. It's likely that my clients will call on me to help them buy or sell, no matter what brokerage firm I am with. The brokerages know that, so they choose to work with agents who will bring the business to them.

WHAT TO EXPECT FROM A LISTING AGENT

When it comes time to list your home for sale, the agent you choose matters more than ever because you will be contractually obligated to work with that person for a set period. The agent will represent your home and your interests to the public and to the local real estate community. You will trust this person with the sale of your home. This person will speak and negotiate on your behalf and become the face of your listing. For all these reasons, you must have confidence in your agent and his or her experience and abilities. It's a huge transaction with a lot of money at stake. You can't afford to make a mistake, so it's more critical than ever to choose your listing agent carefully. Unlike when you bought your home, if your buyer's agent wasn't doing a good job, wasn't as available as you would have liked, or simply wasn't experienced enough, you could walk away—no harm, no foul. As we've discussed, price or show the house the wrong way, and you could be paying the price in the end. Now that you know you need one, what should a listing agent be capable of?

Good Agents Have Their Fingers on the Pulse of the Local Playing Field

Real estate agents do dozens of transactions each year. While you spend your day working in your profession, good local agents are shoring up their knowledge base with vast amounts of market information and equity. This means they know the players and other agents in town, how they work, what their reputations are, and how they like to do business.

Sellers could never know that buyer's Agent Jack will work with anyone and often pressures his buyers into making offers when they aren't really ready to buy, or that Agent Sarah is so busy that she sends her assistants to cover property inspections or to do the contract review, which often means more work for the seller and seller's agent or that Agent Sue works for a brokerage firm that doesn't spend marketing dollars to showcase its listings online. A good local agent would know specifics such as these and many more. This inside knowledge ultimately becomes useful to you in the sales process.

Your Agent Should Be Likable

What's as important as experience, competence, and trust in an agent is something few people consider—likeability. You will be spending a lot of time with your listing agent. Unlike when you bought your home and you were out at homes for sale or in his or her office, this person will be coming in and out of *your* home. In some ways you are letting the agent in not just physically but also emotionally. As I talked about in Chapter 10, a home sale can bring to the surface all kinds of stressors, emotions, and pains. The process can be so daunting and so personal that you need someone around you with whom you are comfortable and candid.

🏠 **EXPERT**   **Lockhart Steele, Founder of Curbed**

"The story of the real estate in last ten years is there is so much more transparency. Agents controlled everything before the Internet, from comps to days on market, they knew the information and controlled it," Lockhart told me. "I think that's flipped on its head now, whether it is Curbed laying out what really goes on inside buildings, or everything the syndicates, like Zillow and Trulia, are doing. The best brokers have adapted to this realty and have blogs. They write about the local market. You can now find smarter brokers in the age of the Internet really get a sense of an agent and whether they know their stuff or not, based on their blogs. Be open to local blogs and go outside blogs run by brokerages. Chances are you will run into someone with a blog who might be a great resource for you, especially since it's important to stay local."

Your Agent Should Engage the Public

Your listing agent will be the face of your home to the public and to other agents and therefore should be likable to them. The agent should be honest, straightforward, and ethical. It pays to have a good reputation among other agents. We are not only marketing and selling your home to consumers but also inviting other good local agents to bring their buyers to see your home and make offers. Most people don't consider this when choosing a listing agent. Someone who is respected in the local community will go a long way toward ensuring a successful sale. Choose someone with a bad reputation, and you could turn off good agents in town and therefore miss their buyers.

Good Agents Have the Inside Track on the Market

Agent caravans, or broker open house tours, are opportunities for agents to invite each other into their listings to preview potential places for their buyer clients. They are basically open houses for agents, and you should expect your agent to host them. This is a great way for a good agent to not only keep up with the market but also get feedback and impressions for colleagues who know what their buyer clients are looking for. Behind-the-scenes information such as this can really serve you in the event you need to make a last-minute change to the price of your listing or are in the throes of a weeklong negotiation with a tough buyer.

Good Agents Are Members of the Local Board of Realtors and Have Access to the Local Multiple Listing Service (MLS)

Every local board of Realtors agrees to collaborate by sharing information, business tools, education, and codes of ethics. Ninety-nine percent of the time, you will meet an agent who is a member of the local board of Realtors. What this tells you is that the agent is dedicated to advancing career knowledge while enhancing your home buying or selling experience.

Good Agents Should Be Experienced

It could be that the agent you want to choose hasn't sold a ton of homes in your neighborhood but has been in the business for years. Or maybe the agent is somewhat new to the business but has represented more sellers than buyers. Experience has much less to do with duration of time in the business than with success rate and focus on the issues that are important and necessary for you.

Good Agents Try to Be Neighborhood Specialists

Although not *as* important as having an experienced agent, having someone who knows your neighborhood can only help. If the agent has sold nearby homes, he or she knows and understands the buyer pool. And, more important, that agent has understanding of the inventory and is very familiar with what has sold or failed to sell nearby.

UNREPRESENTED SELLER: WHEN TO GO FOR SALE BY OWNER (FSBO)

With so much information online these days, many believe that the role of the agent has weakened and that our value is not what it used to be. When it comes time to sell a home, it's common for many people to wonder if they can go at it alone and save the 6 percent commission. Surely it has to be easy. Do the research on your own, check out the comparable sales, learn the market, and figure out the best price. Then you take some photos, write up some nice marketing copy, get some ideas for staging and design, and put your home up online for buyers to find. It couldn't be easier to save what amounts to the biggest selling expense, right?

I have been in front of so many sellers who brought the conversation down this same path. I tell them that they absolutely could sell on their own and that there aren't huge obstacles. Also, I encourage them to try it. For some reason, they nearly always ended up listing with an agent. I think that there are two things that make people hesitate.

★

First, with a home sale, there is always going to be this littlest bit of doubt in the minds of homeowners. *Am I making a mistake? Is there something I am missing? Is this the right price? Could I get more?* Given the high stakes of the transaction, I can only assume that the small amount of doubt holds them back, and they ultimately go the traditional way.

Second, I should be clear that a seller who goes at it alone isn't necessarily saving 6 percent. They likely are saving only 3 percent. And that 3 percent savings probably isn't worth the stress or the hassle of listing your home on your own.

Why are they saving only 3 percent? As I discuss later in this chapter, half of the real estate commission goes to the buyer's agent. Buyer's agents prefer to be paid for their work, and the disincentive from selling a home when they won't be paid may sway them away from presenting your home as viable option to their buyers. Plus, buyers assume their agent won't want to work with them on an FSBO, and few buyers would ever want to work with an unrepresented seller on a large financial and hugely emotional transaction. It would just make them too uncomfortable.

Therefore, by doing it alone, you may just lose market share on a home that would otherwise be perfectly saleable in the market. If you lose market share, you lose eyeballs online and traffic through your open house. The fewer people interested in your home, the less competition, which could have a negative effect on your bottom line. For this reason, I see most unrepresented sellers offering to pay the buyer's commission. In this scenario, the seller deals and negotiates directly with the buyer's agent.

It is critical to remember that real estate is a full-time job. Because of weekend work, some agents work more hours per week than folks with positions in other industries. If you are going to sell your home on your own, you need to prepare to put some time and effort into the research, planning, and execution of your home sale. It could, in some ways, feel like your temporary part-time job. For some people this is very possible, and I've seen it happen successfully through the years.

But I use the word *some*. Not everyone is cut out for it. Dealing with the public, knowing how to answer questions, and emotionally separating yourself from your home, to see it objectively to sell it, can sometimes be easier said than done.

If you are going to go down the FSBO path, I advise you to do your homework, cross every *t*, and dot every *i*. There are certain tasks that we, as agents, take for granted because they are ingrained in our day-to-day work. Because you don't do this for a living, you could be caught off guard or miss something that you didn't realize you should have paid more attention to. If you are unsure, don't move ahead. Take a step back, do some research, and formulate a plan.

HOW TO FIND A REAL ESTATE AGENT

It used to be that you stopped off at the local real estate office or called in on the phone to speak with an agent. Maybe you saw one brokerage that had a lot of for sale signs nearby, or maybe you saw a for sale sign nearby and called that agent to be your listing agent. In this next generation of real estate, there are many ways to find a good real estate agent both online and off-line. Also, I should note that you might actually find your listing agent well before you are ready to sell. As I've already said, the selling process can begin many months, if not years, before you actually sign an agreement or list your home for sale. It is important to note that you don't need to commit to an agent or sign a listing until you are nearly ready to go on the market. Many agents will communicate with, advise, and add value to you for some

---

🏠 **EXPERT** Spencer Rascoff, CEO of Zillow

"In addition to learning what's for sale, days on market, and a home's worth, Zillow's users can read reviews of real estate agents," Spencer told me. "On Zillow right now, there are more than 250,000 reviews of agents."

time before you actually list, under the assumption that you will list with them eventually.

Just like finding any other product or service, there will be, as they say in real estate and in dating, a lid for every pot. Not all sellers are created equal, nor are all agents. There is no right or wrong way to meet an agent. Here are some of the most common ways you can meet someone who is right for you and your situation.

Referrals

You need a good local agent for the job. The oldest and most tried-and-true way of finding a listing agent is by referral. Don't forget that we as agents count on referrals from friends, family members, coworkers, and past clients. A referral from someone you trust works because that agent has a reputation to maintain. If the agent doesn't do a good job for you, it will get back to the person who made the referral. Do you know people at work who recently sold? Ask them about their experiences. Did your old friend just post on Facebook that his home sold? Inquire about whom he used. Do you simply need a referral but don't know anyone who has sold recently? Put it out on social media. Surely someone local in your network or friend list can help.

Online

If you can't get a referral, that's not the end of the world. Pop on to any of the real estate syndicator's websites, and you will be over-loaded with information about local real estate agents. Put in your zip code, and click on "Find an agent," and you can see photo after photo of local real estate agents. Click on their photos, read their bios or their blogs, and look at their client reviews from past customers.

One thing that is helpful to note when searching property listings on some of these websites is that the agent or agents whose photo-graphs are next to a particular real estate listing are not necessarily the agents who represent that seller. Instead they are paid advertisements by real estate agents who do business in that local zip code. If you look closely, it will say something to the effect of, "Contact a local agent" or "Get more information" next to those photos.

Some in the real estate industry have voiced their concern that the listing agent should be displayed more prominently. First, they believe it provides more clarity to the consumer. Second, industry insiders believe that if a consumer wants to make contact or inquire about the property, the listing agent should receive the inquiry. To their credit, the operators of these websites do list the name of the actual listing agent; it is just farther down on the listing.

Open Houses

If you know in the back of your mind that a home sale is in your future, then checking out neighborhood open houses could allow you to accomplish both tasks in one fell swoop. First, you can see what the market is doing and how similar homes are selling. Second, you get to meet many local real estate agents. These meetings are sometimes quick. You may engage an agent, or he or she may engage you. As I mentioned in Chapter 10, the process takes some time and research. Many people do their homework independently before committing to an agent.

As an agent, I know that the open house is chock-full of new client relationships. As a potential seller, notice how these agents conduct themselves. Are they professional? Do they appear to be ethical and honest? Is their marketing or advertising good? Also note how they interact with potential buyers. This person will be your talking head and serve as your representation to the broader community. If someone strikes you as particularly likeable or knowledgeable or as a good marketer, take that person's card. Look him or her up online when you get home. You may end up calling this person a few months later when you're ready. The other good thing about meeting a potential agent at open houses is that it is in person. You can watch him or her and get a feeling, good or bad, based on your interaction, and not hunches or hopes.

Begin with the Brand

Although syndicators have certainly streamlined properties, people are still very much aware of brands. Brokerages and agents alike spend a great amount of effort marketing themselves and engaging directly with consumers through social media. Places such as Facebook, Twitter, and Pinterest have become ground zero for brands to get in front of today's consumers. With beautiful photography, blogs, tips, and advice as well as some fun local statistics, real estate brands can become an integral part of the consumer's day-to-day online life. Today brokerages still place local ads, circulate mailbox flyers, and put up for sale and open house signs throughout the area. Attracting consumers in the traditional off-line method as well as via these new media efforts many times lead sellers to reach out independently to a local agent or brokerage with whom they don't previously have a relationship. Searching that agent's or brokerage's website is also key. In many ways, you not only see the listings that are available through that agent and brokerage but also learn about the agent's abilities, experiences, and success rate, which will only add to your own. Most local brokerage websites also provide buyers and sellers access to houses that are listed with them and with their competitors via the local MLS.

My first listing ever came from a call into my office. The woman was familiar with the brand of the broker I worked with at the time. It dominated the market in her part of town. I rushed over to the home, met with her, and followed up regularly for the next six weeks with updates. She appreciated this and ultimately chose to work with me because of my follow-up and passion. Although she understood that I was new to the business, it helped that I was with a trusted and popular local real estate brand.

Ultimately your decision will come down to the agent. It only helps that your agent works under a brokerage that is well known. People trust brands. In the case of my first listing, I may not have been the most experienced listing agent in the neighborhood, but I was sincere, honest, hardworking, and most of all, communicative. My brokerage definitely helped me land the listings. Conversely, a very strong local agent may have years of experience in one particular neighborhood or all over town as a listing agent, but that agent may work for a smaller brokerage or work independently. In this case, a seller might feel confident enough with his or her experience that the brokerage doesn't matter as much.

NEXT GENERATION REAL ESTATE FACT: COMBINE LISTING AGENT INTERVIEWS WITH THE HOME TOUR

Facing a potential new seller, good local agents will set up two meetings. The first will be for them to tour the home and speak to the homeowners about their situation. The second will be a quick follow-up meeting to present their opinion of value, comparable marketing analysis (CMA), and marketing and sales strategies. If you are a seller, be open to this. You want as much information as possible. Also, don't forget that when it comes time to sell, you will pay this person a lot of money, and he or she will be the face of your home. The agent has to be the right person for the job, so the more face time you have with agents, the more of an opportunity you have to understand how they would represent you.

You need to have an agent come over to tour your home and speak with you about what's going on. They need to see your home physically. A good local agent will want to hear all about both your current and desired circumstances. Putting it all into words could be a helpful first step for you. Note that there should never ever be any cost or obligation involved with asking an agent to come see your home. This is typical for the business.

If you don't have a relationship with an agent from when you bought your home, you need to use the first meeting as the listing agent's interview. Hopefully, you've met this person while out and about before or you've researched him or her online or both. It's common for a potential seller to invite two or more agents over to see the home and present their CMAs. For starters, it's good to get more than one opinion of value. Second, the more feedback you have on your home, the better.

Knock, Knock. Who's There?

You can do all of the research in the world on your own, go to open houses, look at online listings, and research your home's value via automated valuation models. When you were buying a home, it was more of an intangible thing. Although you were looking hard for a home and you focused with your agent on your search process, your criteria, and finding a home, the object of the transaction was somewhere out there.

This time around the object is right there in front of you. You have something to sell. You own it and it is tangible. When you were buying a home, your agent likely didn't spend too much time in your home. It could have been a rental, or you lived with your parents. There wasn't any reason for your agent to see where you lived. Now, in order to take a big step forward and gather the information, you have to invite someone into your home. For some people this is very stressful and emotional.

Remember when you were a kid growing up in the 1960s, 1970s, or 1980s? It was as if everyone had an open-door policy. The doorbell ringing was natural. For many people today, a knock at the door or the ring of the bell could be anxiety provoking or eyebrow raising. Imagine you are even thinking about selling your most prized possession, the place where you've built memories or a home you've spent years renovating. Inviting someone in, a real estate agent, in some circumstances a complete stranger (even if a referral or someone you sort of know) can raise the stress levels. The following are common fears, questions, or concerns of sellers who are getting ready to invite a real estate agent into their home:

- I need to get home and clean.

- Will she think my bathroom is dirty?

- I am embarrassed that my house smells like Fido.

- The kids' stuff is all over the place.

- I haven't renovated my kitchen in 20 years.

The good news about stressing out a bit about concerns such as these is that you are aware or are concerned about some issues that you feel may impede your sale. Instead of being embarrassed about them, bring them to the surface and test your agent's viewpoints by asking his or her opinion about them. Inviting over the local real estate agent is just the beginning of a very intrusive process, and sometimes calling out the elephant in the room could help cut to the chase and facilitate faster selling.

I spoke a bit in the last chapter about CMAs. A CMA not only is a market analysis or a commentary on your home and its value but also serves as the listing agent's résumé; you should expect agents to use the second meeting to show you their CMA of your home. Meeting with you and reviewing the CMA provides agents with an opportunity to demonstrate their level of experience and to tell you how they will sell and market your home.

Through the CMA, potential agents should provide you with an overview of their marketing strategy, plan, and timeline. They can provide statistics on their recent home-selling success and some information about how they would advertise your home.

Knowing where you stand in the marketplace and using that information to make informed financial decisions or plans are sometimes necessary months or years before selling your home. What's also helpful when meeting with an agent is knowing what you would need to do to your home, if anything, before you get ready to sell it. Your home may have the potential to be worth $350,000 based on recently sold homes in your neighborhood that are the same size. Knowing that home X, with a brand-new kitchen and renovated baths, sold for $350,000 and that home Y, in need of a heavy renovation, sold for $250,000 can tell you how you fare and what the potential value is. If your home is sized similarly to home X, no matter how awesome a renovation, it's unlikely that it would be worth much more than home X sold for, unless you were on a larger lot of land or had some tangible value-adding feature.

People who are considering selling their homes in the future would benefit from knowing the intricacies between these homes, not only for information's sake, but also to know what kind of upside opportunity there is in the near future. If you plan to sell in the next year, the agent meeting and CMA could offer you some time and ideas for fix-up work so that you can realize your home's true value.

It's important to note that the CMA provides a would-be seller with data about the value of the home at that moment. Agents also might differentiate between the price they would list your home at and the price they think it would sell for. When it comes time to get more serious about listing a home for sale and putting it on the market, you and your agent will have a series of discussions about the list price and possible sales price. Your agent will update you on the recent comps and may even tell you that your home's value has increased. I'll revisit this situation in Chapter 15.

It's common for sellers to communicate to the agents any concerns they have about selling. Agents may ask the following: Did you previously have termite issues? Are you worried that your neighbor's home is an eyesore? Is your loan amount close to what the proposed value is? Do you have any strange liens on the property or major disclosures items that could affect value? Being open and communicative about these important real estate items up front will allow you to find an agent with whom you feel comfortable and to feel confident to outline a clear strategy for a successful sale.

Use these meetings to ask agents about themselves and their experience. The following are some key and run-of-the-mill questions a listing agent may entertain:

- How long have you been selling real estate?

- What portion of your business comes from buyers and how much from sellers?

- Have you sold many homes in this neighborhood or community?

- Do you work on a team or independently?

- Do you have an assistant who does your showings, or will you be the face of the listing?

- What is your strategy with regard to pricing?

- How will you market my home?

- Where can I find my home listed online if I list with you?

My belief is that sellers, not unlike buyers, choose their agents based on their gut feelings or reactions. You may feel that this person just doesn't seem to be on the same page as you. He or she could have all the best experience in the world and have the best marketing plan, but for whatever reason, you just can't imagine having this person in your life for an unforeseen amount of time. Conversely, there may be a person who hasn't sold a ton in your local community but is experienced and knowledgeable. You just get a good feeling about and trust him or her. They say that in sales, people buy from people that they like. In some ways, you are buying into this listing agent. You also want potential buyers, your customers, to like your agent and therefore buy your home.

Once you find someone you feel comfortable with, you've made a huge first step. Although you are not expected to sign a listing agreement right then, it will be helpful for you to understand the ins and outs of such agreements as well as how the agent is paid.

How Can I Help You Find an Agent?

If you don't like the first or second person that you meet, don't fret. You probably have a good idea about how your home will fare in the market, so keep on the lookout. I often receive web inquiries from sellers all over the nation who can't find a good agent to list their home. They've met with two but just don't feel either of them would be the right person for the job. Getting more serious, the seller doesn't know where to look, what to ask, or simply how to move forward. But they recognize that a good listing agent is important, so they turn to me for a referral via my blog. Having been in the business for so many years, I know exactly what questions to ask. I can pick up the phone, talk to five agents, and within a couple of days find a couple of good local agents.

ENTERING INTO A LISTING AGREEMENT

Among other things, a listing agreement states the commission payable to the brokerage, term of agreement, and agreed-upon list price. Remember that this is a business agreement. These terms are all negotiable, although there are some standards that vary by market.

Commission

I've seen real estate commissions as low as 4 percent and as high as 7 percent. The most common commission is 6 percent. The commission of the sale is not pocketed solely by the listing agent. Here is how it is divvied up in the fictional scenario of Tabitha and Rob.

Tabitha and Rob just sold their home in Boca Raton, FL for $300,000. According to their listing agreement, their listing brokerage's commission is 6 percent, or $18,000. But what many people don't realize is that that commission is then split with the buyer's agent. Therefore, in actuality, the listing brokerage takes 3 percent ($9,000), and the buyer's brokerage takes 3 percent ($9,000).

The first 3 percent is split between the listing brokerage and the listing agent. For easy numbers we'll say 50 percent ($4,500) goes to the agent, and 50 percent ($4,500) goes to the brokerage. The other 3 percent is split between the buyer's brokerage and the buyer's agent similarly.

Term of Agreement

The term of an agreement, also called the listing term, is usually six months. Some owners prefer a shorter listing period. Talk about what is common for your local market. A six-month term does not mean that your home needs to be publicly listed for six months straight. Instead, it grants your agent and brokerage the *exclusive* right to list your home for sale during that time. Quite simply, you can't list with someone else, and you can't sell it on your own. Any home sale that happens during this listing shall go through the agent, and he or she is due a commission for that sale. This means that during the

Buying the Listing

There's a term used in the real estate agent community to describe the actions of an agent who takes an overpriced listing—*buying the listing.* Common among newer agents or less productive agents, buying the listing means that the agent got the listing because he or she told the seller the property was worth more than it actually was. These agents may need the business, want exposure in the marketplace, or simply desire to make themselves look active in the market. Be mindful of an agent who gives you a number that is much higher than what you think or what other agents are telling you. If two agents tell you your home is worth between $475,000 and $500,000 but a third agent tells you it's worth $550,000, as much as that could seem promising and hopeful for you, it should be a red flag. Talk about the high number with each of the agents and ask for an opinion. Don't be afraid to ask the higher-priced agent why he or she thinks that price is achievable. It sounds tempting to list higher. After all, who wouldn't want an additional $50,000? As I discussed in the last chapter, remember that going in too high could risk you six months of little to no activity, only to end up reducing the price to $499,000. Your listing will look stale, and agents and buyers will punish you in the marketplace in the form of a final lower selling price.

term of the agreement, if you have a coworker come look at the house independently, and he makes you an offer, you will still have to pay commission to the brokerage, even if its agent didn't bring the buyer to you.

Sometimes sellers entertain the idea of selling to their neighbor or friend but decide against a private sale. They still want to list the home for sale with an agent; however, now that they are serious, it's still possible that they would sell it to that neighbor or friend. Most listing agreements will allow a seller to list an exception or two for a certain period, so if your cousin Eddie decides to actually follow through and purchase the home from you, he could be an exception. As such, you and the agent can decide how to handle the commission and if any commission should be paid. Be mindful that your agent will spend time and money once your home is listed. It wouldn't be fair for him or her to receive nothing after five months of marketing just because Cousin Eddie comes to the table. Be up front with your agent before you sign the listing agreement. These situations are worked out all the time.

List Price

I never set the list price at the time of signing the listing agreement. Instead I write in "TBD," or "to be decided." I do this because it could be a month or six weeks between the time the agreement is signed and when the home is listed, and we don't want to decide on the price until the last possible moment; however, you and your agent need to be on the same page and in the same price range before you sign.

For example, if an agent and seller agree that the range of a home's worth is something between $475,000 and $500,000, and there is little competition when its time to go live, you might decide to list at $499,000. If three similar homes come on the market the week you decide to list, you might go on at $485,000. Your pricing shouldn't come as a surprise by the time you sign the agreement, but you don't necessarily have to lock in a price until the most recent comps have been reviewed, and you are just about to go live.

Now that you have a partner on board, you are about to delve deeper into the home selling journey. You likely have some big planning and work ahead. Having an agent alongside you in this process will make things so much easier. You now have someone experienced in the market who knows you, understands your concerns, and is familiar with your home. He or she has the experience to take you from your current situation to your desired place. The next step, which in the real estate world is called *prepping*, could happen over the course of just a few weeks or even months but is imperative before you go live on the market.

Prepping Your Listing:
How to Stay One Step Ahead
of the Next Generation Buyer

Would you run a marathon without first seeing the course—hilly, flat, or muddy? Would you interview for a job that you didn't know a thing about? Would you pick up your blind date in a car filled with empty Slurpee cups and back issues of *Girls Gone Wild* magazine? Not unless you want to peter out by mile 4, lose the job opportunity, or purposely send a potential mate running for his or her life. The same goes for putting your house up for sale. A lot of behind-the-scenes activities go into prepping your listing—getting your home ready—to make the best impression it can make. Prepping your listing includes getting into the mind of the buyer, making updates and renovations to the home, doing repairs, revisiting comps, and providing disclosure statements.

At this point, just as you'd want to get into the mind of a potential employer to provide assurance that you can deliver the needed results, now you will need to get inside the mind of your potential buyer. You most definitely can't prep your home without knowing for whom you are prepping. In the next generation of real estate, things have gotten a bit more complex because buyers and their situations are less static and predictable than 30 years ago.

> **🏠 EXPERT** **Spencer Rascoff, CEO of Zillow**
>
> "One mistake sellers make is they don't assess the competition well enough," says Spencer. "You have to think like a buyer and spend time looking at the competition and how you price your home relative to others. Make sure that your listing is well represented on three or four top sites in your city. You don't want to see low-res photos of your home posted on top websites. Test how your house appears on both mobile devices and desktop. Make sure you have your home represented the way you want it to be represented. Check that the specifications and other information are correct because they impact your Zestimate. Owners on Zillow can comment on their Zestimate and upload information. There are Zillow tools that allow owners to merchandize their home. Sellers' default should be to not assume their listing agent is doing all of this for you or properly."

GIVE THE PEOPLE WHAT THEY WANT

Meet Maddie from North Carolina, who e-mailed me in distress. She was planning to move her mom out of her out-of-date family home and sell it. Maddie read online that it makes sense to do small cosmetic renovations before selling because you could actually get more money in the end. Because of this, she was seriously considering replacing the avocado green appliances with new stainless steel ones, refinishing the hardwood floors, and painting the bathrooms. But when she added up all her cost estimates, she wanted help understanding the benefits and risks of spending $5,000 out of pocket. I did some research on Maddie's family home and contacted a local real estate agent to assist Maddie further.

As it turns out, this home was in a tech hub near Research Triangle Park, North Carolina—an expensive area that attracted young, wealthy tech buyers. People were going into these five-star neighborhoods and tearing down old homes to build new mega-mansions. No matter what Maddie did to the house, the improvements wouldn't sway buyers because they had altogether different (and much grander) plans for the home.

Maddie moved her mom out, cleaned up the home, and listed it as is. Had she spent $5,000 to fix up the home, she wouldn't have gotten any of the money back. She had believed, rightfully so, that if she invested $5,000, she would improve the value. Unfortunately, this type of buyer wouldn't pay extra for such amenities, and the home might have sat on the market, overpriced.

The moral of this story is that it's important to know who your buyer is. Can you ever really *know* who exactly will buy your home? Of course not. But with the help of a good local listing agent and wider eyes, you can likely get a sense for who the likely type of buyer will be. You can paint a clearer picture and then plan accordingly.

After you hire your listing agent, you both should ask and answer the following questions before you go on the market to give the people what they want, just as Maddie did:

- Who are our target buyers?
- How will they find our listing?
- What will they look for in their next home?
- What do we have to offer them?
- What do we want to highlight about the home?

NEXT GENERATION FACE-OFF

Every competitor knows the best way to win a game is to get into the mind of the opponent. Now that you've asked yourself who the buyer is, to prep your listing for an appropriate presentation for that buyer, you need to shift your mind-set from one of homeowner to one of product salesperson.

I'll talk about this more in the next chapter on staging, but it's important to realize that once your home goes on the market, it is not necessarily your home anymore. Once you go live for sale, your home becomes a product for sale in a marketplace. The buyers are your customers. You have to know who they are, how they think, and what resources they have to make an informed decision about your home.

Anticipate that the buyer of your home will likely look at every room of your house, review your floor plan, do a Google Street View search of your block, and maybe even check your building permit history, all *before* they ever step foot into your home. They come armed with information and intelligence about you, your home, and your home's sales history. There is no such thing as buyer beware anymore.

A next generation seller knows that the reality is that the world is very transparent and buyers are somewhat in the driver's seat. The information they collect about your house, whether good or bad, can be used in your favor, though, as long as you anticipate what might arise in the buyers' minds. Doing some reconnaissance work in advance will inform you about things you may not have planned for and will allow you to take corrective actions before you go on the market. Otherwise, you may be stuck with a red flag after you have a buyer in contract. The goal is to eliminate as many red flags as possi-

---

🏠 EXPERT   Richard Florida, Senior Editor at *The Atlantic*

According to Richard, sellers today should know that their buyers are extremely tech savvy and have been brought up on transparency of information. They are resourceful and full of inquiries and ideas about what they want and expect from their future homes. In fact, Richard calls this group of people, *The Creative Class*.

Richard told me, "The Creative Class people have a wide range of personality traits, but psychologists find the most highly creative people tend to be high in openness-to-experience, and this partly explains the tendency of highly creative people to cluster in exciting urban areas. Likewise, it explains why the Creative Class now demands neighborhoods and communities that are open, diverse, and thick with amenities (a vibrant arts scene, good restaurants, a safe community, etc.). As you can imagine, the rise of the Creative Class and its economy power and interests have a significant impact on the market for both buyers and sellers."

ble in advance. That's smarter selling and more money in your pocket at the closing.

Here are some things you can do to stay one step ahead of the next generation buyer:

- **Google your address.** You never know what will come up when you Google your address. Are you running a home-based business? Has there been police activity at your home? I received an e-mail from a frantic seller in Millersville, Pennsylvania, who explained that five years earlier his bike was stolen out of his open garage. Although it was his mistake because he left it unlocked and the door open, he filed a police report, which the neighborhood newspaper picked up for its police blotter section. The seller had forgotten about this unfortunate incident and didn't mention it to his agent, but after the buyers Googled the address and clicked the link to the blotter that took them to the theft report, they became concerned about crime and safety.

  Any number of things could come up in a search of your property address. Googling your address ahead of time will allow you to come up with a strategy or communication plan should questions arise.

- **Google Street View your block.** I once took a listing in San Francisco on the ground floor of a three-story building. The windows were right at the sidewalk, and they had bars on them from years earlier. In addition to a new paint job, as part of the prepping process, we decided to build out a small garden on the sidewalk next to the home to create a buffer between people walking on the sidewalk and the home. It would also look pretty. It made perfect sense. Unbeknownst to us, a serious buyer Googled the address and looked on Street View. There was the same home, with a bad paint job and bars on the windows. It looked like a different home altogether. This raised a huge red flag to the buyer about safety in the neighborhood. Other issues may come up, such as neighbors who may have previously operated a day-care center out of their house or some type of perceived neighborhood nuisance that a potential buyer might not see in real time.

- **Research your home at the local building or planning department.**
  Nearly every municipality has online access to public records of
  each property. Before technology saved the day, potential buyers
  had to spend hours scanning the microfiche in the basement of
  town hall to do their research. Today they can do so with just a few
  clicks. What should you be on the lookout for? One example is a
  wrong use code for your home; in essence, is it a legal two-family
  home, but the city says single family? Say you find an old permit
  that was never signed off on. Did you do some work on your home
  three years ago? You assumed your contractor got the right permits
  and got them signed off on, right? Well, that's not always the case.
  This could pose a problem down the road. If you figure it out
  before you list, you can remedy it or present a solution in advance
  of the buyer asking for one.

- **Search the address in the Kids Live Safe database.** According to PR
  Newswire, as quoted in the website "Kids Live Safe" at Kid-
  slivesafe.com, the number of registered sex offenders increased by
  23 percent from 2006 to 2011. Buyers with children will certainly
  find this tool an essential one when thinking about buying a property. And you as a seller might be taken aback once you see who
  might be living in a half-mile radius. Doing your due diligence on
  this sensitive and important issue will help you and your agent cut
  concerns off at the pass.

- **Read the police blotter.** You may be asked to complete some disclosures about your knowledge of crime in your home or in the neighborhood. Although you might assume that it's a safe neighborhood
  because you've never had an issue, it's possible there could have
  been some type of crime nearby. If your neighbors got divorced, for
  instance, and have had reports of domestic disturbances or even
  arrests, surely your buyers will see this on the blotter, so they need
  to be reassured that these were isolated and personal incidents and
  have nothing to do with the property or the surrounding area.

- **Look up your Zestimate.** Nearly all buyers will look up your listing
  online and will come face-to-face with Zillow's Zestimate. Even

though I know this number could be way off, it's helpful to anticipate it. If your home is larger than what Zillow says, you may want to claim your listing there and update the statistics. Be careful not to reveal too much. Sometimes saying or putting out less is actually more or better. I worked with a seller who had, many years earlier, put in a Make Me Move sales price on Zillow. A Make Me Move price allows homeowners to list a price at which they would actually sell their home and then allows a buyer to contact them. In the case of the seller, his old Make Me Move price was $100,000 less than his current list price. That's what's scary about the Internet—once it's out there, and you don't maintain it, it's out there forever. Luckily this seller updated his Make Me Move number before he went live to prevent a perceived lower value. Below is a sample screen shot of listings from Zillow.com. In this instance, we looked at homes in the Sacramento area that have "Make Me Move" prices.

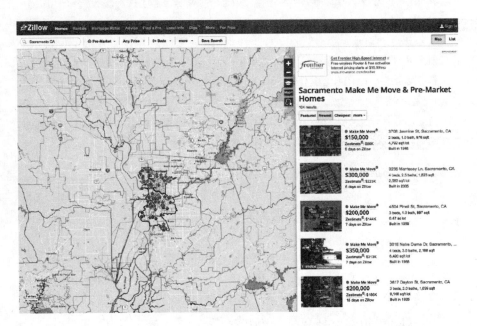

- **Look up your listing and sales history.** A property's sales history, days on market (DOM), or previous sale used to be locked up in the real estate agent's database, and the only person with the key was the agent. Now, it's all out there. Was your home listed a year earlier, but it failed to sell? A buyer will see this and try to understand your history or motivations. If you list the home at too high of a price, the buyers may conclude that you are an unmotivated seller based on the old data and your new listing. Did you buy the home two years earlier for 10 percent less than your list price? Or, as could be the case today, for 10 percent more? Although what matters now is your current list price as it relates to today's market, buyers may try to leverage history to their advantage. In the case that you may seemingly be turning over the property for some easy money after just one or two years, some buyers may take issue. In the case of your taking a loss, buyers may think you are desperate to sell. Put yourself in the buyer's shoes, and be conscious that it's human nature to want to get more but pay less. Then prep your home to prove otherwise.

- **Review the listing from when you bought the home.** Once, a seller who contacted me through my blog bought a home and renovated the kitchen but did it with Uncle Al and didn't take out a permit to move the sink. There was no mention of the renovation anywhere. The buyer pulled up the old listing and noticed that the kitchen sink was on the opposite wall now and that a renovation took place. The buyer next went to the building department website to look up the permit. Guess what she found: nothing. My advice to this seller: You should have disclosed that you did some work without a permit because now the buyer feels that you are not forthcoming. She may be thinking, *What else could be wrong here?*

    This scenario can work in your favor if you bought a home at a much lower price and did a lot to improve it. A buyer can see the before and after pictures alongside your documentation and feel confident that this was a good renovation, all above board and worth the value. If you know what's out there, you can stay one step ahead and anticipate anything.

- **Take a lot of quality photos.** If you looked up the listing from when you bought your home, would you be satisfied with the photos that could still be out there in cyberspace? Today's buyer is high-tech, curious, and research-oriented. Searching is in the DNA of next generation buyers, and they want their questions answered with a touch of a finger. They'll hunt information down themselves, which raises the risk that they'll run into those not-so-flattering photos from the old listing, so give the people what they want: pictures (lots of them), a 360-degree tour of your home, and the ability to navigate your floor plan as they would a video game. The more you show, the more the buyers know, and they will reward you with further inquiries and hopefully a showing or a visit to your open house. Some shortsighted buyers skip perfectly good listings simply because only a few photos are available and mostly of the same room. They think the seller is trying to hide something, and speaking of hiding something, don't. If you fear that your outdated rooms might detract buyers, talk to your agent about staging beforehand. We'll talk more about visually marketing your home in Chapter 14.

- **Know the most recent comps.** Any good agent and seller working together will have studied the comparable houses in the neighborhood before setting a price or listing the home for sale. It's plain common sense. However, sometimes one comp is off the charts, either in a good or bad way. It could have been a home that sold at a huge discount because of a death that occurred in the home or an expensive structural issue. Many times this type of information isn't online or can't be seen by the naked eye. An agent likely wouldn't have put "death on premises" or "needs a new foundation" in their marketing remarks, so some buyers, without access to a good local buyer's agent, may ask about this home or try to use it as a comp when making an offer. Know the backstory of any comps that aren't in line with your list price.

★

These exercises should be done well in advance of listing your home for sale. It could take time to get your contractor over to get that outstanding permit signed off or for you to go to the building department and let it know about an illegal renovation. It could be as simple a remedy as taking out a permit after the fact and documenting it with the city. Doing your own due diligence might require you and your agent to get together and strategize how to deal with buyers who ask these questions or notice these things. Don't forget that your agent, as the face of your listing, will likely be on the front lines fielding these questions or concerns. You should communicate what you find in your research with your agent. The last thing that agents want is to be blindsided because you didn't give them a heads-up.

Although these exercises may seem tedious and time consuming and may not amount to anything valid to your home's listing or sale, it's best to check the boxes. My examples may be extreme, but they help highlight what could happen. The information is all out there today, and there isn't any turning back. You must assume that each and every serious buyer will use whatever information is available to pick your home and your listing apart before making a serious play for it. This is a huge financial, practical, and emotional investment for them. You may have raised your family in this home. The potential buyers may want to do the same.

NEXT GENERATION REAL ESTATE FACT: INSPECT YOUR PROPERTY BEFORE YOU LIST IT

It sounds backward for sure. The buyer pays for and arranges the property inspection, not the seller. You have been in the market before, and you know that the process goes along these lines: Buyers make an offer, sellers accept it, and then the buyers do their inspection. But in the next generation of real estate, the process goes a little differently. Today, it's wise for a serious seller to do a presale property inspection weeks or months before going on the market. As I explained earlier, the seller has to anticipate the buyers' next moves and be prepared. Having an inspection before going on the market will give you the leg up when it comes to pricing and negotiating your home's sale. Doing so is also a sign that you are a fair and honest seller. Here are three reasons why I advise sellers to do inspections *before* they list their homes:

1. **It will help you properly price and market your property.** A presale inspection will help you address glaring home-improvement issues so that you can properly price and market your property. If you know the house needs a new roof, either fix it before going on the market or factor that into the list price. Factoring that into the list price will save you headaches when you have buyers under contract who want to negotiate the price down further or who ask for a credit after the inspector informs them about the roof. Do you know the roof is old but hope the buyer won't notice? That's not the best approach.

2. **It makes buyers more confident in your property.** If you do a presale inspection, make the written report available to potential buyers. Having them see the inspector's report up front will give them the added confidence to make an offer on your property. You'll weed out the buyers who may not be into small fixes, as well.

3. **You'll have the upper hand in negotiations and save time.** The idea of documenting your property's flaws up front may seem counterintuitive to a seller. Ultimately, though, it can give you the upper hand in negotiations. The possibility that a serious buyer won't eventually learn about these flaws is very low. Why not take the high road? Flag the issues from the get-go, and negotiate from a place of strength.

Too often, the scenario I see play out goes something like this: The seller has no inspections or reports. The buyer makes an offer, assuming that the property is in good condition. The seller accepts the offer, the buyer begins his due diligence, the earnest money is deposited, and then the inspections and loan processes begin. Basically the sellers think that you have a deal and that you are moving ahead.

However, then the buyer's inspector discovers a variety of small issues: The electrical panel needs updating, some plumbing needs to be changed, and the heating, ventilation, and air-conditioning system is near the end of its life. The buyer may not be up for home improvements and walks away. Now, after having spent a week or two tying up the sale with this one buyer, the seller is forced to go back on the market. The property now seems flawed in the eyes of buyers, the brokerage community, or anyone who can see the listing history online. Alternatively, the buyer may negotiate a credit of up to $30,000 to accommodate for these fixes—money the seller probably hadn't intended on forfeiting.

If the seller had done a property inspection before going to market, these issues would have been obvious to the buyer before his or her offer, and both parties could have avoided a lot of wasted time and energy.

DISCLOSURE AND PROPERTY HISTORY

One of the main components of proper prepping includes filling out disclosure reports. (See the sample disclosure statement on the following pages.) In many parts of the country, sellers must complete three to five pages of yes or no questions. Additionally, some states, counties, or towns have more specific reports that must be provided to the buyer when a transfer takes place. For example, sellers along the Gulf Coast or the Mississippi River are likely required to provide sellers with a disclosure about flood plains. In California, there is an earthquake hazard report that buyers review before they close on the property. It's the seller's legal obligation to provide this documentation and inform the buyer of property defects or issues, past or current violations, crime, and anything that would affect the value or habitability of the property for future buyers. Your agent will facilitate the property documentation of these disclosures before you list.

In many parts of New York State, sellers can pay an extra $500 in lieu of completing any disclosures. In this case, it's buyer beware. If you are in a place where you don't have to disclose, you can count on the buyers doing extra due diligence on your home. If they find things out or discover issues, it could lead to a deal falling apart and to being forced to go back on the market.

No matter what the law requires, I believe it is good practice for the seller to disclose as much as possible. In some states, lack of disclosure about something that could affect the value of the home could lead to a lawsuit. I always advise sellers to take their disclosures

San Francisco Association of REALTORS®

REAL ESTATE TRANSFER DISCLOSURE STATEMENT
(California Civil Code § 1102, et seq.)
SAN FRANCISCO ASSOCIATION OF REALTORS® STANDARD FORM

THIS DISCLOSURE STATEMENT CONCERNS THE REAL PROPERTY SITUATED IN THE CITY OF _____, COUNTY OF _____, STATE OF CALIFORNIA, DESCRIBED AS _____. THIS STATEMENT IS A DISCLOSURE OF THE CONDITION OF THE ABOVE DESCRIBED PROPERTY IN COMPLIANCE WITH SECTION 1102 OF THE CIVIL CODE AS OF _____. IT IS NOT A WARRANTY OF ANY KIND BY THE SELLER(S) OR ANY AGENT(S) REPRESENTING ANY PRINCIPAL(S) IN THIS TRANSACTION, AND IS NOT A SUBSTITUTE FOR ANY INSPECTIONS OR WARRANTIES THE PRINCIPAL(S) MAY WISH TO OBTAIN.

I. COORDINATION WITH OTHER DISCLOSURE FORMS

This Real Estate Transfer Disclosure Statement is made pursuant to Section 1102 of the Civil Code. Other statutes require disclosures, depending upon the details of the particular real estate transaction (for example: special study zone and purchase-money liens on residential property).

Substituted Disclosures: The following disclosures and other disclosures required by law, including the Natural Hazard Disclosure Report/Statement that may include airport annoyances, earthquake, fire, flood, or special assessment information, have or will be made in connection with this real estate transfer, and are intended to satisfy the disclosure obligations on this form, where the subject matter is the same:

☐ Inspection report completed pursuant to the contract of sale or receipt for deposit.
☐ Additional inspection reports or disclosures:

II. SELLER'S INFORMATION

The Seller discloses the following information with the knowledge that even though this is not a warranty, prospective Buyers may rely on this information in deciding whether and on what terms to purchase the subject property. Seller hereby authorizes any agent(s) representing any principal(s) in this transaction to provide a copy of this statement to any person or entity in connection with any actual or anticipated sale of the property.

THE FOLLOWING ARE REPRESENTATIONS MADE BY THE SELLER(S) AND ARE NOT THE REPRESENTATIONS OF THE AGENT(S), IF ANY. THIS INFORMATION IS A DISCLOSURE AND IS NOT INTENDED TO BE PART OF ANY CONTRACT BETWEEN THE BUYER AND SELLER:

Seller ☐ is ☐ is not occupying the property.

A. The subject property has the items checked below (read across):

☐ Range	☐ Oven	☐ Microwave
☐ Dishwasher	☐ Trash Compactor	☐ Garbage Disposal
☐ Washer/Dryer Hookups	☐ Carbon Monoxide	☐ Rain Gutters
☐ Burglar Alarms	Device(s)	☐ Fire Alarm
☐ TV Antenna		☐ Intercom
☐ Central Heating	☐ Satellite Dish	☐ Evaporator Cooler(s)
☐ Wall/Window Air Conditioning	☐ Central Air Conditioning	☐ Public Sewer System
☐ Septic Tank	☐ Sprinklers	☐ Water Softener
☐ Patio/Decking	☐ Sump Pump	☐ Gazebo
☐ Sauna	☐ Built-in Barbecue	☐ Spa
☐ Hot Tub	☐ Pool	☐ Locking Safety Cover
☐ Locking Safety Cover	☐ Child Restraint Barrier	
☐ Security Gate(s)		

Garage: ☐ Attached   ☐ Automatic Garage Door Opener(s) ☐ Number Remote Controls
Pool /Spa Heater: ☐ Gas   ☐ Not Attached   ☐ Carport
Water Heater: ☐ Gas   ☐ Solar   ☐ Electric
Water Supply ☐ City   ☐ Well   ☐ Private Utility or
Gas Supply ☐ Utility   ☐ Bottled   Other _____
   ☐ Water-conserving plumbing fixtures

☐ Window Screens   ☐ Window Security Bars ☐ Quick Release Mechanism on Bedroom Windows
Exhaust Fan(s) in _____   220 Volt Wiring in _____   Fireplace(s) in _____
☐ Gas Starter _____   ☐ Roof(s): Type: _____ Age: _____ (approx.)
Other: _____

Buyer's Initials   **Seller's Initials**

_____/_____   _____/_____

Are there, to the best of your (Seller's) knowledge, any of the above that are not in operating condition? ☐ Yes ☐ No. If yes, then describe. (Attach additional sheets if necessary):_____

_____

B. **Are you (Seller) aware of any significant defects/malfunctions in any of the following?** ☐ Yes ☐ **No. If yes,** check appropriate space(s) below:
☐ Interior Walls ☐ Ceilings ☐ Floors ☐ Exterior Walls ☐ Insulation ☐ Roof(s) ☐ Windows ☐ Doors ☐ Foundation ☐ Slab(s) ☐ Driveways ☐ Sidewalks ☐ Walls/Fences ☐ Electrical Systems ☐ Plumbing/Sewers/Septics ☐ Other Structural Components
(Describe:)_____
If any of the above is checked, explain. (Attach additional sheets if necessary):_____

_____

_____

Installation of a listed appliance, device, or amenity is not a precondition of sale or transfer of the dwelling. The carbon monoxide device, garage door opener, or child-resistant pool barrier may not be in compliance with the safety standards relating to, respectively, carbon monoxide device standards of Chapter 8 (commencing with Section 13260) of Part 2 of Division 12 of, automatic reversing device standards of Chapter 12.5 (commencing with Section 19890) of Part 3 of Division 13 of, or the pool safety standards of Article 2.5 (commencing with Section 115920) of Chapter 5 of Part 10 of Division 104 of, the Health and Safety Code. Window security bars may not have quick-release mechanisms in compliance with the 1995 edition of the California Building Standards Code. Section 1101.4 of the Civil Code requires all single-family residences built on or before January 1, 1994, to be equipped with water-conserving plumbing fixtures after January 1, 2017. Additionally, on and after January 1, 2014, a single-family residence built on or before January 1, 1994, that is altered or improved is required to be equipped with water-conserving plumbing fixtures as a condition of final approval. Fixtures in this dwelling may not comply with Section 1101.4 of the Civil Code.

C. **Are you (Seller) aware of any of the following?**
1. Substances, materials, or products which may be an environmental hazard such as, but not limited to, asbestos, formaldehyde, radon gas, lead-based paint, mold, fuel or chemical storage tanks, and contaminated soil or water on the subject property .... ☐ Yes ☐ No
2. Features of the property shared in common with adjoining landowners, such as walls, fences, and driveways, whose use or responsibility for maintenance may have an effect on the subject property.................................... ☐ Yes ☐ No
3. Any encroachments, easements or similar matters that may affect your interest in the subject property................... ☐ Yes ☐ No
4. Room additions, structural modifications, or other alterations or repairs made without necessary permits .... ☐ Yes ☐ No
5. Room additions, structural modifications, or other alterations or repairs not in compliance with building codes ..... ☐ Yes ☐ No
6. Fill (compacted or otherwise) on the property or any portion thereof... ☐ Yes ☐ No
7. Any settling from any cause, or slippage, sliding, or other soil problems .... ☐ Yes ☐ No
8. Flooding, drainage or grading problems .... ☐ Yes ☐ No
9. Major damage to the property or any of the structures from fire, earthquake, floods, or landslides........................ ☐ Yes ☐ No
10. Any zoning violations, nonconforming uses, violations of "setback" requirements... ☐ Yes ☐ No
11. Neighborhood noise problems or other nuisances .... ☐ Yes ☐ No
12. CC&Rs or other deed restrictions or obligations.. ☐ Yes ☐ No
13. Homeowners' Association which has any authority over the subject property .... ☐ Yes ☐ No
14. Any "common area" (facilities such as pools, tennis courts, walkways, or other areas co-owned in undivided interest with others) .... ☐ Yes ☐ No
15. Any notices of abatement or citations against the property .... ☐ Yes ☐ No
16. Any lawsuits by or against the Seller threatening to or affecting this real property, including any lawsuits alleging a defect or deficiency in this real property or "common areas" (facilities such as pools, tennis courts, walkways, or other areas co-owned in undivided interest with others) .... ☐ Yes ☐ No
If the answer to any of these is yes, explain. (Attach additional sheets if necessary.):_____

_____

_____

D. 1. The Seller certifies that the property, as of the close of escrow, will be in compliance with Section 13113.8 of the Health and Safety Code by having operable smoke detectors(s) which are approved, listed, and installed in accordance with the State Fire Marshal's regulations and applicable local standards.
2. The Seller certifies that the property, as of the close of escrow, will be in compliance with Section 19211 of the Health and Safety Code by having the water heater tank(s) braced, anchored, or strapped in place in accordance with applicable law.

Seller certifies that the information herein is true and correct to the best of the Seller's knowledge as of the date signed by the Seller.

Seller _____ Date _____ Seller _____ Date _____

Buyer's Initials   Seller's Initials

_____/_____   _____/_____

Copyright © 2012 San Francisco Association of REALTORS®

Page 2 of 3
(Rev. 01/12)

III. AGENT'S INSPECTION DISCLOSURE
(To be completed only if the Seller is represented by an agent in this transaction.)

THE UNDERSIGNED, BASED ON THE ABOVE INQUIRY OF THE SELLER(S) AS TO THE CONDITION OF THE PROPERTY AND BASED ON A REASONABLY COMPETENT AND DILIGENT VISUAL INSPECTION OF THE ACCESSIBLE AREAS OF THE PROPERTY IN CONJUNCTION WITH THAT INQUIRY, STATES THE FOLLOWING:

☐ Agent notes no items for disclosure.

☐ Agent notes the following items:

Agent (Broker Representing Seller)_____ By _____ Date _____
                 (Please Print)   (Associate
                                                  Licensee or
                                                  Broker
                                                  Signature)

IV. AGENT'S INSPECTION DISCLOSURE
(To be completed only if the agent who has obtained the offer is other than the agent above.)

THE UNDERSIGNED, BASED ON A REASONABLY COMPETENT AND DILIGENT VISUAL INSPECTION OF THE ACCESSIBLE AREAS OF THE PROPERTY, STATES THE FOLLOWING:

☐ Agent notes no items for disclosure.

☐ Agent notes the following items:

Agent (Broker Obtaining the Offer)_____ By _____ Date _____
                 (Please Print)   (Associate
                                                  Licensee or
                                                  Broker
                                                  Signature)

V.

BUYER(S) AND SELLER(S) MAY WISH TO OBTAIN PROFESSIONAL ADVICE AND/OR INSPECTIONS OF THE PROPERTY AND TO PROVIDE FOR APPROPRIATE PROVISIONS IN A CONTRACT BETWEEN BUYER(S) AND SELLER(S) WITH RESPECT TO ANY ADVICE/INSPECTIONS/DEFECTS.

I/WE ACKNOWLEDGE RECEIPT OF A COPY OF THIS STATEMENT.

Seller _____ **Date** _____ **Buyer** _____ **Date** _____

Seller _____ **Date** _____ **Buyer** _____ **Date** _____

Agent (Broker Representing Seller)_____ By _____ Date _____
                 (Please Print)   (Associate
                                                  Licensee or
                                                  Broker
                                                  Signature)

Agent (Broker Obtaining the Offer)_____ By _____ Date _____
                 (Please Print)   (Associate
                                                  Licensee or
                                                    Broker
                                                  Signature)

SECTION 1102.3 OF THE CIVIL CODE PROVIDES A BUYER WITH THE RIGHT TO RESCIND A PURCHASE CONTRACT FOR AT LEAST THREE DAYS AFTER THE DELIVERY OF THIS DISCLOSURE IF DELIVERY OCCURS AFTER THE SIGNING OF AN OFFER TO PURCHASE. IF YOU WISH TO RESCIND THE CONTRACT, YOU MUST ACT WITHIN THE PRESCRIBED PERIOD.

A REAL ESTATE BROKER IS QUALIFIED TO ADVISE ON REAL ESTATE. IF YOU DESIRE LEGAL ADVICE, CONSULT YOUR ATTORNEY.

seriously. It's better to be up front than to try to hide something and have it come back to bite you, either in the form of sabotaging your sale or eliciting a lawsuit a year later.

It's also good practice to keep your receipts and evidence of previous work done. Did you have a new roof put in? Provide evidence of that work to the buyers. Why? It will help them be comfortable with the home. If you did hefty renovations, keep copies of all the permits, job cards, and invoices that show that the work was completed and that the city signed off on it. If you added a pool, make sure that it was documented and approved. Doing so will give buyers confidence to know that they are getting a home that is fully up to code and legal.

Some sellers like to itemize the work, dollar for dollar, that they have done to a property to show the buyers how much they spent on a renovation project. I advise against it. It's too revealing and buyers could use that information against you. If they see that you spent $34,000 on a bath renovation that should have cost $10,000 why should they pay three times as much? It just opens Pandora's box and leads to too many questions. If you have some sort of documentation of work done, save it and make it available to buyers if they ask for it, but they don't need to know what you spent.

Did you hire an architect to plan an addition to the home, but you decided against it? Include these plans. Why? Because this could give the buyer some good ideas about expanding the home in ways they hadn't considered. Plus, doing so could prove to add value. If you've already spent the money on the architect, the new buyer could take it from there and do the renovation. You've already paid for the plans, so you might as well use them to help you sell the home for top dollar.

These are just a few examples of ways to disclose information to the buyer. Check with your agent before you do anything because every community is different, and some buyers might respond differently to ideas like these. However, I do believe that the more information you can provide to the buyers *before* they make an offer or while they are under contract, the better chance you have of faster selling.

WHY YOU SHOULDN'T DISCLOSE SQUARE FOOTAGE IN YOUR LISTING

An inch is an inch is an inch, correct? That's what you would think. Therefore, including the size of the home—its square footage—into the listing description would be wise, right? I say no way in the next generation of real estate. What many people don't realize is that the measurement of square footage is not an exact science. I worked with a buyer who had two bank appraisals. The seller ordered one appraisal two years before she sold, and my buyer ordered the other. The measurements were off by 20 square feet. How could this be? Both appraisers measured the same home. Upon further investigation, we discovered that some of the hallways weren't measured correctly and that one appraiser included the mudroom in calculating the square footage, and the other left it out.

You can have 10 different appraisers measure the same house, and although they would likely be in the same range, they could all come in with different numbers. Some appraisers use the good old-fashioned measuring tape and measure each room. I can recall countless times when the appraiser asked me to hold up the tape at one end of the hallway while the appraiser walked away. Others use these new infrared laser machines that measure wall to wall. One time I watched an appraiser use his hands and feet to measure a tough space. There is so much room for error, in most cases the smallest amount.

But there are instances where the discrepancy is more than just a few feet and actually a part of a larger problem. I've seen appraisals include a finished basement that may not be technically finished. The seller thought it was but the buyer did not. Should it be included in the square footage? Who's to say? It would likely come down to whether the basement is legal living space. This opens up a new debate, and before you know it, the buyer is down at the town's planning department, trying to research what it takes to make a basement finished.

Through the years I've seen countless arguments and negotiations over the smallest amount of square feet. Because of this, I advise that sellers not list square footage when selling their homes. If you absolutely must list the square footage, do so with a disclaimer, such as "per tax records," "per appraisal," or "per engineers' reports." If you have a recent appraisal and you want to use that number, provide a copy of that appraisal to the potential buyers with a note or disclosure that this is just one means of measurement.

What you don't want to happen is what happened to Trudy in 2006 in San Francisco. The seller of a newly constructed, large home insisted that I include the square footage of the home because the county records showed the square footage at 1,500, less than half the size of the actual home. The previous owner had done a giant renovation and expansion. Naturally Trudy wanted every buyer to know that her home was actually 3,450 square feet because she had a copy of an appraisal from when she purchased to prove it. I pushed back, saying that any buyer would realize the expansion was done and that the county records were wrong. We ultimately agreed to include it, with a copy of the measurements page of the appraisal. Furthermore, I made my own disclosure that measuring square footage is not an exact science and that buyers shouldn't take this as the final number.

Two months into the listing, Trudy received and accepted an offer. The buyers had all their inspections and were completing their loan swiftly when the buyers' agent called. The buyers' bank's appraisal was 50 square feet less than the seller's previous appraisal, and the buyers wanted to knock off some money from the agreed-upon purchase price.

Now, the home hadn't gotten any smaller since the buyers had put in their offer. It was the same home with the same number of bedrooms and bathrooms. It's just that this appraiser came in with a lower number. At the end of the day, this was an emotional reaction on the part of the buyers. Because of the discrepancy between the appraisals, the buyers believed that they had overpaid for the house and believed that the seller had misrepresented its size, despite the copy of the appraisal and my own warning that it was only one form of measurement.

Square Footage in New Construction

Did you buy your home new? If so, you definitely want to keep reading. Builders use engineers and architects to make the plans to build their homes. Generally when drawing out the floor plans and designs for the home, the engineer will use the "walls out" approach to calculate the sizes of the rooms. This means that he or she measures to the exterior walls. Well, developers submit these same plans to the county, and the county will likely use the square footage listed there as the basis for the tax records. A seller of a newly built home will see the tax records showing, say, 2,250 square feet.

However, imagine all of that space between the exterior and interior walls. It adds up, and a buyer's appraiser will measure from the interior walls and come in with a lower number. I advise sellers of homes bought by a developer to look at the size of their home closely. Find the appraisal from when you bought. You may not have even noticed, at the time of purchase, the difference between the size from the tax records and the actual appraisal size, but the next generation buyer surely will.

★

I am not advising you as the seller to obsess about your home the way you would a third date. I don't tell you these stories to scare you away. Instead, I want you to understand what is out there, how today's buyers use technology, and the types of things coming up in real estate transactions because of so many changes in the world. My advice is to be proactive, do your homework, and put your best foot forward. Doing so will eliminate red flags once you have the buyer under contract. I advocate for faster selling.

Seeing Is Believing: Transforming Your Home with the Art of Staging

"**A**ll the world's a stage," wrote Shakespeare. For many of us, our home is our world. Now that your home is for sale, what kind of stage will you put it on, how will you present it, and what does the audience want to see? These are the types of questions you should ask yourself as you take a good, hard, long look at how your house shows, meaning does it have curb appeal and does it have what I call couch appeal?

Before you decided to sell your home, its décor and *knick-knacks* reflected who *you* are. Your couch appealed to you. Now that your home is a product for consumer consumption, the inside should reflect who the buyers *can be* if they would only buy your home. Maybe your sunken-in couch won't necessarily *appeal* to today's potential buyers, even though you worked hard to have it molded to your form. Believe it or not, something as simple as an old rickety couch can potentially throw off potential buyers. Think about it this way: Your hopes and dreams may have once depended on buying this home (or lying on that couch), but now that promise needs to be communicated to potential buyers. How? Through the art of staging.

I was late for dinner and told my father I was late because I had spent the entire day staging one of my client's homes. The last time my dad bought a house was 1988, so it is not surprising that he asked me if I was filming a commercial! Relatively speaking, the concept of staging is a new one; it is one that television shows, blogs, and syndicator websites have really popularized. We've come a long way from *Lifestyles of the Rich and Famous*.

Although you might have heard of the term, many people are still a little confused as to what it all entails. Fret not. Staging isn't always about spending a ton of money, taking all of your furniture out, and bringing in a truckload of museum-quality furniture. In fact, staging can be fun and economical and require just a little bit of effort on your part. If you take nothing else away from this chapter, just know that for the next generation seller, staging is more crucial than ever.

🏠 EXPERT   Richard Florida, Senior Editor at *The Atlantic*

"Aesthetics are extremely important," Richard told me. "Our research indicates that the higher people rate the beauty of their places or communities, the higher their overall level of personal satisfaction. Human beings crave physical beauty. We look for it in so many of the things that surround us, and especially in the communities and places we live."

THE PSYCHOLOGY OF STAGING

Have you ever noticed that a bedroom seems larger once you put a bed in it? Or that a front door painted red has an inviting rustic charm? Or that a well-lighted room can put you in a good mood? As a real estate agent, I too have noticed these details and many others. A lot of people do not consider themselves visual. Therefore, it's a lot to ask of them to walk into a cluttered, musty, or frankly, gauche home and simply picture the couch here, imagine installing French doors, visualize lifting the rugs and replacing the floor with tile, or consider making this private by putting in a pocket door. Oh, believe me, I've seen it all, and it's all true. But still, most of the time, my mostly good suggestions fall on deaf ears.

What's more surprising is that it is even more challenging to ask a buyer to walk into a completely empty home and figure out how it would look and function with furniture in it. It might seem contradictory to, on one hand, advise my sellers to de-clutter and get rid of personal items, photos, collectibles, and so on, yet on the other hand, tell them that it's more difficult to sell a house when it's empty. But the latter is true. The reason? An empty home feels, well . . . *empty.*

First, many people say that a home without any furniture appears sterile, cold, or lifeless. This has an effect on buyers. Spending more than 10 minutes in a home where you can hear your echo will remind you of those feelings. It's human nature to more vividly recall how you felt after leaving somewhere than the actual details about the event. Maybe you don't remember the colors of the latex balloons at senior prom, but you certainly remember if you had the time of your life or sought therapy afterward. The same goes with buyers. They will remember if they felt great or icky when leaving a house, so when it comes to moods, your home should put people in good ones!

Second, many buyers, absent furniture, artwork, or fixtures in the home, lack the imagination necessary to see themselves and their belongings there. With Facebook, Instagram, and other photo-sharing sites so commonplace in the lives of the next generation buyer, the importance of visual appeal has skyrocketed in the past ten years. But long before that, somewhere, at some point in the past, some person had the genius idea to bring in some furniture and stage a home to help buyers literally see the home's potential. When this first unknown staged home hit the market, an entirely new industry was born. In many parts of the country, home stagers, interior designers, and reality television shows are seeing huge success in business or ratings.

You'll see this a lot with new construction. Usually the model home is decorated pristinely with the perfect hues on the walls, the lighting just right, and all the bells and whistles of the twenty-first century. Music might be playing through the ceilings, thanks to the nifty Wi-Fi stereo system, or the tray ceiling may be accented with a painted pattern that matches the curtains. You've seen dozens of beautiful spaces such as these, and they're hard to resist. Buyers who are looking for a three-bedroom, stand-alone house on a large lot could wind up wanting to make an offer on large town house in a condo complex, simply because they fell more in love with the décor than the space itself! That's the power of staging.

FROM COUCH APPEAL BACK TO CURB APPEAL: PROPERTY PRESENTATION AT ITS MOST POWERFUL

Buyers are learning a lot from blogs and reality television about real estate, so they approach their process with the expectation of a Hollywood ending. What they see online and on television is what they think they can get. Therefore, you have to work to make your home show its best; otherwise, potential buyers might not come see it. Don't forget, in 1988, when my parents went to see homes for sale, they didn't know what to expect. They likely didn't see pictures, floor plans, or virtual tours. Why? They didn't exist. Buyers then went to see homes either based on the descriptions in the newspaper or at the suggestion of their agents, who may have toured the home as a way of previewing for their buyer clients.

Buyers have more than one decision to make today. It's not about deciding if they want to make an offer on your home. Based on what they see on the Internet, they will decide whether they even want to go and see your home in person. What if your home is really great? What if it is a good fit, and it would actually work for that buyer? If the home doesn't show well and isn't presented to the market properly online, you could miss an opportunity to get a buyer in the door.

First Impressions: The Online Listing Is the New Drive-by

In this next generation of real estate, there may not be time for the buyer to do the drive-by. Today's buyers first see a home listed for sale online. They receive an e-mail alert about a new listing from their agent, or they happen to see the new listing themselves while doing their own search. Decades ago, would your parents have listed their home before they had the exterior painted or the front lawn mowed? Probably not. Before they listed the home, they likely spent some time and money on curb appeal to make the home look appealing from the street, especially because the street was their best advertising method.

> **🏠 EXPERT** **Maxwell Ryan, Apartment Therapy, www.apartmenttherapy.com**
>
> "We deal a lot with photographs," says Maxwell, "and interiors can be challenging. When photographing your home's interior, have as much natural light as possible. Believe it or not, sunny days are the worst days to take out your camera. The best light to photograph in is filtered light or an overcast day. This allows the lens to open more, which brings more light in, and produces vivid colors."

Today, if your agent is a next generation real estate listing agent, he or she should have three major considerations when it comes to your online listing photos:

- **Use high-resolution photos.** High-resolution photos are those that display best online and have the highest quality. Properly lit, high-resolution photos are the only type of pictures you should use in a home marketing campaign. As with any sales effort, it's important to put your best foot forward. If your agent suggests taking property photos with a smartphone, it should be a red flag. These pictures are fine for informally sending photos quickly back and forth between agents and buyers, but they don't measure up to what an experienced photographer with a good camera can achieve. Request that your agent hire a good photographer. If he or she refuses or doesn't know one, you should initiate the process and pay for it. However, your agent should pay for property photos.

- **Make sure the photos are uploaded when the listing goes live.** It's true that you never get a second chance to make a first impression. Many buyers see homes for the first time from automated e-mail alerts they receive from their real estate agents. Imagine a busy buyer seeing your listing come across in an e-mail in the midst of his or her busy workday. The buyer opens the e-mail, clicks on the link, and there is your listing—but no photos. I can't tell you how frustrating this is to my clients. In a market with high inventory, this could be a huge missed opportunity. If three other e-mails come later that day with competing houses and great photos, the buyer may simply not go back to your listing or see your home in person. One less buyer could translate into more days on the market and ultimately less money.

- **The home should be in open house condition at the time of the photo shoot.** Next generation sellers should spend as much time prepping and cleaning for their photo shoot as they would for the open house. Take this as an opportunity to control certain variables to ensure the best shoot. Is the light best in the morning? Schedule the photo shoot then. Turn on all the lights, if necessary, and make sure your animals' cages and little Johnny's toys are hidden away. These photos are not only the buyers' first impression but the basis on which they make their decision—to inquire or not. Serious buyers will also go back to your photos once they've seen the house in person. What if they had a good feeling about the house once they were there but then went to look at photos and there were either too few or poorly taken photos? These small intricacies could turn the buyers off and send them on to the competing property.

Don't piss off next generation buyers. As I've discussed, these buyers are high-tech and like to search, research, and gather as much information as possible. They expect lots of photos and virtual tours but not under false pretenses. One of the worst things sellers can do is

EXPERT   Barbara Corcoran, Real Estate Expert

Barbara says, "Sellers need to realize that web appeal is the new curb appeal. It's so important to stage a home, get professional photos taken before listing, and make sure those photos are on every great home site out there—Zillow, Trulia, Realtor.com, Yahoo! Real Estate, as well as on your local listing sites. Spending $200 to $500 to get a professional gallery of thirty to forty photos always pays."

entice the curiosities of potential buyers and have them show up and see a completely different home. If they end up liking your home and move forward with an offer, your negotiations may start on the wrong foot. Good faith goes a long way. As I say, "Share openly; you'll get more back in return."

TURNING YOUR HOME INTO A PRODUCT

You've seen those furniture catalogues with the best pieces, perfectly placed, with matching pillows, a throw blanket draped over the couch, and an oversized, colorful rug. These are the images that some people conjure up when they think of staging. Your home doesn't need to show like the Pottery Barn catalog cover, nor do you have to spend a fortune prepping your home for sale. But you have to consider this: Once your home goes on the market, it is no longer your home but rather a marketable product in the eyes of a potential buyer.

Consider the example of Mickie, who had to sell her house. It had been on the market for almost five months, and her now ex-husband and she were being forced to cohabitate. She e-mailed the details of her conundrum to me and asked for help. The house, a four-bedroom expanded cape with a finished basement and wraparound deck on a 100 x 150 lot, was priced well for Ramsey, New Jersey, but still only a few buyers had come through and not one offer. "There is this lime green bathroom," Mickie wrote, "that *I* can't even stand to look at. In fact, when we bought the house, it was hard for me to envision how my then husband would refinish it, but he said he could."

Because she hated the bathroom, she never used it or gave it any tender loving care. The door was always kept shut. It was completely empty, without shower curtains or doors, with exposed cracked tiles, and without guest towels.

Among other things, I advised her to set a budget of $150 and make a run to a department store: The mission was to buy bathroom accessories. Mickie was grateful but totally skeptical about how such an act could help move a $465,000 house, but she was desperate. If all it took to get started on her new life was a soap dish and a towel rack, she was all in.

When Mickie got to the store, she noticed that there were interesting color combinations showcased on the walls of the bathroom section: purple and lime green, blue and lime green, white with lime green, and green with lime green. She was in luck. It seemed that for this season lime green was the new black!

She hurried home with her lavender and white shower curtain, silver and white fixtures, and an incredible oversized lime shaggy rug. She hung a $17 white shelf and placed a few lit candles on it, along with a black-and-white picture she took of a giant rock she once saw on the Jersey shore and a lavender diffuser that set off a spa-like smell.

She wrote afterward, saying that no matter what happened, she loved her new bathroom! She said, "Too bad I didn't think to do this for myself when it was mine."

You can probably see where this story is going. Yes, Mickie and her ex wound up getting an offer—a great one—soon after. Now, of course, I will never say that there is a correlation between Bed Bath & Beyond and selling a home, but for $150, wouldn't it be worth the shot?

Even with the littlest budget, there are things that you can do to put your home's best foot forward, just as Mickie did:

- **Depersonalize.** Like any product for sale, you want your home to stand out and be as appealing as possible. This means depersonalizing it and making improvements to show the home in as neutral a light as possible. You want buyers to walk through your home and imagine *themselves* living there. You *don't* want them thinking they're walking through someone else's home. This means taking down old family photos and diplomas and designs or objects that are personal to you. You want this buyer to make an offer. You don't want to offend her. Packing away religious artifacts, political objects, or anything controversial is the way to go.

- **Emotionally detach.** You have to move on emotionally before you can move on physically. As I said in Chapter 10, someone who is not ready to sell can make huge mistakes that will affect a sale down the road. Know that it's normal and highly likely that you'll experience strong feelings when prepping your home for sale. Taking down your wedding photos, boxing up memorable objects, and painting over the fire truck mural in Johnny's bedroom, all to shine the best light on your home and make it appealing as a product, will cause stress and leave a lump in your throat. I find that this is actually the toughest part for sellers, instead of the closing. It's when the home transitions from their home to their listing that emotions swirl.

Be mindful of this and allow yourself to express the feelings. Acknowledge that selling a home is stressful and emotional. This will be especially difficult if you've been in your home for many years. Acknowledging this up front is a great first step. Allow yourself to grieve if you need to, but keep focused on what lies ahead: a new chapter. I find that many sellers find solace in a new beginning and look forward to moving on so much that they are motivated to make the home sale a huge success.

- **Declutter, clean, and paint.** I tell sellers that the best investment they can make in the home prep process is the cost of a storage unit. The less-is-more approach applies to setting the stage for a home sale. Don't have room in your garage for belongings? Rent a storage locker while you are in transition. Have tons of furniture or big pieces? Taking things out of your home, providing the appearance of more space, is the smartest task a seller can do. Will it be annoying not to have your favorite recliner around while your home is listed? Maybe. Is it worth it to you in the end? That's for you to decide.

  A coat of paint is the next best thing. A fresh coat of paint is great for the senses. It smells new and makes the walls clean. What more could you ask for when putting your home on the market? Well, if you must ask, I like some new carpet or refinished hardwood floors, but that's likely not in everyone's budget.

🏠 *EXPERT*　　Maxwell Ryan, Apartment Therapy,
　　　　　　　　www.apartmenttherapy.com

We know that so many people today are too busy to feel confident about doing a lot of maintenance to a house, and since so many next generation buyers are looking for low-maintenance solutions, it can be challenging if you're trying to sell a home with an expansive lawn. For sellers in this scenario, Maxwell suggests, "Dress up your house from the outside to make a big difference. Add planters in front, pots of colorful flowers to break up all the green of the lawn, and add even more pots in the event the lawn *isn't* green! Adding mulch is a great way to tidy up a space in no time."

NEXT GENERATION REAL ESTATE FACT:
WHEN ALL ELSE FAILS, CALL IN THE PROFESSIONALS

When a seller has the budget to do some serious preparations, the home in its present condition just needs some serious help, or both, it's time to call in the professionals. Your real estate agent likely has some contacts for good local stagers, as well as lots of tradespeople who specialize in quick cosmetic improvements. Calling these folks in doesn't mean you don't have a nice home, and it's not an insulting suggestion on the part of your agent. Instead, think of it as smarter and faster selling in the next generation.

Calling in the services of a stager doesn't necessarily mean that some person will show up with a truckload of furniture. In fact, stagers are just interior designers who either have easy access to, or own lots of, good furniture. It's the interior design services that you will pay for. When most people think of an interior designer, they think of the well-dressed characters designing homes with million-dollar price tags in swanky sections of New York City or Los Angeles. Well, you'll be surprised to know that there are dozens of local designers in your community who could offer their services to help transform your home into a product that your buyers will covet.

People assume that hiring a designer is an expensive proposition. I'm here to tell you that it's not the case. A designer can come in and charge by the hour, depending on your location and the extent of help you need. Tip: Look for design students at a local arts school. They likely want to build their portfolios and will work with a home seller at a fraction of the cost of a full-time designer.

A smart seller will be open to some form of interior design or staging options. Here are some ways you can benefit from working with a designer or stager:

- **By-the-hour fluff staging:** Fluff staging, as we say in the business, means the designer will work with your own stuff and fluff things up. By far the most affordable way of using a stager, you can get a ton of bang for the buck by paying a designer by the hour to work with redesigning your own stuff, taking some things away, and moving others around. Designers can consult with you on paint colors if you decide to paint or suggest small changes, such as lampshades or area rugs. Typical inexpensive improvements include painting kitchen cabinets or changing out light fixtures. After a few minor changes, coupled with furniture shuffling, moving some things to the basement, and a trip to Home Goods, and you will be ready for the big leagues.

- **Partial staging:** A stager or designer can come in and do just a little bit of work, a partial staging. For example, maybe, in your day-to-day life as a homeowner, you use one bedroom as your messy office, but to attract the right buyer, your agent suggests showing it also as a bedroom. Buyers want more bedrooms. A stager may bring in a daybed and small dresser to help show this room as an office *or* a bedroom. You may want to get rid of your oversized sectional sofa and have a stager bring in something smaller to give the appearance of a bigger family room. Do you have some rooms that seem bare, cold, or sterile? A partial stager can bring in carpets, curtains, or throw pillows to give any room some life. Some economical art on the walls can also add some color and design to any room.

- **Full staging:** This is staging in its most grandiose form. A stager will bring in an entire home's worth of furniture, right down to the towels, bath mats, and fancy olive oil or fake fruit for the kitchen table. Full staging costs more because stagers need to hire the moving truck and use their furniture, but agents around the country highly recommend full staging an empty home. Imagine the buyer's first impression when they simply see photos of empty rooms versus when they see your home fully staged. Can't afford full staging? See if you can leave some of your furniture behind or even rent some furniture as a way of saving money.

Before you list your home or enlist the help of designers or stagers, work with your agent to understand what buyers are looking for. Are the buyers in your local community persnickety? Do many of the homes for sale get staged or are small renovations completed to appeal to buyers? If so, then you would have to seriously consider spending some time and money. If you live in a community where staging or design work just isn't common, that doesn't mean you shouldn't do it. To the contrary, if you are up for it, this could be your chance to beat out the competition. See what other homes for sale in your price range look like. In the months or weeks leading up to a home sale, see how other homes show. If you live in a community where people don't spend an ounce of energy on presenting their homes well, then your listing can rise to the top and sell faster.

Showtime! Tips and Tricks
for Going Live on the Market

You've arrived. This is the moment you have been planning for, for nearly a year, maybe more, hopefully less. You considered selling your home, ran the numbers, thought about timing, and weighed the pros and cons of selling your home. You've done all the research and maybe even hired a team to help you get the home ready to show. The day you go live on the market, it's showtime!

As you prepare to go on the market, you and your agent should nail down the following:

1. Final list price

2. Approval of listing photos and marketing copy

3. Potential showing schedule

FINAL LIST PRICE

As I've said from day one, or more precisely, from page one, determining the list price (and the eventual sale price) of your home is not an exact science. In the days leading up to going live on the market, you and your agent should be hyperaware of the competition. How many homes are for sale nearby that are comparable homes to yours? How do they show and how are they priced? As a next generation seller, you will work with your agent to review these listings online, look at their sales history, analyze their photos, and know their pros and cons, as they relate to your home. Then, you should go to the open houses or even make appointments and see these homes. If a new and comparable listing comes on the market that shows better than yours and is better priced, you might think twice about trying for that high list price. Nothing should be a surprise at this point. Also, remember that you have the final say, although your real estate agent likely has a very strong opinion.

🏠 EXPERT   Vera Gibbons, Personal Finance Expert

"About three-quarters of the sellers I have been in contact with think their agents price them too low," Vera told me. "The people who are not quite ready to sell overprice their home. But since people like shiny and new listings, thinking they are getting the latest on inventory, sellers can really shoot themselves in the foot if they list too high and stay on the market too long."

When Cash Causes Cold Feet

Although I advocate for a home being priced right and showing well from the get-go, the fact of the matter is, nobody wants to sell a home for too little or feel like he or she left any money on the table. It's common for a seller, at the last minute, to get a little bit nervous and give the listing a shot at the higher price. This discussion likely has happened over a longer period, but when it is time to go live, things get serious.

If you are uncertain about the price, or you and your agent are a little bit off on where to ultimately list, talk about it. Randy, a seller in Wolcott, Connecticut, was concerned that his agent was pushing for a list price that he thought was too low. They had always had a small difference of opinion on price. Everything else was great, and this was the right agent for Randy. He said so himself. But it was time to list, and Randy wanted to list at $225,000, against the wishes of his agent, who suggested no higher than $199,000. Randy just didn't want to miss the chance that there might be a buyer who would offer $215,000.

Any experienced agent can document countless conversations such as this, and they make sense. It's the seller's property and financial (and sometimes emotional) decision. Randy thought he stood to lose much more, up to $25,000. His agent would lose only a small portion of that amount—3 percent of $25,000 was nothing in comparison. When Randy came to me for advice, I asked him a series of questions to assess how serious he was about selling. Did he have a place to move to? Was there a real reason for the sale? How long had he considered selling? How much time had he spent preparing the home for sale? Randy was moving for a job and had already lined up a short-term lease close to where his new job was. He had packed up much of his house and invested $1,000 in painting and cleaning up his home. I thought he was a serious and motivated seller and suggested Randy plan to drop the price to $199,000 if there wasn't any activity, let alone offers, within four weeks.

My advice is this: If you have a doubt about listing too low and you just can't get past it, agree to try it at the higher price. But have a plan in place! Your first few weeks are generally your strongest and the time when the most serious and active buyers see your home. If, after a certain period, you don't have the right kind of activity—second showings, calls with questions, or open houses where people are hanging around—then you should reduce the price and market with language such as "Price Reduced." Use the reduction to get your home in front of buyers and your agent back in touch with other agents. If done well and timed right, a price reduction can breathe some life into a listing. Also, it shows that you are a serious and motivated seller. A buyer may see that you simply tried at a higher price but then made the smart adjustment in response to the market. How long should you wait to reduce? That depends on your local market. Talk about it with your agent. The conversation should be an ongoing one.

I believe that, in a good agent and seller relationship, a price reduction shouldn't ever be a surprise, a big conversation, or the elephant in the room. Like the preceding example, agents and sellers should talk about price early as a preemptive strategy. If your agent isn't doing it, bring it up early and often. Ask yourself how you would feel if you received an offer within a week of going on the market. Would you wonder and obsess over this offer and wonder if that same buyer would have offered $10,000 more if the list price were higher? Nobody wants to have seller's remorse. What's the best way to avoid it? See and feel for yourself that the market didn't respond to your higher price. If a month goes by without any action at the higher price, then there you have it. At least you saw it and felt it on your own. Your agent can tell you all day long that the price is too aggressive and that it won't work. Sometimes sellers need to have that experience on their own.

APPROVAL OF LISTING PHOTOS AND MARKETING COPY

A lot of the marketing and promotional materials are built and put together at the very last minute. Why? Because a typical seller simply doesn't get their home in tip-top shape, ready to list and sell until the last minute, until they absolutely have to. The listing photos are at the center of all marketing materials, including website copy, web layout in the case of a property website, real estate brochures for the open house, and any mailers. So when the sellers are nearly ready to go on the market, that's usually when the photo shoot takes place.

Just know that it's probably going to be a scramble to get everything up and going. It's not out of the question to ask your agent if you can approve the photos and marketing materials. Some agents may push back, feeling as if you are second-guessing them, but if you have a good relationship, this shouldn't be an issue. Be mindful that your agent has probably spent some time and money on the marketing materials, so speak up sooner rather than later. Last-minute changes or additions could push things back or cost money.

POTENTIAL SHOWING SCHEDULE

You thought that cleaning, de-cluttering, and making your home into a product were hard, right? Now comes the harder part: maintaining

EXPERT — Maxwell Ryan, Apartment Therapy, www.apartmenttherapy.com

"When getting ready to show a house, whether for an open house or by appointment, the most important staging tip—and the easiest—is to make sure there are at least three points of light in a room," advises Maxwell. "Most homes are under lit, and our experience of space is driven by how our eyes read a room. Proper lighting expands a house visually, and since people want to buy a home they can literally expand into, lighting can help potential buyers feel the potential of a room. Spend money on fixtures, like table lamps, desk lamps, light that is below the eye level, and don't forget to make sure they're turned on!"

that look for days, weeks, or months of showings. Potential buyers and their agents could reach out to want to see your home at a moment's notice. You tend to get the most requests for showings in the first couple of weeks. Because of this, you may want to work with your agent on a possible showing schedule for the first few weeks.

Plan for at least a few open houses. Although some agents believe that open houses are a waste of time and that real and serious buyers come through private appointments during the week or on the weekend, I believe that open houses are simply there for a reason: to provide easy access to potential buyers. If your agent pushes back on having open houses, talk about it. See more about the open house later in this chapter.

If, in your community, open houses do not happen every single week, and private showings by appointment are more appropriate, work around that. Just know that your agent can call you at a moment's notice and want to show your home. You may decide certain times work better than others. If you know that the kids are at school and that both parents are out of the home Monday, Tuesday, and Thursday between nine and noon, see if your agent can make those days and times work.

Five Biggest Turnoffs When Touring a Home

Having toured hundreds of homes through the years, agents have come to loathe certain sights. They sometimes leave houses wondering whether the seller even knew a showing was scheduled for that day. Here are five huge turnoffs agents and their buyer clients see when touring homes and how to avoid them:

#5 Pets and Their Stuff

Pets bring so many great things to a family and home, but no potential buyer wants to see a dirty litter box next to the breakfast table or Fido's bitten, saliva-filled bone on the sofa in living room.

When your home is for sale, nobody needs to know that a pet lives there. Potential buyers who are allergic to dogs or cats will be turned off immediately, and the mere presence of a pet will send some buyers right out the front door. Have a plan in place to keep the pet remnants at bay, the home tidy, and your pet's stuff out of sight. It may seem like a burden, but if you are serious about selling, this is of utmost importance.

#4 Toys and Baby Supplies

Selling your home when you have children—especially a newborn—can be trying and stressful. For the most part, buyers can appreciate that keeping the home tidy under such circumstances is a challenge, and they are forgiving. But it is important to make an effort before showing the home.

If possible, have a toy chest or large closet dedicated to storing your kids' stuff. Also keep in mind that buyers have a hard time with the more sanitary or personal items associated with infants. Leaving breast milk, a breast pump, or dirty baby bottles on the kitchen counter could make a buyer feel that the home isn't clean or sanitary. If you have a newborn, put a plan in place, and allow 20 minutes to store baby items before a showing.

#3 Cluttered Counters and Dirty Dishes

Kitchens and bathrooms help sell a home. Most people spend the majority of their time in the kitchen, and buyers will want to spend some time in yours. If the counters are crowded with the blender, coffeemaker, toaster oven, and other items, it will appear that there is little counter space, or worse, that your kitchen lacks cabinet space. Also, last night's spaghetti stuck on plates piled in the sink is sure to turn buyers off. Clear the countertops and put away the dishes before leaving home on the day of a showing.

#2 Personal Items and Toiletries

Don't stop with the kitchen countertops; the same holds true for bathroom countertops as well. Clean the toothpaste off the sink, and put away your prescriptions, open body lotion containers, toothbrushes, and dirty towels. Buyers want to feel clean in the bathroom, and although it's clear that they won't be the first to use this bathroom, they don't need to be reminded that they will be taking over a bathroom someone else has used.

#1 Toilet and Toilet Seat

Imagine serious buyers touring your home. They've fallen in love with the chef's kitchen and are already planning where they would put the television and how their sectional couch would fit in the living room. Then, they stumble upon your bathroom to find the toilet seat up and not clean (or worse, not clear!).

The last thing anyone wants to see is a dirty toilet, so make sure the toilet seat is down at all times. Will buyers be scared off otherwise and not move ahead with an offer? Probably not. But you want them to fall in love with your home, not be turned off.

Twenty percent of home sellers make one or more of these mistakes. As a next generation seller who knows what not to do, you won't become a statistic.

Unfortunately, when you have someone very serious, no matter how tough your situation, you need to cater to him or her. Especially in times when the market is slow and homes don't sell immediately, it can be hard to judge who is a serious buyer and who is just coming to see your home as a part of some big tour. Although I encourage making the home available to show anyone as much as possible, if things are tough, definitely accommodate buyers who are on their second and third showings before someone who has never seen it. Be up front about your situation with your agent. He or she is the gatekeeper, and a good listing agent will know when to push.

I once worked with some sellers who had a three-year-old, a newborn baby, and two dogs. The wife was just back from the hospital, and the thought of leaving the home for some stranger to walk through infuriated her. However, they were under the gun to sell the home. They made a strict showing schedule up front and agreed to work within those time frames. I made sure to communicate this to agents and buyers. Was it harder for some buyers to see the home? Sure. But did a serious buyer make an effort to get there during the proposed times? Absolutely.

A good real estate agent should show up before every showing to make sure that the home is in showing order. Good agents will get to showings ten minutes early. This way they can do a quick inventory and walk through the home to make sure that everything is in order. I also understand that it isn't always possible. Sometimes buyers and their agents will tour a home using a lockbox or there simply won't be enough time because a showing request was last minute. Be mindful of your home's condition when you leave it in case you do get one of these last-minute requests and need to allow the house to be shown on the spot.

NEXT GENERATION REAL ESTATE FACT: OPEN HOUSES ARE NECESSARY

I believe that the open house is the gold standard in real estate. Born out of the need for buyers—in the days before the Internet, online photos, dedicated property websites, and virtual tours—to have access to actually view homes for sale, some agents argue that open houses are a waste of time, that real buyers don't go to open houses, or that open houses are simply a time for the nosy neighbors, unmotivated buyers, or random folks doing a drive-by to poke around. As discussed, all of these people have been known to poke around, and I've even encouraged, you, the next generation seller, to visit open houses in your area!

Busy listing agents claim that serious and motivated buyers make appointments to see the home privately, with their agents using a lockbox or by appointment with their agents. I will say that, yes, there is some truth to this. Serious buyers will come with their agents to see the home by appointment.

But serious buyers don't just show up in a puff of smoke. They become serious over time by researching homes on their own, both online and off. These buyers need open houses to get into the market, to learn the types of homes, to understand pricing, and to educate themselves as to whether they should buy and as to what they get for their money. It's all part of the process.

Open houses are built into the real estate industry as framework by which buyers and sellers work to buy and sell homes. If nobody did open houses, buying and selling homes would be quite different. Those same listing agents who complain about the open houses would then complain that they are constantly running around, showing their properties to buyers who aren't serious. The open house can weed these folks out.

If you haven't read the buyer's section of this book or you have never been a buyer for some reason, know that home buying takes time. Most buyers spend up to nine months looking at properties online or at open houses by themselves before engaging an agent. Then they spend another three months actively looking with their agents. Take a look at the bar chart on the following page for an idea of how many homes the typical buyer previews before settling down.

Could a serious buyer use the open house as his or her first showing? Yes. Also, someone who has already made an appointment could

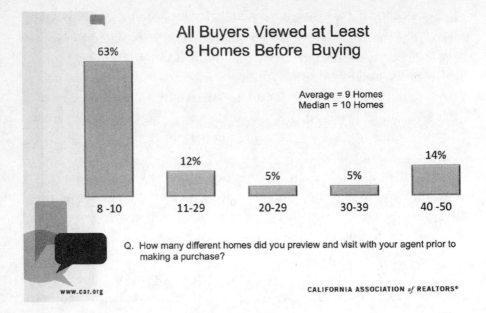

All Buyers Viewed at Least
8 Homes Before Buying

Average = 9 Homes
Median = 10 Homes

63%

12%   5%   5%   14%

8 -10   11-29   20-29   30-39   40 -50

Q. How many different homes did you preview and visit with your agent prior to making a purchase?

www.car.org   CALIFORNIA ASSOCIATION *of* REALTORS®

use your open house as an opportunity to visit a second or third time. Finally, open houses could be good for the seller. Instead of having to clean the home and run out 5 times during the week, the 2-hour open house on Sunday could allow as many people as possible to show up and take their time. Some sellers prefer lumping all of the showings together at once to make this easier. If you're not showing on a Sunday, consider a weekday evening showing. In the next generation of real estate, the rules have changed and Sunday doesn't *have* to be the day. It's all about accommodating buyers but making things somewhat easy on sellers.

I believe that, for the sake of the real estate search process, open houses are par for the course and integral to home buying and selling. Don't be surprised if you hear your agent push back. Every community is different. Talk about the best ways to get your home exposed once you are on the market.

May I Be at the Showing?

The short answer? No.

As tempting as it is, sellers being present when a home is being shown to buyers is not advisable. No matter how helpful you think it will be and no matter how well you think you can best describe the features of the home, I say that you should never ever be present at the showing. Here are three reasons why.

- **Buyers feel awkward in sellers' presence.** Many homebuyers do not feel comfortable opening closet doors, investigating cabinets and pantries, or feeling for drafts in the doors and windows in the presence of a homeowner. Serious buyers want to uncover everything about the house that they can in a short period. Too many times, I have seen buyers be overly cautious about delving into the property and dishonest about their reactions and criticism, or their intense excitement over the property, when the seller is there. When buyers don't feel completely comfortable to explore, they may miss the intricacies of a property, or they might not give the home a fair chance. That's bad news for everyone.

- **Sellers tend to offer too much information.** Honesty is always the best policy, of course, but don't forget that this is a sales process and that saying less is usually more. Suppose a potential buyer asks the seller about the neighbors. "Oh, we love our neighbors!" the seller answers. "We have an open-door policy with them. They've got these adorable twin boys who are so much fun. It's one big, constant block party!" Although some might like this idea, others who value their privacy will be turned off.

- **Sellers can be sensitive and emotional, which can cost them money.** The questions buyers and sellers ask sometimes can seem callous, when really they are looking for information about the product. For example, a seller at an open house overheard a buyer touring the home, which had dark-colored walls and floors and heavy window coverings, ask his agent what it would cost to refinish the floors and paint the place. The seller, who preferred the dark, found the questions insulting and immediately went on the defensive. When a low offer came in from that buyer, the seller couldn't help but think that the buyer was trying to discount the price to pay for those cosmetic changes. The seller refused to budge on price. In this instance, emotions got the best of the seller. Ultimately, the seller lost a buyer and a good offer. The final accepted sales price came in less than that offer by $7,500.

Exceptions to the Rule

Occasionally it helps for the seller to be present during an open house or showing. After weeks on the market without any offers, especially with a property that needs serious cosmetic or staging work, it might be helpful for the seller to attend the open house—anonymously. He or she can hear directly from buyers that the paint job is off-putting, how the place feels too much like a bachelor pad, and so on. The real estate agent may have been trying to tell the seller these things all along, but sometimes, independent confirmation is necessary before the seller will take action.

I once sold a home at the top of a hill. There was a steep walk from the driveway to the front door, which proved to be a major objection among potential buyers. The seller, a triathlete, just couldn't grasp why buyers would seriously object, and he wouldn't budge on the price. By being present (briefly) at one open house, the seller witnessed buyers arriving breathlessly, saying snide comments, such as, "If I bought this home, I could cancel my gym membership." He got the message and agreed to drop the home's price significantly.

★

If you've gotten this far in the home-selling process, you've likely spent hours, weeks, and months thinking about the sale. It's important to put your best foot forward. Right before and when you first go on the market is the most critical time for you as a seller. It surprises me day in and day out and year after year how so many small mistakes are made when a listing goes live. Being "just listed" happens only once. You have to maximize this opportunity. Double-check and triple-check everything, and work closely with your agent.

This is also when your agent should start to shine. If you have a good relationship with your agent, lean on him or her for last-minute help or support and count on him or her for honest feedback. If you are uncomfortable about the smallest little thing, bring it up sooner rather than later. The last thing you want is something small to be building a rift between you and your agent and have that affect your ability to negotiate when your buyer comes along.

If all systems are go and you've given it your best shot, then the wheels are in motion. Next up: how to handle an offer . . . or maybe more than one!

Closing Time:
How to Negotiate, Accept,
and Close a Buyer's Offer

You've planned for this, but receiving an offer can be both exciting and scary. When it comes time to negotiate that offer, it could be tense and frustrating and sometimes drawn out for days or weeks. You must keep your eye on the prize. If you are serious about selling, you've done so much leading up to this point. This is your chance. The end is near.

The buyers can offer whatever they want, but likely they are serious and will write their offer with the advice of their agent. When an offer comes in, the seller has three options: accept it as is, reject it completely, or counter some part of the offer. The latter is usually what happens. The offer will likely include three major components.

- **Price:** This is the one sellers want to know about first.

- **Due diligence and inspection period:** The length of this period varies by community, but the buyers will have some amount of time to inspect the property, sign off on your disclosures, and do their due diligence before moving forward. The buyer can walk away from the contract, pretty much for any reason, during this period. The shorter the time frames, the stronger the offer.

- **Appraisal and loan period:** Nearly every buyer needs to get a loan.

As you know, the banks don't simply give loans without doing their own due diligence, both on the buyer and your property. This takes time. You want to make sure that a bank has already preapproved the buyers before they make their offer. If not, these may not be your buyers.

HOW TO KNOW IF YOU ARE DEALING WITH A BUYER WHO IS THE REAL DEAL

Your agent presents you the offer. It's not quite what you'd hoped, and you're unsure of how serious the buyers are about your home. Although you may see it as an insulting lowball offer coming out of left field, you should still look closely at this offer while considering some of the questions below. We often say in the business that your first buyer is nearly always your best buyer. Take your first buyer's offer very seriously. I can't tell you how many times a seller disregarded an early offer only to wish that buyer were still around two months later.

- Who is the buyer?

- How long has the buyer been looking?

- Has the buyer written other offers nearby?

- Is the buyer working with a good local agent?

- Does the offer come with a preapproval letter?

- How much is the earnest money deposit, also known as good faith deposit?

- Is this offer a number that is close to the number your real estate agent initially suggested?

This offer could very well be a good offer from a serious buyer. Pay attention to how your agent responds to this initial buyer and, no matter how off the offer seems, take note.

WHAT IS THE EARNEST MONEY DEPOSIT?

Buyers will put up some amount of money into a third-party escrow account once you have a signed contract. This is their good faith or earnest money deposit. In much the same way a deposit on a vacation rental is nonrefundable, the buyers forfeit this money if they don't have a legal way to exit the contract. Although the buyers can cancel through inspections or disclosures contingencies, it's nice to know that they are putting this money up, should something go wrong at the last minute. The earnest money deposit could be as little as $1,000 but up to 3 percent of the offer price. Ask your agent what is strong or weak for your market. The more the buyers put up, the more serious their offer. They can get this money back if something serious comes up, and they need to exit the contract via one of the contingencies. But just putting this money up shows they are serious.

In Texas, buyers have something called an option fee. They can pay money to have the unrestricted right to cancel the agreement, typically within 10 days. In this case, if two buyers make similar offers, one with a $500 option fee and the other with just $50, you have to believe that the $500 buyers are serious. They are willing to lose $500 in this transaction. Money talks.

Buyers who are completely in the game, approved for a mortgage, and actively engaged with their mortgage lender or broker are the real deal. Maybe they've even written an offer or two before. They've narrowed down their search parameters, spent months learning the market, and pricing and checking the comparables. Real dealers are often the ones who write the first offer a seller receives on a property, and that's why sellers should take their offers seriously.

Furthermore, a real dealer's offer may not come in within days of a property going on the market, but it will come from an informed buyer who is knowledgeable of the market. If a home is priced too high and a month or two goes by without an offer, the real dealer is watching the listing and waiting to see how the market responds. If real dealers note that there aren't any offers on it and that there is no activity after some time, they will come in with a low offer, which actually may be a good offer.

As difficult as it may seem to contemplate an offer much lower than your asking price, serious sellers should look at all the signs leading up to it and consider if this is the offer to accept. Trust your agent, and even better, trust the saying, "The first buyer is always your best buyer."

NEGOTIATIONS ROUND 1

A real buyer has stood up, and now you want to negotiate their initial offer. Any parts of the offer are negotiable, and it is up to you and your agent to know where and when to negotiate things. Every market works differently so my advice is always general. I once wrote an offer for a home in California for a buyer who was preapproved and had the loan all teed up. The inspections were done within 24 hours of signing a contract because he had prearranged the inspection appointment. Similarly, the appraisal was done in three days. The loan was approved in 10 days, and they closed in 15 days. This was the quickest closing, with a loan, ever. Would this work in Shreveport, Louisiana? Probably not.

Ask your agent what the signs of a strong offer are in your market. Be open to working with the buyer. Nine times out of 10, the final contract terms are much different from the buyer's original offer. Do not be offended by any part of the buyer's offer. I know that this is your house, and there are a lot of emotions attached to it. However, at this

---

🏠 EXPERT   Vera Gibbons, Personal Finance Expert

Vera Gibbons says that nearly 50 percent of purchase decisions is based on the first minute of buyers being inside a home. "Because of this, it is important for sellers to entertain all offers, especially the first one, because the first is usually the best. The buyers have liked what they have seen and didn't need more than sixty seconds to get serious. Buyers who know what they want when they see it go a long way when it comes to closing a deal," advises Vera.

point in the game, it's just business. If you react, you could make a mistake that will come back to haunt you.

The offer and counteroffer process can go on for hours, days, or weeks. If you have multiple offers at once, you can be assured that you will have your buyer under contract sooner rather than later. If you take my advice and identify if the buyer is the best buyer, then you will work with that person to come to terms. If the buyer senses that you are serious, he or she will move quickly. Know your limits, and don't feel compelled to respond immediately.

When to Take a Step Back

Sometimes it takes a good night's sleep to evaluate not only the offer but also your current situation and your motivations. There are times when the buyer and seller are on the same page, and they come to terms quickly. The buyer knows what he or she wants and goes for it. The seller knows what he or she needs to do and accepts it. But the negotiation could go back and forth a few times and ultimately come to a standstill, usually over money. I've seen dozens of negotiations fall apart over as little as a few thousand dollars. It could be that the buyer has really gone to his or her max through a few rounds of negotiations and doesn't feel the price is worth it or affordable, or the seller simply doesn't want to see the property go for that price. If you are a seller and you are close, ask yourself and your agent, "Is this the right buyer, and is it the right price? Is it really about this last $3,000, or is there something else brewing here?" Many times sellers get cold feet toward the end of the negotiations. By agreeing to the final and last term, you are making this final. It's a huge decision. If you are not ready to sell this house, your unwillingness will show its face here.

I say, in cases like this, it often makes sense to take a step back. You may be resisting going down that last $5,000, but maybe the buyer really wants the home. I've seen over and over how just a few days' time away from the negotiation table can make a world of a difference. For you, a few days away may involve some sleepless nights or fear of being on the market for another month, if this buyer walks. You could dream of actually closing this chapter and moving on if you make it work with this buyer. If you step away, you will have a chance to let the situation seep in deeper and allow other parts of your life to weigh in on the decision.

Conversely, a few days away may scare the buyers into thinking that someone else may come in with a better offer, or they may dream of your home and raising their family there and get so excited about it that they decide to cave in. I always advocate for a few days away from the table. Things happen. Also, note that I've seen situations where weeks go by, the buyer makes another offer or two on another home but misses out, and the buyer decides to come back and meet the seller. In contrast, the seller doesn't have any showings for two weeks and gets scared. The seller calls the agent and asks him or her to reach out to that buyer's agent to see if the buyer is still around. If so, the seller may take the buyer's final offer.

UNDER CONTRACT

Once you've accepted an offer, you are in escrow or under contract. Your agent may put up the pending sign or change the listing online to "Pending," "Active Contingent," or something to that effect. It's likely that there is no getting out of it now. Although the buyers have contingencies or outs in the agreements, it's not common for a seller to have them. This is why so many sellers hesitate or hold back on accepting the final offer.

Although I don't want your buyer to do it, many buyers feel comfortable knowing that they can exit the contract if something goes wrong. That's not the case with the seller, so imagine how you would feel if, the day after you sign the buyer's contract, you receive another offer? Would you have seller's remorse? It's possible, so I encourage my sellers to ask themselves these questions:

- Will I have remorse if I sign this contract?

- Am I really ready to sell?

- Do I have a plan in place, assuming this moves forward as the contract reads?

- Do I have any doubts about selling to this buyer?

Creative Ways to Make a Deal Work

Negotiations go back and forth and don't always have to focus so much on price. If possible, speak to your agent and try to uncover ways that you can use terms to help seal the deal. Are you moving into a rental home and able to close quickly? Ask the buyer for a quick close in exchange for the lower offer price. Do you need to go and buy a home with the funds from this sale? Maybe you agree to take a lower price but ask for a longer closing period, or if you need the cash quickly but still need time, ask the buyer to close quickly so that you pay off your mortgage and settle your debt. But in addition to the quick close, ask your buyer to allow you to rent back the property for a specified period after the closing. That way you can satisfy your bank's mortgage, but aren't under the gun to move out quickly. You may, in fact, be able to close on your new home while you are living in your old home, albeit as a renter.

Another way to make a deal is to buy down the buyers' mortgage rate. When interest rates go up, home buying becomes less affordable for some buyers. A rate increase could affect their monthly bottom line. Sellers should be mindful of this. After using a mortgage calculator or talking to a mortgage lender, buyers may wonder if they can afford the monthly payment. Sometimes, for the cost of 1 percent of the loan amount, buyers can get a better interest rate, up to a half a point, and lock it in for 30 years. This may be a smart idea if rates are rising and the buyer prefers to pay an out-of-pocket cost up front as opposed to over time. If you and a buyer are $10,000 off on price, it could be possible that, for only $4,000, you can offer a credit to the buyers that they can use to go toward getting a lower mortgage rate. Buyers focus so much on their monthly payments these days that a lower mortgage interest rate could actually make the monthlies, and therefore the home, more affordable. This can be a much cheaper solution for a seller.

The Seller's One Out: An Offer Contingent on the Sale of a Property

Sometimes buyers will make an offer on a listing, but they need to sell their current home in order to close on the purchase. I see this situation only in strong buyer's markets. The way this works is that the buyer and seller can come to terms and actually have a signed contract. They can have their inspections and get their loan moving along but aren't able to close until the buyer's home closes. In this scenario, the sellers reserve the right to keep showing the property and even accept an offer from another buyer. If they do, they have the right to give the buyers notice (generally 48 to 72 hours) that they would like to cancel the contract. The buyers can give up and walk away, because their home hasn't sold, or move forward. This gives the seller the option to sell to someone else.

INSPECTION PLANNING AND STRATEGY

In a perfect world, you are a next generation seller and have already presented the buyer with a property inspection report and some property disclosures to review. Because of that, the offer will reflect the buyer's knowledge of the property. Aside from liking the floor plan and the condition of the bathrooms, the buyer knows about any potential flaws or issues with the home, so making an offer shows that he or she must really be serious.

Most likely, even if you've had inspections done in advance of listing, many buyers will want to have a second inspection, done by someone of their choosing, just to cover their bases. Don't be insulted by this. A buyer is spending a lot of money, and if that person is willing to spend a few hours of a day and pay a few hundred dollars on an inspection for a property that was previously inspected, you have to believe that he or she is serious. Note that the property inspector is liable to the person who hired and paid for the inspection, so if your inspector missed a major issue with the electrical system, he or she is not liable to your buyer. Many buyers want to cover themselves for these reasons.

The inspection can be stressful and agonizing for a seller. Someone is there in your home with an inspector checking your home out from top to bottom. It's helpful to note that the buyer is still getting to know the home at the time of the inspection. The buyer gets another hour or so in your home to let the idea settle in or to get to know your home better. Make sure the home still shows well.

Make it easy on the inspector. Tell your agent where everything is, and make things such as systems in the basement or the garage easily assessable. Your agent is there to represent you. In the next generation of real estate, I encourage my sellers to be by their phone and ready to answer a call or a text. Something always comes up during the inspection: a question about a water stain, a malfunctioning stove, or a key to the unfinished part of the basement that doesn't unlock the door. If you've had work done on the property recently, make evidence of that work available, or point out to your agent what was done. Without that evidence, sometimes all that an inspector can do is see what's there and speculate as to what happened in the past.

NEGOTIATIONS ROUND 2

Additional negotiations are par for the course with any inspection, particularly in a slower buyer's market, but not so much in a seller's market. The buyer always finds fault with the home and asks for things to be fixed or for credits back at closing. Many sellers anticipate this. If you and the buyer fought over the last $5,000 during the initial contract negotiations, you can be sure it will come back during the inspection, in the form of a new furnace or a credit to fix the small leak in the hot water heater. The conflict is never just about the furnace or the electric.

Some buyers believe that once they get a home under contract, they have the upper hand in negotiations. A next generation seller will plan for this by having inspections up front and fully disclosing all there is to know about a property. Try to make the listing bulletproof by putting everything on the table early on.

No matter how much effort you put into disclosure, problems can still come up. I say that if you are serious about selling and you are this far along in the process; give the buyer something to make him or her feel good about the sale. If you nickel and dime the buyer for every last penny, you risk losing the sale. How would you feel if you and the buyer were arguing over a couple of thousand dollars and the person walked away? I advise sellers to throw a bone to the buyers. They can see it as a goodwill gesture and as a way to ensure a smooth closing.

Of course, I don't want to spend your money for you, but I think it's good practice to keep this option open. Also, understand that a credit at closing, say for their closing costs, is sometimes easier than fixing appliances. If you are trying to move out of your home, possibly the last thing you want to do is deal with getting a leaky hot water heater repaired, only to have the buyer want to come and inspect the repair. Offering buyers a credit will give them more cash at closing and is simply more meaningful to them.

NEXT GENERATION REAL ESTATE FACT: BE AWARE OF THE LOAN AND APPRAISAL CONTINGENCY

I tell my sellers, "The deal isn't done until the last contingency has been removed." Many sellers believe that once they have a signed contract, the home is sold and they can start packing up and moving on. Not so fast. As I mentioned earlier, the buyers have some contingencies, such as disclosures and inspections, that need to be met, and if they are not done so satisfactorily, the buyers are free to exit the agreement. In the next generation of real estate, there has emerged a hyperawareness around the loan contingency, particularly the appraisal. Although it has always been a part of the escrow and sales process, the appraisal has grown to become one of the largest concerns and the biggest threats to smarter buying and faster selling.

Most buyers today need a loan to close. They likely come to you with an offer the bank already preapproved. The bank knows about their income, debt, and credit, but now that the buyers want to buy your home, the bank wants to make sure that the home is worth what the buyers have agreed to pay and that there aren't any major issues with the property. That's the job of an independent third party the bank hires, known as an appraiser. An appraiser visits the property, measures and assesses it, and writes a report with an opinion of value. The appraiser reviews recently sold comparable homes and factors those sales into the report. Much like determining the square footage and the market value of a home, the appraiser's findings are not an exact science. What happens if an appraisal comes back with a value less than what the buyer and seller agreed on in the contract? The buyer's appraisal or loan contingency allows the buyer to decide not to go forward with the sale, and the deal could be over. This was a rare occurrence before 2009. Historically, the property appraisal came in right at the contract price. From time to time, we saw the appraisal come in less and sometimes come in a little more.

Before 2009, the appraisal was something that happened in the background, a part of the process you weren't active in. It was a box that you checked. The buyer's lender called up its favorite local appraiser, likely someone it had had a good relationship with for years, and received a report within a few days. If the buyer wanted to move quickly, it's possible that the appraiser could make a point to get the appraisal done as soon as possible, instead of waiting. There were rarely appraisal issues because the appraiser generally appraised the home at the contract price. However, in the years leading up the mortgage meltdown and housing crisis, lenders started giving out loans to anyone with a pulse. They also allowed homes to be financed with zero money down. This is when the appraisal business started going sideways. During that time, there were situations in which the appraisers and mortgage folks (as well as real estate agents and buyers or sellers) were working in cahoots to get a property to appraise at a high number just to get a deal done. Because they were being guaranteed appraisal orders from their favorite mortgage or real estate agent, home appraisers were signing off on home prices that weren't worth what buyers were offering. Some mortgage professionals sometimes turned a blind eye to get a loan through and make a commission. However, everything changed after May 2009 with the passing of the Home Valuation Code of Conduct (HVCC).

This code stated that a loan broker or banker could no longer contact the appraiser directly. Instead, the Home Valuation Code of Conduct (HVCC) instituted an intermediary who ordered the appraisals. These intermediaries are called appraisal management companies (AMCs). After the law passed, the lender now submitted a request for an appraisal through the AMC, and the AMC in turn contacted an appraiser to set up an appraisal appointment. It sounds like a valid fix to a broken issue. Well, in theory it sounds good, but in practice, it has helped derail thousands of purchases and refinances across the country. Here's why.

The AMCs, in the business of supplying appraisals, hired and sent out the cheapest appraiser to do the appraisal. A good local appraiser, knowledgeable in the market and with 10 years or more of experience, might charge $500. The AMCs want to pay only $250, so they find an inexperienced appraiser or someone from two counties away to do the appraisal. The combination of poor appraisals and unintended negative consequences of HVCC resulted in appraisals coming in too low. They went from one extreme to another.

How Home Appraisals Can Kill Your Sale

As I mentioned in the buyer's section of this book, I once listed a large single-family home in San Francisco with a small legal studio in-law unit below. The home was owner-occupied. The owners used the studio for guests and family members. Also, the home had beautiful views. The seller received an offer within a month, standard for that market. The AMC-hired appraiser, who said he'd never been in that neighborhood, appraised the house by comparing the property to two-unit, tenant-occupied, investment properties with low rents. Not surprisingly, the appraisal was off by $100,000.

Had the appraiser been local, he would have understood that there was a trend in the area for larger homes with legal in-law units. He would have looked for comparable sales of single-family homes, and he would have found great comps priced higher than the contract price. Instead, he searched by two unit buildings and came up with investment properties with the same amount of square feet as my client's home.

Additionally, had the appraiser been local and experienced, he would have understood that San Francisco has strict rent control laws, which brings down the value of tenant-occupied homes. Some of the comparable homes he used in his report were buildings with very low rents and therefore low sales prices. Finally, he'd have understood that homes with views tend to sell for upward of 10 percent more than homes without views in that market.

In this scenario, the clients lost their buyers and had to go back on the market to find a new buyer. They eventually did, but the price was $25,000 less than the first buyer's offer. Having been off and then back on the market, the new buyers thought there was an opportunity to negotiate. The new buyers' appraisal came in at the asking price, $75,000 more than the appraiser's price from three weeks earlier. Sometimes a low appraisal scares off buyers, as in the preceding scenario. Even though they were willing to pay the asking price, they believe that if the appraiser values it less, then it must be worth less. Well, this makes sense. Buyers who aren't experienced in real estate sales would assume that this appraiser knows the profession. What buyers don't understand is that with the recent HVCC law and AMC appraisers, low or inaccurate appraisals often do not reflect market value. The buyers, sellers, and their agents need to be watchdogs in these cases.

Ways to Prevent Bad Appraisals from Wrecking Your Sale

Nowadays it is very difficult to prevent bad appraisals because much of the control lies with third-party AMCs. Even though it is the buyer who needs the appraisal for his or her loan, the appraisal can have a drastic effect on the sale of the property. Therefore, the sellers and their agent need to prepare. Generally, the appraisers will call the listing agent to make an appointment for the appraisal. If your agent gets a call from a phone number with an area code from 10 towns away, this could be the first sign of trouble. Here are ways to prevent an appraisal from ruining a sale.

1. **Have your listing agent talk to the appraiser before the appointment.** When I list a home, I always ask appraisers where they are from and where they do the majority of their appraisals. I also ask them how long they've been in the business. I do this to sense whether there could be an appraisal problem. If I sense the appraiser is inexperienced for whatever reason, I will show up to the appraisal inspection with comparable sale data printed out. I've even gone as far as printing out the details on the past five sales, presenting them to the appraiser, and pointing out how each of them differs. It is a very fine line here, and I don't in any way advocate antagonizing the property appraiser. But it is imperative for the buyer and seller to work together.

2. **Dispute the appraisal.** Because of the influx of inaccurate or bad appraisals and unqualified appraisers, many banks have created appraisal dispute processes. If your appraisal comes in low, but you and your buyer still want to move ahead, the buyer may submit, through his or her agent and mortgage professional, additional or different comps. The bank's underwriting department will review these in light of the questionable appraisal and issue a decision.

    When doing this, your agent should present a clear and informative package. I once submitted an entire package of comps as part of an appraisal dispute process on behalf of my buyer. Working with the listing agent as a team, we included a map of each of the locations of four comps and highlighted the sales dates and features of each home. We also included a side-by-side comparison of each home with respect to the home the buyer wanted to purchase. The more information you give to and the easier you can make it on the bank, the better your chance at getting the loan approved. Sometimes the bank's decision is in favor of the sellers. Other times the loan is rejected.

3. **Ask the buyers to split the difference.** Other times, in the case of a bad appraisal, the buyers still want to buy the home. They understand the bad appraisal and believe that the home is worth the higher price. In this case, depending on how much lower the appraisal is, they will agree to bring more cash to the table to make up the difference. I've seen times when both the buyer and the seller contribute to make the deal work. If the appraisal is off by $10,000, the buyer will come in with a larger down payment, in this case, $5,000, and the seller will agree to lower the price by the same amount. This $10,000 can save the deal. Sometimes it's better to do this than go back on the market. Being aware of the problem and talking about it with all parties is a good start.

4. **Ask the buyers to start over with a new bank.** A final option, if negotiating and settling the issue quickly is not possible, is to have the buyers start over with a new bank. I've seen it hundreds of times; a

---

EXPERT Jonathan Miller, CEO, Miller Samuel Appraisers

"The role of the appraiser has changed from Trusted Advisor to Deal Enabler to Deal Killer," Jonathan told me. "Before HVCC came on the scene, appraisers were hired by a bank, which was comfortable with its network of appraisers, trusted their experience, and worked with them to enable a deal. After HVCC, the ability of the bank or mortgage brokers to hire from their pool of appraisers was taken away and replaced by the hiring of unknown appraisers, who most of the time do not have local market knowledge. With little information on the home, appraisers come in often too low on their reports, which can wind up killing the deal for everyone involved."

To help sellers in the next generation of real estate navigate the often-elusive appraisal process, Jonathan's tips are as follows:

1. **Appraisers report to the bank, not the buyers.** The biggest misconception on the part of buyers is that the appraiser works for them in a mortgage transaction. After all, the appraiser is only necessary

because the buyers are the ones borrowing money. Couple that with the fact that the buyers are paying for the appraisal, it's easy to misunderstand. Regardless of who is paying the appraiser, from the appraisers' standpoint, they work for the party that engages the appraisal—the bank. While the borrowers pay the bank the appraisal fee, it's the bank that flows the money through and pays the appraiser. Ultimately, the bank is the party that requires the valuation of the property to determine whether it will lend. To be completely accurate, the appraiser actually works for the AMC, who, in turn, works for the bank. The appraiser is one step removed so there is no influence. The buyer's agent and the buyer don't have any interaction with the appraiser. Buyers need to work closely with listing agents, since they are the ones who accompany the appraiser on the walkthrough.

2. **Don't smother the appraiser during the walkthrough.** Sellers should be sure that their agent gives the appraiser space. I have seen many cases where the listing agent is nervous about what my valuation might be and feel the need to walk through the house with me, pointing out things that don't usually affect an appraisal report. However, it's not a bad idea to offer the highlights of the home to appraisers, especially if they are unfamiliar with the market, which is why I advise agents to have a "one sheet." This sheet should include a bulleted list of the features of the home that the sellers consider must-knows for the appraiser. This way, sellers have their say without crowding or offending the appraiser, and the appraisers keep their personal space personal.

3. **Every home as a story. Tell it.** Since financial reform HVCC was born, 3 out of 4 appraisers that come to a home do not have local market knowledge. This disconnection changes the volatility and role of appraiser from form filler to deal killer. If buyers and sellers are concerned that the appraiser will not have an accurate picture of the home and/or the neighborhood, my advice is to tell the story of the home. So many people hide behind the comps, but it must be considered that there are circumstances behind the data of those comps. A home's value can be determined by circumstantial things. For instance, a hus-

band and wife may have been looking for a home for four months with nothing in their price range, which is why when a home was suddenly listed in their range, they offered the list price for fear they would lose it. Or one of the comps might have a lower selling price, but the fact is the buyers were paying all cash and the sellers preferred a lower sale price with no contingencies than a higher one with contingencies.

Knowing such stories are important to the appraiser and should be included or attached to the one-sheet the listing agent hands to the appraiser along with the comps the agent pulled. Include short, objective clinical points about comps. Don't use words like "special," or "lovely," or any subjective points. If the appraiser is a good appraiser, he or she will verify the information. Banks review 10 percent of the batches they are issued, so state the facts directly.

buyer's appraisal comes in low, the buyer and seller decide to extend the loan contingency and escrow times, and the buyer starts over with a new bank. The loan is then approved 15 days later, without any problem with the appraisal.

CONTINGENCIES REMOVED: MOVING TOWARD CLOSING

Once the day comes and the buyer has signed off on everything, it's time to celebrate. Today's transactions happen faster than they did a generation ago. Much paperwork is sent and approved electronically, banks wire money, and many steps are removed from the process. Once buyers have gotten their big contingency out of the way, the loan or appraisal contingency, they are days or just a week away from closing.

The Walk-through

The buyers will likely do a walk-through either on the day of the closing or a few days before. This is their chance to look at the home, make sure any agreed-upon repairs were completed, and see that the home is in the same state it was in during their inspection. The buyers will likely go in and check the place out from top to bottom. Don't leave any surprises. The last thing buyers want is three shelves full of old, rusty paint in the garage or your tool bench that was too heavy to move.

My advice is to have the home cleaned and cleared out, or else you'll risk holding up the closing. Imagine if you were buying this home. What condition would you want to accept it in?

I advise sellers (although many do it on their own) to leave a nice card, small gift, or bottle of wine behind as a gift to the buyers. You'll never know when you could need them in the future. Particularly when a transaction or the negotiations got tough, it's nice to end it on a high note. I've seen sellers have horrible postal mail issues after they moved. The postal service kept sending mail to their old homes. The sellers had to keep reaching back out to the buyer, and it was annoying. Luckily for the sellers, their transactions ended on a high note—with a gourmet food and wine basket.

Closing Time!

As I told the buyers in Part II, closings are a little different in every state. In places such as Arizona, Nevada, Alabama, and California, the buyers and sellers never meet in person. The buyers sign their loan and closing papers on one day, and the sellers sign theirs separately. In places such as New York, Connecticut, and Texas, the buyers and sellers sit around the table on the day of the closing. There is less responsibility and paperwork to sign as a seller at the closing. You don't have loan documents to pore over, unlike the buyer who is getting a loan. For the most part, all the seller needs to do is sign the deed over to the buyer.

Your signature will have to be notarized. You may have to sign some documents showing that you've paid off your mortgage and settled the debt with your lender. Before you go in to sign your closing documents, you should receive an estimated closing statement from your escrow officer or attorney, if you are in a state where attorneys do closings. Assuming these numbers work well, you'll likely have the money from the proceeds of the sale wired into your account at the end of the day of the closing or the next day.

It's common that a home sale goes off without a hitch. There could be a small issue here or there; perhaps the buyers want a credit back or need to extend their time to get their appraisal done.

★

In the next generation of real estate, I advise sellers to think ahead and plan in advance. Work with a good local agent, and do your best to anticipate any and all issues . . . before you list the home, before you release the results of an inspection report, before you accept an offer, before you negotiate a credit with the buyer, and before you make the final decision that will bring you one step closer to moving on to the next stage of your life.

Real Estate Technology Companies and Services

Technology has had a huge impact on all things real estate in the past fifteen years. And, its not just about searching homes online or using the Internet. Dozens of company have come up with fixes to issues that make it easier, smarter, or simply better to buy or sell a home. The list in this appendix includes next generation real estate technology companies and/or services that have impacted real estate today.

Rentenna • www.rentenna.com

Rentenna's core technology analyzes data on rental properties and their immediate surroundings to produce property-level "RentennaScores" (0–100 ratings) that provide consumers with an objective measure by which to compare their rental options. Through its scoring system, Rentenna aims to bring context and transparency to the infamously opaque world of real estate search. Rentenna's data set is robust, with over 1 million historical listings analyzed, over 180,000 properties scored, and over 250 million discrete data events analyzed to date.

Postable • www.postable.com

Thank You cards, made easy. Postable is the free and easy way to get people's mailing addresses and a totally new way to write customized thank you cards, or any type of card for that matter. Postable makes it incredibly easy to write and mail beautiful thank you and holiday cards that will show your family, friends and clients that you care. All you have to to is type your cards on the site and Postable prints (on luxe stock), stuffs and mails them for you directly. Voila! With Postable, it's never been easier to show someone you care.

nest. Nest • www.Nest.com

Nest is focused on reinventing unloved but important home products, like the thermostat and smoke alarm. The company focuses on delighting customers with simple, beautiful and thoughtful hardware, software and services. The Nest Learning ThermostatTM and Nest Energy Services offerings address home energy consumption, and Nest Protect: Smoke + Carbon MonoxideTM will help keep people safe. Nest products are installed in more than 90 countries and the Nest Learning Thermostat has helped save more than 1,000,000,000 kWh of energy to date

thumbtack Thumbtack • www.Thumbtack.com

At Thumbtack we know how hard it can be to find the right person for the job, let alone the right person who is available, nearby, and within budget. Instead of wasting time searching, browsing and playing phone tag, just tell us what you need. We'll deliver you multiple quotes from our network of vetted home improvement pros within 24 hours.

MyCityWay MyCityWay • www.mycityway.com

MyCityWay's mobile consumer apps and interfaces provide a live, personalized view into more than 100 cities worldwide. The local discovery and search platform integrates content from more than 120 sources based on location, relevance and other real-time criteria.

Walk Score® — Walk Score® • www.walkscore.com

Walk Score's mission is to promote walkable neighborhoods. This is one of the simplest and best solutions for the environment, our health, and our economy. Our vision is for every property listing to read: Beds: 3 Baths: 2 Walk Score: 84. We want to make it easy for people to evaluate walkability and transportation when choosing where to live.

BuyerMLS — BuyerMLS • www.buyermls.com

BuyerMLS is an online marketplace where real estate agents can anonymously list their buyers' wants and needs and listing agents can search for potential matches for their available properties. The company offers a version for brokers, which enables them to keep a database of anonymous available buyers for all their agents to search and use.

Floored — Floored • www.floored.com

Floored creates interactive 3D models for all types of real estate, including homes. By leveraging the latest 3D camera technology and recent advances in computer vision and graphics research, it replaces 2D floor plans, photographs, videos, panoramas, and 3D renderings while providing an interactive experience.

HomeZada — HomeZada • www.homezada.com

HomeZada's online and mobile software helps homeowners organize and manage their home. Homeowners can plan, budget and organize home improvement projects; inventory and track all of their personal possessions and fixed assets; and keep a personalized calendar with key maintenance guides, tasks and automatic reminders. HomeZada's professional solution allows real estate agents to easily create digital home profiles for their buyers, then transfer the data to them after closing.

keyzio   Keyzio • www.keyzio.com

Keyzio is an online marketplace where any homeowner in the country can claim their home, and any prospective buyer can indicate interest in buying a home—even if it's not for sale.

closing time   Closing Time by Amitree Inc. • www.closingti.me

Closing Time, a product by Amitree Inc., is the first tool to help buyers navigate the closing process so that it can be quick, easy, and free of surprises. By organizing the dozens of mission-critical tasks into a simple, easy-to-understand checklist that is fully customized for each buyer's unique situation, buyers can close with far less stress. Buyers and their agents can try out Closing Time for free at www.closingti.me.

RealScout   RealScout • www.realscout.com

RealScout offers agents a full-featured search portal that allows home buyers and their agents to search the MLS not only by needs (e.g., bedrooms, bathrooms, price, square feet), but also by wants (e.g., open floor plans, high ceilings, large backyards, natural light). Buyers and their agents can also search active listings by photos of a particular feature.

updater   Updater • www.updater.com

Updater offers relocating families and individuals a one-stop shop where they can easily update all their accounts and records with their new address, schedule utilities to be turned on, and file their official USPS mail forwarding form. Updater offers branded, white-label versions of its technology for real estate professionals to offer their clients.

Index

A

Accidental landlord, 190–192
Address, looking up on Google, 230
Adjustable-rate mortgage, 89–90
Agent advertising, 57–59
Agent-buyer relationship, understanding, 60–62
Agent(s)
  benefits of local, 64–66
  breaking up with, 128–129
  communication style with, 101–103
  delay in contacting, 36
  engaging to sell, 203–204
  for help finding tenants, 191
  how to find buyer's, 54–57
  how to find seller's, 214
  how to work with, 59–60
  listing, what to expect from, 209–212
  questions to ask, 60
  role in transaction, 134

  seller's relationship to, 207–209
  what to expect from, 48–54
AMC, 147, 281
  consequences of, 148–150
American dream, 19
Appraisal management company (AMC). *See* AMC.
Appraisal, 145–147
  disputing a bad, 150–152
  interfering with sale, 281–284
Appraised value, 201–202
Appraiser, 135
Attorney, role in transaction, 134–135
Auctions, 169–170
Automated valuation models (AVMs), 37, 42, 44, 198, 199, 203

B

Bank negotiations, for lowering monthly payments, 192

Board of Realtors, 49, 211
Boiler, inspection and, 156
Breakeven Horizon Chart, 28
Building department,
    researching your home, 231
Building records, 143
Building/planning department,
    231
Buyer
    determining a serious, 271
    versus seller, 180–183
Buying the listing, 224
Buying versus renting, 25

C

California Association of
    Realtors, 36, 102
Closing, 159–160, 287
CMA, 203, 218, 220–221
Commission, 223
Communication style,
    establishing with agent,
    101–103
Comparable homes, 234
Comparative marketing
    analysis (CMA). *See* CMA.
Compromise, home-buying
    and, 99–101
Construction, new. *See* New
    construction.
Contingent on sale of property,
    277
Contract, 136–137, 275
Corcoran, Barbara, 7, 20, 22,
    88, 125, 127, 250
Courthouse sale. *See*
    Foreclosures.
Creative Class, 199, 229

Credit report, 85
Criteria, home-buying, 94–95,
    97
Curb appeal, 248

D

Data collection, 37
Days on market (DOM), 181,
    232
Declutter, home staging and,
    253
Depersonalize, home staging
    and, 252
Direct lender. *See* Mortgage
    professional
Disclosure, 237, 241
    common, 140–141
    using Internet to ascertain
    missing, 142–143
Disclosure review, 137–138
    property inspection and,
    138
Disclosure statement, 238–240
Distressed sales, due diligence
    and, 173–175. *See also*
    Foreclosures; REO; Short
    sales.
Draining/grading issues,
    inspection and, 157

E

Earnest money deposit, 272
Electrical requirements,
    inspection and, 157
Emotional attachment, to home
    for sale, 185–186
Emotional considerations,
    home-buying and, 31–33

Emotionally detach, home
staging and, 252–253
Escrow, 272
Escrow deposit, protecting, 160
Escrow officer, 135

F

Facebook postings, what not to
do, 124
Fair Isaac Corporation, The
(FICO), 85
Federal Housing Authority
(FHA), 67
Federal Housing Finance
Agency, 193
FHA loan, 90–91
Financial considerations
home-buying and, 25–27
preapproval and, 78–79
Fixed-rate loan, 92
Flint, Pete, 7, 51
Florida, Richard, 7, 199, 229, 246
For sale by owner. See FSBO.
Foreclosures, 165–166, 169–170
Foundation/structural issues,
inspection and, 157
FSBO, 212–214
Furnace, inspection and, 156

G

Gibbons, Vera, 7, 21, 24, 71, 258,
273
Good faith estimate, 81, 83
Google Earth, 143
Google Street View, 142, 230

H

HARP, 193

Home Affordability Refinance
Program. See HARP.
Home equity, 27
Home tour, interviewing listing
agent during, 218, 220–222
Home tour turnoffs, 262–263
Home Valuation Code of
Conduct (HVCC). See
HVCC.
Home value, researching,
196–201
Home-buying
emotional considerations
and, 31–33
financial considerations,
25–27
practical considerations and,
27–31
Home-buying process, reasons
for starting, 20–22
Home, living away from, 13
Hot water heater, inspection
and, 157
Hotpads.com, 25
HVCC, 146–147, 148, 281

I

IDX, 40–41
Inspection planning, 277–278
Inspection. See Property
inspection.
Inspector, 135, 153, 155. See also
Property inspection.
Interest-only loan, 87–89
Internet Data Exchange (IDX).
See IDX.
Investment, real estate as a
long-term, 34

K

Kids Live Safe database, 143,
231
Kidslivesafe.com, 143, 231

L

Landlord, accidental, 190–192
Lending Tree, 74
Lifestyle changes, 14
List price, 111–114, 202
    final, 257–258
    listing agreement and,
        225–226
    uncertainty about, 258–260
Listing agent, benefits of
    forging relationship with,
    118–120, 121–122
Listing agreement, 223–225
Listing history, 232–233
Listing term, 223–225
Living alone (trend), 15
Loan, finalizing, 144–145
Loan and appraisal
    contingency, 279–280
Loan approval/commitment,
    152–153
Loan types, 76, 86–91
    Fixed rate, 86, 92
    Interest-only loan, 87–89
    Adjustable-rate mortgage,
        89–90
    FHA loan, 90–91
Local considerations, buying
    home and, 26
Location, buying and, 94

M

Make Me Move, 41, 122

Market value, 189, 201–202
Marketing copy, approving, 260
McBride, Greg, 8, 29, 77, 79,
    144, 153, 168
Miller, Jonathan, 7, 147, 152, 284
MLS, 38, 39–40, 49, 101, 103,
    181, 197, 211
Mortgage banker. *See* Mortgage
    professional.
Mortgage broker. *See* Mortgage
    professional.
Mortgage calculator, 23
Mortgage lending, evolution of,
    91
Mortgage professional, 70–73,
    135
    how to find, 72
    what to expect from, 75–76
Multiple agents, myth of, 62–63
Multiple listing services (MLS).
    See MLS.
MyFICO, 85

N

National Association of
    Realtors, 39
Negotiations, 132, 273–275, 276,
    278–279
    walking away from, 133
New construction, 114–117
    square footage and, 244
Next generation trends, 13–15

O

Offer
    components of, 270–271
    making a bad, 126–128
    preparing the, 125–126

submitting, 129–130
terms of, 130–133
Oil tank, inspection and, 157
Online, finding an agent, 57,
    215–216
Online listing, 248–250
Online MLS, 39–40
Online mortgage banking,
    74–75
Open house
    finding an agent at, 55–56,
        216
    necessity of, 264–266
    to research home value,
        200–201
    types of people who attend,
        109–111
    visiting, 106–109
Option fee, 272
Owning, renting versus, 13–14

P

Paint, home staging and, 253
Patience, home-buying and,
    105–106
Photos, 233–234
    approving, 260
    online listing and, 249–250
PITI, 76
Plumbing, inspection and,
    156–157
Police blotter, 144, 231
Practical considerations, home-
    buying and, 27–31
Preapproval versus
    prequalification, 77–78
Price
    buying and, 94–95

wrong, 184–185
    See also List price; Sale price.
Pricing, understanding, 201–203
Property history, 237
Property inspection, 131,
    153–154
    before listing, 235–236
    disclosure review and, 138
    misconceptions of, 154
    what to look for, 155–158
Property presentation. See Curb
    appeal.
Purchase offer, 136

R

Rascoff, Spencer, 7, 41, 57, 69,
    214, 227
Rates, 80–81, 84, 144–145
Real estate agent. See Agent.
Real estate market
    comparison of past and
        present, 11–16
    driving forces, 16
    overview of past to present,
        1–5
Real estate syndicators. See
    Syndicators.
Real estate transactions, people
    involved in, 134–136
Realtor.com, 37, 38, 197
Referrals, 11
    finding an agent through,
        54–55, 215
Renovations, inspection and,
    158
Renting, 191–192
    versus owning, 13–14
REO, 166

what to know, 170–173
Roof, inspection and, 155
Ryan, Maxwell, 8, 42, 249, 254, 261

S

Sale, resisting, 187, 189
Sale price, 202
Seller
    learning about the, 121–122
    unrepresented, 212
    versus buyer, 180–183
Seller pricing, 113
Settlement statement, 160, 161–163
Short sale, 164–165, 192–195
    what to know, 167
    stigma, 168–169
Showing
    by appointment, 104–105
    poor, 185
    presence of seller at, 267–268
Showing agent, 108
Showing schedule, 260–261
Size and specs, buying and, 95
Smarter buying, 20
Square footage, 95–96, 98, 242–243
Stager, professional, 254–256
Staging, 245–256
    psychology of, 246–248
Steele, Lockhart, 7, 44, 65, 210
Suburban exodus, 14
Syndicator's search, getting most out of, 41–43
Syndicator's websites, imperfection of, 43–44

Syndicators, 37–38
    for researching value, 197–200

T

Tax professional, consulting, 191
Technology, impact on real estate, 14
Tenant
    choosing the right, 191
    treating well, 192
Title officer, 135
Trulia.com, 37, 38, 197
Truth-in-lending disclosure statement, 81, 82

U

Unrepresented seller, 212
Urban expansion, 14

V

Value. *See* Home value.

W

Walk-through, 158–159, 286–287

Z

Zestimate, 37, 41, 123, 198, 199, 231–232
Zillow(.com), 28, 37, 38, 41, 122, 123, 197, 198, 199
Zillow Digs, 197
Zillow's Breakeven Horizon Chart, 28
Zillow's Mortgage Marketplace, 74